F. X. (Francis Xavier) Weninger

On the apostolical and infallible authority of the Pope

F. X. (Francis Xavier) Weninger

On the apostolical and infallible authority of the Pope

ISBN/EAN: 9783742869142

Manufactured in Europe, USA, Canada, Australia, Japa

Cover: Foto ©Lupo / pixelio.de

Manufactured and distributed by brebook publishing software (www.brebook.com)

F. X. (Francis Xavier) Weninger

On the apostolical and infallible authority of the Pope

ON THE
APOSTOLICAL
AND
INFALLIBLE AUTHORITY
OF THE
POPE,

WHEN TEACHING THE FAITHFUL,

AND

ON HIS RELATION

TO

A GENERAL COUNCIL.

By F. X. WENINGER, D.D.

MISSIONARY OF THE SOCIETY OF JESUS.

SECOND EDITION.

NEW YORK:
D. & J. SADLIER & CO.
CINCINNATI:
JOHN P. WALSH.
1869.

CONTENTS.

Introduction.. 7

I.

TESTIMONY OF HOLY SCRIPTURE

CONCERNING THE PRIMACY OF ST. PETER, AS INVESTED WITH INFALLIBLE AUTHORITY IN MATTERS OF FAITH. 19

II.

TESTIMONY OF THE HOLY FATHERS

FROM THE BEGINNING OF THE CHRISTIAN ERA, UNTIL THE DAYS OF ST. BERNARD, PROCLAIMING THE SEE OF ST. PETER AT ROME, TO BE THE HIGHEST TRIBUNAL IN MATTERS OF FAITH................................ 32

III.

TESTIMONY OF ALL THE GENERAL COUNCILS OF THE EAST AND WEST,

DECLARING THE JUDGMENT OF THE CHAIR OF ST. PETER AT ROME, TO BE THE INFALLIBLE RULE OF FAITH..... 100

IV.

TESTIMONY OF THE POPES THEMSELVES,

ASSERTING THEIR PREROGATIVE AS THE SUPREME AND INFALLIBLE JUDGES IN MATTERS OF FAITH............. 154

V.

TESTIMONY OF THE POPES EXERCISING THIS PREROGATIVE.

THE POPES OF ALL CENTURIES, DEFINITIVELY BY THEIR OWN AUTHORITY, CONDEMNING HERESY AND ERRORS. 176

VI.

TESTIMONY OF THE MOST CELEBRATED THEOLOGIANS AND UNIVERSITIES,

SINCE THE TIME OF THOMAS AQUINAS, MAINTAINING THE INFALLIBILITY OF THE POPE, WHEN SPEAKING "EX CATHEDRA".. 198

VII.

TESTIMONY OF PRINCES AND PEOPLES,

ACKNOWLEDGING THE AUTHORITY OF THE ROMAN SEE TO BE THE HIGHEST TRIBUNAL ON EARTH, AND THE ROMAN PONTIFF THE INFALLIBLE JUDGE IN MATTERS OF FAITH.. 218

VIII.

THE "RATIO THEOLOGICA,"

OR THE EVIDENCE OF THE TRUTH OF OUR THESIS BY THE FORCE OF LOGICAL CONSEQUENCES................... 248

OBJECTIONS REFUTED... 279

INTRODUCTION.

THERE are already, within the reach of all, standard works upon the Divine Institution of the Papal Supremacy. The same can not be said of the several prerogatives, consequent on the Supremacy. And yet, in these unstable times, when the eyes of the whole world are directed toward the Holy See, as toward the only safeguard and stronghold, not merely of the Church, but even of Christianity, it were desirable to have at hand able treatises, setting forth, in detail, the rights vested exclusively in the Sovereign Pontiff.

Now, among these, none is capable of eliciting a more intense interest than his Apostolic Authority, as the divinely commissioned teacher of the Church. We thought, therefore, that we should meet a general want, by submitting to the public the present unpretentious volume, in which it has been our humble aim to collect an invincible array of arguments in support of the point in question.

But, before entering upon our task, we must premise a few remarks.

In the first place, we assume to establish the infallible authority of the Pope within those limits only, which are covered by the very title of the book, namely, in matters of faith and morals. We claim no such privilege for the Head of the Church in scientific questions, except in so far as these touch, directly or indirectly, upon the "deposit of faith," and upon its preservation.

Secondly, we ascribe no such infallibility to the utterances of the Pope, except when he, as we say, is speaking "*ex cathedra*," which means, when the Pope is teaching the faithful as the Head of the Church, and the expounder of her doctrine. We admit that, when he expresses his opinions as a private theologian, he is liable to err, but not when he solemnly pronounces upon the teaching of the Church.

By upholding the Infallibility of the Pope, thus understood, we, by no means, derogate from the authority of the other prelates of the Church. Their dignity, as the legitimate successors of the Apostles, is not at all impaired by this privilege of the Sovereign Pontiff, because they do not represent the Apostles in the *Apostolate*, but in the *Episcopate*. As Bishops their dignity is tantamount to that of the Bishop of Rome, from whom, nevertheless, they have received their jurisdiction over that portion of Christ's flock, entrusted to their charge; not because the Pope alone possesses the plenitude of the Episcopal character, but because he alone represents the Prince of the Apostles.

The Infallibility of the Pope flows altogether from his Primacy, and is shared by no other Prelate, because no one of them can lay a claim to the Apostolical authority, transmitted by Peter to his successors.

The prerogative of the Bishop of Rome does

not, then, detract from the dignity of the other Bishops; on the contrary, it redounds to the honor of the entire order. For, after all, it is a Bishop, and no one but a Bishop, who is invested, with an attribute, so divinely sublime, and shared by no mortal. The Episcopal dignity is a *conditio sine qua non* for the Vicar of Christ, who is not consecrated by a distinct Order, when decked with the tiara, but, on being legitimately elected, and consecrated Bishop of Rome, succeeds, at once, to all the powers of the head of the Church and becomes the infallible judge, in matters of faith.

For further illustration, upon this point, we refer the reader to what we purpose to say, more diffusely, in the Chapter entitled *ratio theologica*, or theological consequences.

Concerning the aim of such a work, it may not be amiss to anticipate an objection, which might possibly be urged by some very able theologians devoted, heart and soul, to the interests of the Holy Church. We are fully aware, that there are some, who scruple to entertain any doubt upon the question, but who, nevertheless, deem it ill-advised and unsuited to our times to direct public attention to claims, calculated, as they fancy, to alienate those not yet received into the household of the faith. While appreciating the motives, by which these zealous laborers in the vineyard of the Lord are actuated, we beg leave to dissent from their views, and respectfully invite attention to our reasons.. We are fully persuaded:

That it is utterly useless, at this late day, and especially among our enlightened, free-minded and good-hearted countrymen, to dissemble our personal convictions. The armies of Truth and Error are drawn up in the sight of the whole world, and prepared to meet, in a decisive combat, for the very life of Christianity. It is time to define our position more accurately, and to let our enemies feel our strength and the utter impossibility of engaging us in any compromise. They themselves are fully satisfied, that the question at issue, is not the admission or the rejection of this or that particular article of the Creed, but the existence or the extinction of the Church and of Christianity itself. They know very well, that all their schemes must prove abortive, unless they succeed in destroying or, at least, in weakening the influence of the Head of the Church. Accordingly, they bring all their engines of attack to play against the authority of the Roman Pontiff, with the view of effecting a breach in this bulwark of Catholic Unity.

Under these circumstances it is the urgent duty of all true sons of the Church, to strengthen, as much as in them lies, the devotion of the faithful toward the Head of the Church. The sympathies of the Catholic world are evidently with our suffering Father. Thence that solicitude to protect the patrimony of St. Peter from the desecration of the invader; thence that generosity in furnishing pecuniary aid; thence that ardor for enlisting among the indomitable Papal Zouaves.

But, if we manifest so much earnestness, in the defense of his earthly territory, shall we make no efforts to stay the inroads of malice on his spiritual realm? He may lose his temporal possessions, without the slightest detriment to the Unity of the Church, so long as his subjects remain in his Communion and acknowledge his supremacy as the infallible teacher, in matters of faith. But he can not surrender one tittle of his spiritual sovereignty, with which Christ has invested him. The invasion of the Papal States ceases, at intervals, but the attacks, made on Catholic Unity, are uninterrupted. The enemies of truth are never asleep; but, in our times especially strive, with insidious artifice, to undermine the outworks of the Church, which consist in the ready submission of her children to the judgment and decision of Christ's Vicar, the successor of St. Peter, Pope Pius IX.

Our Holy Father, alive to the growing danger, has more than once met it, by solemnly asserting his right, as the divinely commissioned teacher of mankind. Even in the first years of his eventful Pontificate, he proclaimed the Dogma of the Immaculate Conception; and recently, again, he startled an unbelieving world by his syllabus, which hurls its anathemas, regardless of policy, against all doctrines dangerous to the faith. These acts argue an exercise of supreme Authority, which call upon us, especially in this country, to clear them from the charge of Papal arrogance and usurpation.

It is worse than useless, to disguise our real sentiments, in the face of facts, which stamp themselves upon our whole outward deportment, and which reveal to reflecting minds the real nature of our conduct. All see how we act and how we must act, if we wish to remain in Communion with Rome. The Pope teaches and *defines*, without previously convoking a Council or asking the formal consent of anybody; and the clergy of every order, as well as laymen of every condition, are obliged to conform, and do conform, precisely as Pius IX, in his capacity of Head of the Church, so teaches and *defines*. Such a submission, without a belief in the Papal prerogative for which we contend, would be the sheerest hypocrisy, and an eternal stigma on the sacred character of the Episcopacy. It would argue a cringing acquiescence, dictated by no interior conviction of duty, but prompted by a sort of exterior necessity or force. For, a sincere exterior submission is incompatible with an interior dissent. The mere "obsequious silence," so often affected by the Jansenists, is an unmistakable evidence of insincerity, and can only tend to set up the hypocrites, as a laughing-stock to the enemies of the Church. It reminds us of the ostrich, who hides his head in the sand, as if thus he could escape the eyes of his pursuers, though his whole body is visible. Such conduct betrays a craven disposition, which is neither honorable nor calculated to inspire confidence; while, on the contrary, a noble, open, bold bearing, conscious of the invincibility of truth, must eventually gain even upon the bitterest antagonists of our Holy Faith.

We shall therefore state, with precision of style and solidity of logic, our reasons, for submitting to the doctrinal utterances of the Holy See. Nor shall we be deterred from putting forth our convictions, in all their strength, through a fear of giving rise to misunderstanding. Such an objection, if it had any force, would hold equally of many other tenets of our Holy Religion. Is there a single dogma of Catholic belief, which has not been misconstrued, and assailed with a volley of stereotyped calumnies, from the dawn of the so-called Reformation up to the present day?

In publishing this treatise we have not in mind those who, like Pilate, ask "what is truth," and then turn their backs upon Christ; but, at the same time, we ought to satisfy the earnest doubts of such, as are desirous to put their conscience at ease, upon the teachings of Holy Church. Now, of such men there is a large number in our own country. Let us then teach these, why the Catholic world subscribes, so readily, to the utterances of Rome; and we may hope that a large number of our dissenting brethren, convinced of the solidity of our religious convictions, will soon join us, and tread, in our company the way of salvation, under the guidance of the divinely-appointed shepherd of souls.

With respect to the division of the work, we have but little to add, because we simply refer the kind reader to our Table of Contents. The very nature of a theological treatise, such as it is our aim to make the present, renders it desirable to set out with the arguments from Scripture, and then to pass over to those drawn from tradition, arranged in the order of their relative importance and their chronological succession; finally adding the force of the so-called *ratio theologica*, by studying the deductions, at which our own reason must arrive, when arguing, with logical severity, from what is otherwise known to be a matter of faith.

As to quotations, in which this volume must of necessity abound, we shall always give the most important words in Latin, with the view of making the work more interesting to professed theologians, and to other readers of classic tastes and acquirements. We shall also give, at least the substance of every passage, in English, for the benefit of such, as are not familiar with the Latin idiom.

Readers of the latter class will be pleased to learn, that the unity of the work suffers nothing, from the omission of the original Latin texts, because they are reproduced, either literally or substantially, in the vernacular.

May the book, under the protection of the Immaculate Queen of the Apostles, attain completely its aim, and draw nearer around the chair of St. Peter all those, who are partakers of the Holy Ministry in the Church of God.

May it inspire every Catholic reader with more filial devotedness toward the Holy Father, and strengthen his religious convictions; and may it also command respect of the outsiders, by showing that even those articles, which Catholics believe, and which are especially looked upon as superstitions and results of the dark ages, victoriously stand the light of the most severe criticisms of faith and reason.

THE AUTHOR.

CINCINNATI, Feast of St. Peter, 1868.

I.

TESTIMONY OF HOLY SCRIPTURE

CONCERNING THE PRIMACY OF ST. PETER, AS INVESTED WITH INFALLIBLE AUTHORITY IN MATTERS OF FAITH.

If the authority and power of teaching the faithful with infallibility the way of salvation was divinely conferred on St. Peter and his successors in office, we naturally look for striking incontrovertible evidences to that effect, in those passages of Holy Writ, which record the institution of the Primacy.

But, before citing either the words of Holy Writ or those of the Fathers, we ought to remind our readers, that it is not our object to prove the Primacy in general, except in as far as it brings with it, when united to the teaching authority, the inherent prerogative of Infallibility in matters of faith. We deem this observation of importance, in order to guard against the supposition that we force our conclusions.

The first words, which attract our notice, are those addressed to St. Peter, after he had solemnly declared his belief in the Divinity of Christ: "Blessed art thou, Simon Bar-Jona: because flesh and blood have not revealed it to thee, but my Father who is in heaven. And I say to thee, That thou art Peter, and upon this rock I will build my Church; and the gates of hell shall not prevail against it. And I will give to thee the keys of the Kingdom of heaven: and whatsoever thou shalt bind upon earth, it shall be bound also in heaven: and whatsoever thou shalt loose upon earth, it shall be loosed also in heaven."*

It is evident from this passage, that Christ invested Peter as the Head of the Church with infallible authority in questions of faith; for its obvious import certainly is, that Peter stands in the same relation to the Church, which is grounded on faith, as the foundation does to the entire building. Now, if the foundation gives way, the whole superstructure must soon crumble into ruins.

All the Fathers understand these words in the

* Matth xvi: 17.

same manner, and look upon the immovable *faith* of Peter as the rock meant by Christ. St. Cyril of Alexandria, expounding this passage, declares: "To my mind it appears evident that the rock, here intended by Christ, is nothing else than the *disciple's unshaken faith*, on which the Church was built, that it might not be in danger of falling or of surrendering to the powers of darkness." "*Petrum opinor nihil aliud, quam inconcussam et firmissimam discipuli fidem vocavit, in qua Ecclesia fundata est, ut non laberetur et esset inexpugnabilis inferorum portis.*"*

St. Gregory of Nazianzen avers: "Peter is called a rock, and the foundations of the Church are planted in his faith." †

St. Ambrose reasons as follows: "Faith is the groundwork of the Church, because of the faith, and not of the person of Peter, it was said, that the gates of death should never prevail against it." ‡

St. Augustin remarks: "He (Christ) called him Peter, that is, the rock, and praised the foundations of the Church which was built on the Apostle's faith. "*Nominavit Petrum, et laudavit firmamentum Ecclesiæ in ista fide.*" §

---

* Lib. iv de Trinit.   † Or. de moder. ferv. in disp.
‡ De Incarn. C. v, No. 34.   § Tract ii. in Joan, No. 20.

St. Epiphanius says: "Peter was made for us a living rock, on which, as on a foundation, the faith of the Lord rests, and on which the Church is erected." "*Qui quidem solidæ Petræ instar nobis exstitit, cui velut fundamento Domini fides innititur, supra quam Ecclesia modis omnibus ædificata est.*"*

The same idea is forcibly reëchoed in the words of St. Chrysostom, who remarks: "He (Christ) did not say *Petrus*, but *Petra*, because He did not build His Church upon the man, but upon the faith of Peter." "*Non dixit supra Petrum; neque enim supra hominem, sed supra fidem ejus, scilicet Petri ædificavit.*" †

St. Leo the Great, sustains precisely the same views: "Peter," suggests he, "so pleased the Lord by the sublimity of his faith, that, after being admitted to the fruition of bliss, he received the solidity of an immovable rock, on which the Church was so firmly built, as to bid defiance to the gates of hell and the laws of death." "*Tantum in hac fidei sublimitate sibi complacuit, ut, beatitudinis felicitate donatus, sacram immobilis Petræ susciperet firmitatem, supra quam fundata Ecclesia portis inferi et mortis legibus praevaleret.*" ‡

---

* Hæres. 59. No. 7. † I. Sermon. Pentecost. ‡ Serm. 51. al. 94, c. 1.

CÆSARIUS, the Cistercian, appositely thus paraphrases the same passage: "On this rock, namely, on the unshaken faith, to which thou owest thy name, I will build my Church."*

Now, if this reasoning holds of Peter, it holds with equal propriety of his successors. For, according to the reasoning of all the Fathers, the privileges which were conferred on St. Peter for the direction of the faithful, are the inalienable prerogative of the Holy See, because the authority vested in the Head of the Church was to subsist through all ages, even unto the consummation of time. Certainly Christ did not build His Church upon Peter, for the good of Peter, but for the welfare of mankind.

Pope Leo, therefore, contended for an acknowledged prerogative, when he so emphatically asserted: "The order of truth remains unaltered, and Peter, preserving the firmness of a rock, has not abandoned the helm of the Church. His power is perpetuated in his See, and his authority still challenges obedience. In my lowliness, then, you ought to recognize him, whose authority is not impaired, though transmitted to an unworthy heir." "*Manet dispositio veritatis, et B. Petrus, in accepta fortitudine*

---

* Hom. de. Cath. S. Petri.

petræ perseverans, Ecclesiæ gubernacula non relinquit—cujus in sua sede vivit potestas et excellit auctoritas. In persona itaque humilitatis meæ ille honoretur, cujus dignitas etiam in indigno hærede non deficit."

Hundreds of Fathers have supported the same doctrine, in the Oecumenical Councils, and have solemnly declared that Peter abides in the person of his successor. "Through Leo, Peter has spoken," exclaimed the Fathers of the Fourth General Council. Those of the Sixth General Council expressed the same conviction, couched in the following unequivocal terms: "It appeared to us paper and ink; but through Agatho Peter has spoken. Therefore, we leave it to thee to decide what is to be done, because thou standest upon the immovable rock of faith." *"Charta et atramentum videbatur; at, per Agathonem, Petrus loquebatur. Tibi, itaque, quidquid gerendum sit relinquimus, stanti super firmam fidei petram."*

Supported by the voice of tradition and the teachings of the Fathers, St. Anselm, who had taken up the gauntlet against the antipope, Guibert, furthermore invokes the evidence of historical facts: "Whilst even Patriarchs have erred and apostatized from the faith, the Roman Pontiff, though attacked and assaulted, has stood unmoved in his stronghold, because heaven and earth shall pass away, but not the words of Him who said: 'Thou art Peter; that is the rock, and upon this rock I will build my Church.'"—"*In ejusdem fidei fundamento, licet pulsatus, licet concussus, tamen stetit immobilis. Coelum enim et terra transibunt, verba autem ipsius non transibunt, qui dixit: 'Tu es Petrus, etc.'"* *

It is of no little interest to listen to the train of reasoning suggested, by the above text, even to a Bossuet. In a discourse addressed to the French Bishops, assembled in Council, the eloquent orator speaks thus: "This noble confession merited for Peter the honor of being selected as the foundation stone of the Church. But the power, conferred by this choice upon a mortal man, can not be supposed to have ceased with Peter, because the foundation of a building, designed to last forever, can not be subject to the ravages of time. Therefore Peter will always live in his successors, always speak from his chair. Such is the doctrine of the Holy Fathers, such the declaration of the six hundred and thirty Bishops, assembled in the Council of Chalcedon. St. Paul, who had been rapt up into the third Heaven, bowed to the decisions of Peter, to give an example to after ages. A like dispo-

---

* Lib. cont. Pseud. Pont. Guib.

sition, to abide by the infallible oracles of the Holy See, must ever distinguish the faithful sons of the Church. Every one, no matter how learned or how holy, even though he were another Paul—*'etiamsi alter Paulus quis videretur'*—owes unfeigned allegiance to Peter. The Church of Rome, taught by Peter and his successors, never saw errors spring up in her bosom. She has always preserved her virginity; and therefore her faith of Christianity, and Peter still continues to be, in his successors, the foundation of the Church. Such has ever been the verdict of the General Councils of Africa, of Greece, of France, of the whole Church* 'from the rising of the sun to the going down of the same.'"*

Another decisive declaration of Christ, in support of this Papal prerogative, we find in the Gospel of St. Luke, Chapt. 22d: "Simon, Simon, behold Satan hath desired to have thee, that he may sift thee as wheat. But I have prayed for thee, that thy *faith* fail not: and thou being once converted, confirm thy brethren—*Rogavi pro te, ut fides tua non deficiat, et tu aliquando conversus, confirma fratres tuos.*" †
After this sacred assurance and solemn injunc-

* Sermon sur l'Unité.   † Luke xxii: 31, 32.

tion nobody, who believes in Christ, will question the Infallibility of Peter. Now, if, even in the primitive days of Christianity, the doctrinal Infallibility of the head of the Church was, in a certain sense, necessary for the Church, how much more necessary must it not be, in after ages? If, when Tradition was still recent and the Apostles were still alive, Christ wished some one to strengthen His followers, in the faith, can we reasonably suppose that, after the lapse of centuries, when the Church is obliged to maintain so fearful a combat against error, He would not provide His Church with an infallible doctrinal tribunal? In matters of faith, which excludes even the possibility of error, nothing less than an infallible authority can sufficiently strengthen the believer against the many assaults, to which he is exposed. Every Pope may therefore say, with Innocent III: "Were I not strong in the faith, how could I confirm others in the faith? Yet this belongs to my office, as is evident from the words of Christ: 'I have prayed for thee, that thy faith fail not: and thou being once converted, confirm thy brethren.'" *

"*Nisi ego solidatus essem in fide, quomodo alios possem in fide firmare, quod ad officium meum*

* Inn. serm. ii, de Cons. Pont.

noscitur specialiter pertinere, protestante Domino: Ego royavi pro te."

Bossuet again expresses himself as follows, in his Meditations on the Gospels: "The mission of confirming the faithful was not given to Peter only, but was attached to his office, which, according to the intention of Christ, was to last forever. Peter must always abide in his Church, in order to 'confirm his brethren'—*Semper in Ecclesia Petrus debuit existere, qui fratres confirmaret.*" Even in his Defense, we read: "It is in virtue of their office, that Peter and, through him, his successors have received the command of confirming their brethren—*Hoc ergo ex officio Petrus habet, hoc Petri successores in Petro acceperunt, ut fratres confirmare jubeantur.*" *

"Christ prayed for Peter," remarks the same author, "not because he was less solicitous for the rest of the Apostles, but because, in the language of the Holy Fathers, He, by strengthening the head, wished to prevent the members from staggering." †

"The Church," writes St. Francis de Sales, "is always in need of an unerring strengthener, to whom we may address ourselves; of a founda-

---

* Lib. x, Def. c. 3. † Med. 70 and 72 day.

tion, which the powers of hell, and particularly those of *error*, can not overthrow; of a shepherd, who can not lead her children astray. The Holy Father is therefore invested with the prerogatives of St. Peter, which are not attached to his person, but to the office." *L'église a toujours besoin d'un confirmateur infallible, au quel on puisse s' addresser, d'un fondement que les portes d'enfer et principalment d'erreur ne puissent renverser, et que son pasteur ne puisse conduire a l'erreur ces enfans. Les successeurs donc de St. Pierre ont tous les mêmes privileges, qui ne suivent pas la personne, mais la dignité et la charge publique.*"

And again, when he compared the Popes with the High Priests of the Old Covenant, he remarks that the former, as well as the latter, bear on their breasts the sacred *Urim* and *Thumim;* that is, *Doctrine* and *Truth*. The saint assigns as a reason, that no right was given to Agar, the handmaid, which was not conferred, in a still more eminent degree, on Sarah, the wife.

After the Resurrection, Christ, having heard Peter's triple protestation of love, formally installed him as head of the Church, saying to him: "Feed my lambs, feed my sheep."*

* John xxi, 15, 16, 17.

Now, as the food here meant is the doctrine of salvation and sanctification, and as Christ could never expose His whole flock to the inevitable danger of being led to noxious and fatal pastures, by those whom he had set over them as the supreme shepherd, we are warranted in the inference that as vicars of Christ, Peter and his successors can not fall into any doctrinal error. "From the shepherd I expect protection for the flock," writes St. Jerome to Pope Damasus. Nothing, indeed, is more natural or proper. Remark, moreover, that, according to the manifest declaration of Christ, this flock comprises not only the lambs, but also the sheep. Hence all the Fathers concur, with the great St. Eucharius, in interpreting the above text to mean, that not only the common faithful, but also their pastors, are bound to listen to their chief Pastor, the successor of Peter, the Vicar of Christ. "He has made Peter not merely an ordinary shepherd, but the shepherd of shepherds." "*Sed et pastorum ipsum constituit pastorem.*" *

Therefore, as, according to the first two texts, nobody can be a member of the true Church, unless he yields obedience to the teachings of St. Peter, who speaks by the mouth of the Sovereign Pon-

---

* Hom. in vig. Sti. Petri.

tiff, so, according to the present text, nobody can belong to the flock of Christ, unless he is nourished, with the food of doctrine, by the chief shepherd, who can always distinguish the sweet and wholesome pasture of faith from the rank and poisonous weeds of error.

These are consequences, at which the thinking mind readily arrives, without at all straining the words of Christ, into an unnatural meaning. Indeed they flow so necessarily from universally admitted principles, that they appear more like self-evident truths, than like deductions, seen by the reflected light of logical sequence.

Yet, the strength of this scriptural argument is greatly augmented and wonderfully illustrated by the testimony of Tradition, transmitted to us, without interruption, by the writings of the Holy Fathers, to which we shall now appeal.

II.

TESTIMONY OF THE HOLY FATHERS

FROM THE BEGINNING OF THE CHRISTIAN ERA, UNTIL THE DAYS OF ST. BERNARD, PROCLAIMING THE SEE OF ST. PETER AT ROME TO BE THE HIGHEST TRIBUNAL IN MATTERS OF FAITH.

It is not a little gratifying, to meet even in the Apostolic age, with evidences in proof of the Supreme Authority exercised in matters of faith, by the successors of St. Peter.

Hermas, a disciple of St. Paul's, mentioned in the Epistle to the Romans, Chap. xvi, wrote a book entitled "Pastor," which seems to have been held in great esteem, by contemporaries. The author himself tells us, that he was ordered to send his work to Clement, at Rome, that the Vicar of Christ, to whom it belonged to decide all questions bearing upon the dogmas of faith, might circulate the treatise among the other Churches, should he think it for the interest of religion. Now, at the time of Hermas, St. John the Evangelist was still alive. Yet, the writer was not called upon to submit his work to the aged Apostle, but to Clement, the successor of St. Peter. What a striking example of the Supreme authority, in matters of faith, exercised by the Roman Pontiff. We can not but hail, exultingly, the entire conformity, in point of doctrine and practice, between the first days of the Christian era and our own times.

St. Ignatius, likewise a Bishop of the Apostolic age, and a disciple of St. John's, states, in his letter to the Romans, that the doctrinal decisions of the successors of St. Peter are authoritative. "*Quæ docendo præcipitis.*" But he, that, by merely teaching a certain doctrine, can lay another under the obligation of teaching the same, must evidently possess supreme judiciary power to decide between right and wrong, true or false. This authority of the Roman See, recognized at so early a date, has plainly no other origin or warrant than the divine institution of the Primacy, as invested with that privilege.

St. Polycarp, the disciple of St. Ignatius, purposely went to Rome to learn from Pope St. Anicetus, what rule he was to follow in fixing the time for the celebration of Easter. Such a journey, undertaken by one of the oldest Bishops of the Church, evinces his solicitude to draw the waters of truth from their fountain source. Were there not other Apostolic Sees much nearer than that of Rome? Aye, was he not a disciple of Ignatius, the disciple of John the Evangelist? Yet men, taught by Bishops of the almost Apostolical age, the wisdom of faith, bend their steps toward the Eternal City, in order to assure themselves of the faith and discipline of the first among the Churches.

St. Irenæus, the disciple of St. Polycarp, writes upon this subject: "All the Churches must depend on the Church of Rome as on their source and head." "*Omnes a Romana Ecclesia necesse est pendeant, tamquam a fonte et capite.*"* The reason, which he assigns, is the preëminent superiority—the "*potior principalitas*"—of the Church of Rome. This precedence in ecclesiastical matters, acknowledged at so early a date, can be ascribed to nothing but the supremacy of St. Peter, who fixed his residence at Rome, and, by his prerogative of Infallibility, made it the incorruptible channel of Apostolic tradition. "*Ad hanc enim Ecclesiam necesse est omnem convenire Ecclesiam, in qua semper ab his, qui sunt*

---
* Iren. lib. 3, adv. hæres.

undique fideles, conservata est ea, quæ ab Apostolis est, traditio." "If we remain firm in our allegiance, to the See of Peter," proceeds the Saint, "we shall easily disconcert the malice of those, who, either through conceitedness or bad faith, broach new-fangled theories, at variance with sound doctrine." "*Confundimus omnes eos, qui sibi placentia, vel per vanam gloriam vel per cæcitatem et malam sententiam, præterquam oportet colligunt.*"* The words of this venerable Father of the primitive Church are decisive. Even the fastidious Quesnel bowed his head before the authority of this great Father, who, passing from the East to the West, was a living witness to the faith of the Greek as well as of the Latin Church.

TERTULLIAN, who, like Irenæus, belongs to the second century, styles the Church of Rome a blessed Church, in which the Princes of the Apostles sealed the *faith* with their blood, and from which all authority emanates—"*unde nobis quoque auctoritas præsto est. De præser. c. 27.*" That this authority referred, in a special manner, to matters of doctrine, and served as a rule of faith to all the Christians of his time, we may gather from the following declaration of the same Father: "I learn," says he, "that a very peremptory decree has been issued. The Sovereign Pontiff, the

* Iren. l. 5. adv. hæres.

Bishop of Bishops, declares, '*Audio edictum fuisse publicatum, et quidem peremptorium Summus Pontifex, Episcopus Episcoporum dicit:*'"*

In this connection, we can not but refer to the illustrious Confession of St. Hypolitus, whose history is thus briefly summed up in the Roman Martyrology: "At Antioch, the martyrdom of St. Hypolitus, a priest, who offered his neck to the executioner, with the words, 'We are bound to profess that faith, which is preserved in its purity by the See of Peter'—'*eam fidem dicens esse servandam, quam Petri Cathedra custodiret.*'"

ORIGEN, who flourished about the same time († 253), adds the tribute of his mighty genius to that of the other early writers. "Consider," remarks he, "what must be the power and authority of Peter, the *living rock*, upon which the Church was built, and whose decisions have as much force and validity as oracles emanating from the mouth of Christ Himself. "*Ut ejus judicia maneant firma, quasi Deo judicante per eam.*" †

ST. CYPRIAN († 258) writes to his friend, Pope Cornelius: "All heresies and schisms have sprung from a disregard for the one Priest and *Judge*, to whom Christ has delegated His power. For if, in compliance with the intentions of our Lord, every member of the Christian Community

* Lib. de Pudic.   † Orig. Caten.

TESTIMONY OF THE HOLY FATHERS. 37

yielded a docile obedience to the representative of God, the unity of the Church would never be rent." "*Nec unus in Ecclesia ad tempus sacerdos, et ad tempus judex vice Christi cogitatur, cui si secundum magisteria divina obtemperaret fraternitas universa, nemo Ecclesiam scinderet.*" *

The same author indignantly exclaims: "They dare approach the chair of Peter, without reflecting that to the Romans no error can have access." "*Ad Petri cathedram navigare audent, non cogitantes eos esse Romanos, ad quos perfidia non possit habere accessum.*" † "One God," he exclaims, "one Christ and one Church, founded, by the Lord, upon Peter." ‡

Other portions of the Saint's writings are, if possible, even more explicit still. In a letter, addressed to a certain Anthony, he identifies the Pope with the whole Church. "You desire me to forward your epistle to Cornelius, because you wish to satisfy His Holiness that you live in communion with Him, that is, with the Church." "*Te secum, hoc est, cum Ecclesia Catholica communicare.*" §

The same spirit runs through his letter of felicitation to Pope Lucius, who had been delivered from prison. After pouring out his generous

* Epist. iv ad. Corn. Pont. † On Novatian and his adherents.
‡ Epist. 48 and 49. § Epist. 43.

soul in words of congratulation, he gives it as his conviction that Almighty God specially interposed in favor of the Pontiff, to show *heretics*, which is the true Church and who is the one designed by Heaven as the chief Pastor of souls.

St. Athanasius († 373) writes to Pope Felix II: "You are the destroyer of the heresies, which devastate the Church; you are the teacher and guardian of sound doctrine and unerring faith." "*Tu profanarum hæresum depositor, doctor et princeps orthodoxæ doctrinæ et immaculatæ fidei existis.*"

The Fathers assembled in the Synod of Alexandria remind the same Pope that the Church, which they represent, has always solicited and obtained assistance from the Holy See, because the chair of Peter was established on an immovable foundation, and designed, by Christ, to serve as a model for all other Churches, and as a pivot, upon which they rest and turn. "*Ipsa enim firmamentum a Deo fixum et immobile percepit, quoniam ipsam formam universorum lucidissimam Dominus Jesus Christus vestram Apostolicam constituit sedem. Ipsa enim sacer vertex, in quo omnes Ecclesiæ vertuntur, sustentantur, relevantur.*" *

---

* Epist. Syn. Alex. ad Felicem II.

In a work, which owes its authorship to Moehler, and bears the title "*Athanasius the Great, and the Church of his time,*" we find the following pertinent reflection: "As the Pope succeeds to the authority of Peter, and thus becomes the head, with which all the members form an organic whole, the several Churches should be guided, in matters of faith, by his controlling care. When the Arian heresy devastated the fairest fields of the Church, and, with the malignity inspired by hatred, aimed its missiles, in a special manner, against Athanasius, all the Catholics, no less than this noble champion of the truth, instinctively looked toward the Holy See for support. Thence resulted a marvelous union of forces. Those who advocated the divinity of the invisible head, appealed to the visible head, and, when assured of his favor and countenance, they cheerfully returned to their homes to offer the remainder of their lives as a holocaust on the altar of the faith. Thus the history of Athanasius is like an epitome of the history of the Primacy, at that epoch. The record of his fortunes and his devotion is not a mere episode, a bare recital of isolated facts, but an abridgment of the most momentous events, which are felt, in their effects, by the remotest posterity."

The thought so happily expressed by this learned author, is well exemplified in our own times, when again the eyes of all Catholics instinctively look upon Pius IX, who, by his energy, is daily strengthening the bonds of Catholic unity.

In a letter of ST. BASIL's († 378), forwarded by the Deacon Sabinus to Pope St. Damasus, we read the following: "To your Holiness it is given to distinguish the adulterated and spurious from the pure and orthodox, and to teach, without alteration, the faith of our forefathers." The holy Doctor then subjoins: "We pray and conjure your Holiness to send letters and legates to your children in the Orient, that we may be confirmed in the faith, if we have followed the path of truth, or be reproved, if we have gone astray. There is no one but your Holiness, to whom we can turn for help." "*Pietati tuæ donatum est a Domino, scilicet ut, quod adulterinum est, a legitimo et puro discernas et fidem patrum sine ulla subtractione prædices.*"*

OPTATUS, the learned and well-known Bishop of Melevi († 390), is the author of a book, entitled "*Contra Parmenianum,*" in which he invokes, against some erratic spirits of his day, the au-

---

* Ep: 71, 74, 77.

thority of the Roman See, established by St. Peter. "Thou knowest," remarks he, "and thou darest not deny, that at Rome, Peter established the Episcopal Chair, which he was the first to occupy, thus securing to all the blessings of perfect unity." "*In qua una Cathedra Unitas ab omnibus servaretur.*"*

The Donatists themselves, conscious of the prevailing belief, which regarded Rome as the infallible teacher of Christian nations, seeking to give to their errors the semblance of orthodoxy, maintained, at the center of the Christian world, a bishop of their own choosing, to make the faithful of Africa believe that Rome tolerated their errors, and remained in communion with them.

The views, entertained by St. AMBROSE († 397), on the prerogative of the Roman See, are manifest, as well from his verbal declarations, as from his personal relations with the Sovereign Pontiff. In a letter, which he, in concert with other Bishops, addressed to Pope SIRICIUS, the saintly Prelate gives utterance to the following sentiment: "In the pastorals of your Holiness, we recognize the care of the shepherd, who watches the entrance of the sheep-fold; who protects from

* Contr. Parmenianum.

harm the flock intrusted to him by our Lord; who, in fine, deserves to be followed and obeyed by all. As you well know the tender lambkins of the Lord, you keep guard against the wolves, and like a vigilant shepherd, prevent them from dispersing the fold." "*Dignus, quem oves Domini audiant et sequantur; et ideo, quia nosti oviculas Christi, lupos deprehendis et occurris quasi providus pastor, ne isti morsibus perfidia sua feralique ululatu dominicum ovile dispergant.*"

But the unity of the fold, here referred to, demands above all unity of *faith*.

In compliance with an ordinance from the Pope, the holy Doctor forbade the troublesome Jovinians the Episcopal city of Milan.

In a funeral oration on his brother Satyrus, he eulogized the zeal of the deceased in the cause of the Roman Church, and alluded, with undisguised satisfaction, to his custom of inquiring from all, whom he chanced to meet, whether they were in communion with the See of Peter. If Satyrus discovered that they had failed in this respect, he rebuked them, because he considered that thereby they had cut themselves loose from the communion of the whole Church.

In his forty-seventh sermon, the Saint advanced the principle: "Where Peter is, there is the Church." "*Ubi Petrus, ibi ecclesia.*" If this axiom is once admitted, it is plain that Peter and his successors, when acting as vicars of Christ, can never err in doctrinal decisions. If they could, the Church herself would be in error. But this supposition destroys the very idea of the church. Therefore, according to St. Ambrose, Peter and his successors can never lapse into error.

A passage in the eleventh sermon of the Holy Bishop bears upon the same point: "Peter is the immovable basis, which supports the entire superstructure of Christianity." *"Petrus, saxum immobile, totius operis Christiani compagem molemque continet."* The Church of Rome, he exclaims, may have sometimes been tempted, but it has never been altered. *"Aliquando tentata, mutata nunquam."* *

St. Epiphanius, at the end of the fourth century, and St. Chrysostom, at the beginning of the fifth, fully acknowledged this sovereign tribunal in matters of faith. The latter's appeal to the center of unity has been justly styled by Dr. Rothensee the most forcible and eloquent exposition which the golden-tongued orator could have made of his belief in the apostolical authority of the Pope as the Supreme Judge in the Church.†

* Lib. 2, de fide ad Gratianum.
† See also the striking declaration of the same Father on the same subject, Hom. ii. in Act. Ap. Hom. 24 in Matth. xi, Lib. ii. de Sac. c. i. Hom. in Ps. 50 and 51.

St. Jerome († 420), whom the Church calls, in her liturgy: "the greatest expounder of the Sacred Writings," thus addresses Pope Damasus: "I hold fast to the chair of Peter, upon whom the Church is built. Decide as you please; if you order, I shall not hesitate to profess my belief in three hypostases." "*Beatitudini tuæ i. e., Cathedræ Petri communioni consortior; supra illam Petram ædificatam ecclesiam scio. Discerne si placet; non timebo tres hypostases dicere, si jubebis.*" Meanwhile I shall declare to the whole world: "If any person is firm in his allegiance to the chair of Peter, he is of my mind; for I hold with the successors of the fisherman. He that does not gather with you scatters; that is, he that is not of Christ is of Antichrist." "*Qui tecum non colligit, spargit; hoc est, qui non est Christi, Antichristi est.*"

In his treatise against Ruffinus, he bursts forth into this brief profession of faith: "The Roman Church can not countenance error, though an angel should come to teach it."

St. Augustin († 430), reminding the Donatists of the unbroken succession of the Roman Pontiffs, thus addresses them: "Number all the High Priests who followed one another in that sacred lineage; every one of them is that rock against which the gates of hell shall not prevail."

"*Ipsa est Petra quam non vincunt superbæ inferi portæ.*"*

He disposes, in a very summary manner, of the endless quibble of the Pelagians, by reminding them that two councils had already referred the matter to Rome, and that an answer had been returned: "Rome has spoken; the question is settled." "*Roma locuta est, causa finita est.*"†

On another occasion he writes to the Pelagians: "By the briefs of Innocent, all doubt upon this subject has been removed." "*Litteris Innocentii, tota hac de re dubitatio sublata est.*"‡

In a treatise against Julian he says: "Why do you call for an investigation, since it has been already made by the See of Rome?" "*Quid quæris examen, quod jam apud Apostolicam sedem factum est.*"§

In his 157th letter he remarks: "The Catholic faith derives so much strength and support from the words of the Apostolic See, that it is criminal to entertain any doubts concerning it." "*In verbis sedis Apostolicæ tam antiqua atque fundata, certa et clara est Catholica fides, ut nefas sit de illa dubitare.*"

In his work on the "Unity of the Church," he discourses in eloquent terms on his relations

---

* In Ps. Contr. Don. † In serm. de verb. Apost.
‡ Lib. ii, c. 3, contr. 2, ep. Pel. § Lib. ii, adv. Jul.

with the Vicar of Christ. "In the Catholic Church," writes he, "I attach myself to the chair of Peter, because the Lord intrusted to him the care of the faithful, and because his authority has descended, through an uninterrupted line of successors, down to our times. The divine Shepherd said: 'My sheep hear my voice, and follow me.' This voice speaks to us, in the clearest manner, from Rome. Whosoever does not wish to stray from the true fold must hearken to this voice." "*Vox ejus de Romana Ecclesia non est obscura. Quisquis ab ejus grege errare non vult, hunc audiat, hunc sequatur.*" *

Thus spoke Augustin, perhaps the most profound thinker among the Holy Fathers, and the best interpreter of his own convictions.

With a transcendent genius, which shrunk from no scrutiny, he threw light upon the obscurest question of divinity, and unraveled the most intricate subtilities of dialectics; yet, when Rome had once returned its infallible verdict, he bowed to the oracular response with the same unquestioning docility with which the humblest pupil would listen to the explanations of his tutor. His testimony alone speaks volumes in favor of the question, which we have undertaken to discuss.

* De unit. Eccl., c. xii.

The Holy Doctor had instilled the same principle into his two distinguished disciples, PROSPER and FULGENTIUS, of Ruspa. The former sings as follows in his poem, "*De ingratis:*"

> "*In causam fidei flagrantius Africa nostræ
> Exequeris; tecumque suum jungente vigorem
> Juris apostolici solio fera viscera belli
> Conficis et lato prosternis limite victos
> Gemino senum celeberrima cœtu
> Decrevit, quæ Roma probet, quæ regna sequantur.*"

In the same poem occur the well-known lines:

> "*Sedes Roma Petri, quæ pastoralis honoris
> Facta caput mundi, quidquid non possidet armis
> Religione tenet.*" *

In Prosper's writings, "*Contra Collatorem,*" we find this passage: "Pope Zosimus had added strength to his decisions, and armed, with the sword of St. Peter, the right hand of all the prelates." "*Papa Zosimus sententia sua robur adnexit, et ad impiorum detruncationem gladio Petri dextras omnium armavit antistitum.*" Does not this sound like the language which, at the present day, we would all hold when speaking of Pius IX?

"We trust," writes our author, in the same

---

* Carm. de ingrat.

work, "that, what happened in the case of Innocent, Zosimus, Boniface, and Celestine, will again happen in the case of Sixtus; and that, as, with the help of God, they were able to repulse the open assaults of the visible wolves, who leaped upon the fold in broad daylight, so he may defeat the secret designs of the invisible wolf, who prowls about for prey under the cover of night."*

FULGENTIUS, the other disciple of the illustrious Bishop of Hippo, thus consoles the afflicted Church of Africa: "Let not your courage fail; have recourse to Rome, the mother of the true faith. What Rome believes, all Christianity believes." †

Quite as remarkable as the above is the testimony of Maximian, the Patriarch of Constantinople, whose love for the Holy See found vent in the following expression: "From the farthest extremity of the globe, the confessors of the true faith look up to the Pope, as to the sun. God has raised him to the instructor's chair, with an indefeasible right of occupying it forever. All, therefore, who would learn the divine lessons of religion, must consult him." "*Cui cathedram magisterii, perpetuo privilegii jure concessit, ut*

* C. l, x, xll.   † Lib. de Incarn.

quisquis divinum aliquod sive profundum nosse desiderat, ad hujus præceptionis oraculum doctrinamque recurrat."*

St. Cyril († 444), alluding to his relations with Nestorius, writes to Pope Celestine: "We did not publicly break off all intercourse with *Nestorius*, before advising with your Holiness. We, therefore, conjure you to acquaint us with your desire, that we may make it our rule of conduct, and may know, beyond the shadow of a doubt, whether in future, we are to hold correspondence with him, or to dissolve, at once, all connection. For, as members of the mystical body of the Church, it is incumbent on us to follow our head, the Roman Pontiff, who holds in trust the deposit of Apostolic faith. From him we must learn what we are bound to believe, think, and hold." "*Inde nostrum est quærere, quid credendum, quid opinandum, quid tenendum sit.*" †

"The Bishop of Rome we shall venerate and consult, before all others, because he alone is commissioned to reprimand, to correct, to ordain, to dispose, to bind and to loose, in place of Him, who has established him in his office and delegated to him alone the plenitude of authority.

* Ep. ad Orientales.   † Hard. viii, 1829.

All, therefore, do him homage, and the prelates of the earth obey him, as Christ." "*Ipsius solius est reprehendere, corrigere, statuere, disponere, ligare et solvere loco illius, qui ipsum ædificavit, et nulli alii quod suum est plene, sed ipsi soli dedit; cui omnes, jure divino, caput inclinant, et primates mundi tamquam ipsi Jesu Christo obediunt.*"*

St. Peter Chrysologus († 450), writes to the heresiarch Eutychius: "We entreat you to harken especially, to the decision of the Pope at Rome, and to abide, with all readiness, by his final sentence; because Peter, who lives and governs in his own See, returns to those, who consult him, the answer of truth." "*Quoniam B. Petrus, qui in propria Sede vivit et præsidet, præstat quærentibus fidei veritatem.*" †

The testimony of the two ecclesiastical historians, Socrates and Sozomenus, both Greeks, likewise belongs to this century and, for obvious reasons, claims a special notice in our pages. Socrates affirms that without the sanction of the Bishop of Rome, "nothing of importance can be done in the Church of God." ‡ But nothing certainly is of more vital importance than decisions concerning the dogmas of faith.

---

* Lib. Thesaur. † Ep. ad Eutych. inter Acta Conc. Ephes.
‡ Socr. ii, 8, 15, 17, and iv, 37.

Sozomenus testifies, that whatever is done without the approval of Rome is null and void. "*Irrita esse, quæ præter sententiam Episcopi Romani constituuntur.*" *

Let us listen to the words of the illustrious Doctor and ecclesiastical historian, THEODORET, (†460) Bishop of Cyprus, whose diocese was one of the largest in the East, numbering no less than 800 parishes. Having been deposed and excommunicated by the local Synod of Ephesus, and thrown into prison by order of the Emperor, he laid his cause before the Holy See, and sought redress for his grievances, at the hands of the Pope, whom he styles the Father of Christians and the *judge in matters of faith*. Mark, how he justifies this course of action: "If St. Paul, the herald of the faith, appealed to St. Peter, for the solution of the difficulties, which disturbed the tranquillity of the Christian Church at Antioch, how much more does it behoove us to have recourse to the Apostolic See, in our troubles?" "*Si Paulus, præco veritatis, ad magnum Petrum cucurrit, ut iis, qui Antiochiæ contenderent, ab ipso afferret solutionem, quanto magis nos ad apostolicam sedem vestram currimus.*"

In allusion to this subject, Gerbert makes the

* Soz. iii, 8, 9, and vi, 39.

appropriate reflection, that, like so many others in the first ages of the Church, Theodoret did not appeal to the Pope as to a powerful man, but as to the successor of St. Peter.

While his case was still pending, he besought the Cardinal Renatus to urge the Holy Father to decide the question. "For," writes he, "the See of Rome has the headship and direction of all the Churches throughout the world; and that for many reasons, but especially because she has never been tainted by heresy nor governed by a man of dangerous tendency in matters of faith."
"*Habet enim Sma. illa Sedes omnium per orbem ecclesiarum ducatum et principatum, multis quidem de causis, atque hac ante omnia, quod ab hæretica labe immunis mansit, nec ullus fidei contraria sentiens in ea sedit.*"*

It was for the same purpose, that Theodoret, about this time, addressed a letter to the Archdeacon of Rome.

So general was the belief in this prerogative of the Holy See, that it was embodied even in the Rituals of the Church. You may take up

---

* Further on we shall see that Leo the Great did not disappoint the confidence reposed in him. In the present chapter, in which it is our purpose to sum up some of the most remarkable passages from the Holy Fathers, we designedly avoid all citations from the Popes, in order to present them, under one head, hereafter.

the old Missal, edited by Muratori and Peter Bellarini. Turning to the Mass for the feast of S. S. Peter and Paul, you will find in the Preface the following words: "God has so firmly established the Apostolic See, on the ground-work of truth, that it can never be moved by the shocks of falsehood; and, therefore, in conformity with the designs of Heaven, all the faithful devoutly embrace the doctrine taught by that See, to which the government of the whole Church has been confided." "*Ut in veritatis tuæ fundamine solidata, nulla mortifera falsitatis jura praevaleant. Quæ (Ecclesia), te dispensante, devota subsequitur, quid Sedes illa censuerit, quam tenere voluisti totius Ecclesiæ principatum.*"

Similar expressions occur in the 20th Mass, which represents the See of Rome as the one, to whose guidance God has intrusted the whole Church, and whose teachings He requires to be implicitly followed every where. "*Ut quid hæc prædicasset, ostenderes ubique servandum.*"

The Church of Spain, having met in the Council of Tarragona, 465, wrote to Pope Hilary: "We rely on that faith, whose encomium was pronounced by the mouth of the Apostle, and wait for an answer from that See, whose decrees have never been tainted with error." "*Ad fidem recurrimus apostolico laudatam ore, inde responsa quærentes, unde nihil errore, sed pontificali totum deliberatione præcipitur."*

About the same time, St. Avitus, acting in the name and with the authority of all the Bishops of France, expressed the belief of the whole Gallican Church, in a written communication, addressed to the Roman Clergy, relative to the election of Pope Symmachus: "When any doubt occurs about the Papal election, not one Bishop only, but the whole hierarchy appears to be wavering."

In another letter to Rome, the Saint avers: "Whenever any difference arises, in Church matters, it is our duty to abide by the decisions of the Sovereign Pontiff, and, as members of the Church, to follow our head." *"Ut membra sequentia."* Then he adds: "The truth is known to us, in so far only, as the Roman Pontiff, in virtue of the prerogative of his authority, is pleased to explain himself to those that apply to him." *"Tantum mihi veritas innotescere poterit, quantum se Romanæ urbis antistes, auctoritatis privilegio, expetentibus respondisse gaudebit."*

In the homilies of this Holy Prelate, the same thought occurs again and again.*

Should the present volume chance to fall into

---

* Galand, x, p. 746.

the hands of non-Catholics, we would respectfully invite their attention to the fact, that all the citations, hitherto given, are taken from writers, who flourished during the first five centuries of the Christian era; a period, during which, according to the admission of nearly all Protestants, the doctrine of the Catholic Church was still the unadulterated teaching of the Apostles. It seems to us, therefore, that even the most skeptical reader can take no exception to these testimonies, or raise objections, which might tend to invalidate the arguments based upon such premises.

Herewith we enter upon the sixth century, in which the first authority of note is POSSESSOR, the Bishop of Africa. His opinion is clear, from a letter in which he thus addresses the Holy Father: "Whom can we ask, with greater right, for strength, in our wavering faith, than the incumbent of that See, whose first head received his appointment from Christ himself, with the words: 'Thou art Peter, and upon this rock I will build my Church.'" "*Aut a quo magis nutantis fidei stabilitas expectanda, quam ab ejus Sedis præside, cujus primus a Christo rector audivit: Tu es Petrus.*"

How significant this evidence, which comprises, as in a nutshell, not only the right, by which this prerogative is vested in the successors of St. Peter, but likewise the matter upon which it is exercised, and the reason which renders it indispensable to the Church of God.

About this time, the learned Archdeacon Ferandus, of Carthage (†505), wrote to a scholastic of Constantinople: "We are ready to learn and not to teach. If you are anxious to know the truth, you must address yourself to the head of the Apostolic See."

In a letter to the Deacon Pelagius, the same writer calls Rome the head of the world—"*cacumen mundi;*" not, of course, in civil, but in ecclesiastical matters, inasmuch as the approval and confirmation of the Holy See are necessary, to give to the decisions and enactments of Synods any binding force. He expresses the same conviction, in a work, entitled "*Compendium Canonum Ecclesiasticorum.*" Voices from the East proclaim the same conviction.

STEPHEN, the Metropolitan of Larissa, in Thessaly († 532), maltreated by Epiphanius, the Patriarch of Constantinople, determined to expose his grievances to the Pope. But, detained in prison and unable to sue for the coveted favor in person, the appellant Prelate dispatched Theodosius of Echina, one of his suffragans, to lay before the Pope a written petition, wherein he says: "No ecclesiastical rank can set aside the authority given to you by Christ, our Savior and Chief Pastor." "*Nullus ecclesiasticus ordo illam vestram, quæ a Salvatore omnium et primo Pastore Vobis est collata, potest excellere potestatem.*"

Stephen stood unmoved by the clamors of partisanship, and in justification of his course flung into the face of opposition the belief of Christendom. "In the recognition of the Holy See, all the Churches of Christendom acquiesce." "*In cujus confessione omnes mundi Ecclesiæ requiescunt.*"

His proxy held the same sort of language before the Pope in Rome.

Not less striking, in some of its features, is the testimony borne to the truth by the African Bishop, FACUNDUS HERMIANENSIS († 553), in his book "*Pro defensione trium Capitulorum.*" Though an avowed schismatic, he plainly and repeatedly acknowledges the Holy See as the supreme tribunal in matters of faith.

The same belief is learnedly set forth in the writings of the severe British moralist, GILDAS, who died, according to Usher, 570.* In a scathing treatise, entitled "*Increpatio in Clerum,*" he solemnly declares, that the fullness of the Episcopal authority resides in the See of Rome, and

* De primord. Eccl. Brit.

thence flows through *all the branches* of the ecclesiastical hierarchy. Now, if it be true that the Holy See is the source and spring of all ecclesiastical authority, she must be so, in a special manner, in doctrinal matters.

The conduct of the courageous Abbot, COLUMBANUS († 515), is likewise illustrative of the same views, with respect to the present question. Like many others, he was desirous to obtain a definite settlement of the question relative to the Easter celebration. Accordingly he addressed Pope Boniface by letter, and humbly submitted his ideas to the consideration of the Holy Father. Thus, after referring to the traditions of the Scotch and Irish Churches, he subjoined, as though fearful of forcing his personal convictions on the attention of the Holy See: "We state these particulars in order to impart information, and not with the view of influencing the decisions of your Holiness; for that were simply ridiculous." "*Nec loci namque nec ordinis est, ut magnæ tuæ auctoritati aliquid quasi discutiendo irrogetur, et ridiculose, te Petri Apostoli et clavicularii legitime Cathedram insedentem, mei occidentales apices de Pascha sollicitent.*"*

In another letter relative to the question of

---

* Galland, xii, 345.

the "Three Chapters," (*de tribus Capitulis*), he writes to the Pope: "I assured the Irish, that the Roman See would never give its support to one who advocated heretical doctrines. Use, then, your sovereign authority, and place yourself at the head of the armies now mingling in the contest for truth. For on you the issue of the contest depends." "*Ad te namque totius exercitus Domini periculum pertinet. Te totum expectat, qui potestatem habes omnia ordinandi.*" "We have no hope," writes he, "except in the power and authority, which you have inherited from St. Peter." "*Quia unica spes de principibus es, per honorem potens Petri Apostoli.*" And again: "Though Rome is celebrated for many other reasons, it is great in our eyes, by reason of that chair alone." "*Licet enim Roma magna est et vulgata, per istam Cathedram tantum apud nos est magna et clara.*"

Like Prosper, Columbanus remarks that the supremacy of Christian Rome is acknowledged, where the dominion of Pagan Rome has never been felt. "Never," suggests he, "did the Cæsars plant the imperial standard on the shores of Ireland; but your Holiness reigns over the islands of the sea, as well as in your capital. We are a province of the new Rome, which the presence of the Vicar of Christ has almost transformed into a heavenly abode." "*Et, si dici potest, prope cœlestes estis.*"

The historian Bercastell informs us, that, at this epoch, in particular, the approving looks of the Christian community were centered upon England, Ireland and Scotland, whose respectful attachment to the Holy See discovered itself, in the numberless pilgrimages that were set on foot. The highways and thoroughfares betweeen England and Rome always were alive with a devout multitude of all classes and conditions. Laymen and monks, priests and bishops, even princes and kings, such as Ceadwalla, Renred and Offa bent their steps toward the Eternal City, to do homage to the Vicar of Christ.*

The Oriental Churches of this period were no less devoted to the Holy See, whose infallibility they recognized, with unquestioning submission. Thus, in a synodical letter written by SOPHRONIUS, immediately (636) upon his accession to the *Patriarchate of Jerusalem*, the distinguished Prelate declares, that the rescript of Leo is a rule of faith, which together with all the papal bulls and briefs he and the other Bishops of the East receive, regard, and respect, as emanating from Peter himself.

* Berc vi, 274.

TESTIMONY OF THE HOLY FATHERS. 61

These sentiments were openly indorsed by all the orthodox Prelates, who subsequently deputed STEPHEN, the Bishop of Dora, to solicit the assistance of the Holy See against the dangerous sect of the Monothelites. On his arrival, the Bishop presented a memorial setting forth the troubles that afflicted the Eastern Church, which breathed throughout a spirit of child-like confidence in the Vicar of Christ. "With David we could wish," say the petitioners, "to have the wings of a dove, that we might fly to you and implore you to heal our wounds. Peter, from whom you hold the plenitude of Apostolical authority, was not only commissioned to keep the Keys of Heaven and to feed the lambs of the Lord, but was moreover endued with indefectible faith and commanded to confirm his faltering brethren. Thus he was empowered to exercise over all the authority of God become incarnate for all."

"Under this conviction," added Stephen, "Sophronius conducted me to Calvary, and, on the spot sanctified by the awful mystery of the Redemption, gave me this solemn injunction: 'Speed thee, in all haste, to the Apostolic See, on which the foundations of the true faith rest.' '*Ubi orthodoxorum dogmatum fundamenta existunt.*' 'Urge the Vicar of Christ to pronounce his judgment, with that Apostolic prudence, which is from God, in order that we may weed the Church of the novelties, which have of late sprung up amongst us.' In compliance with this order, I am come hither, to prostrate myself at your feet, supplicating and imploring you to stretch out your hands and shield the imperiled faith of Christ's little ones." "*Propter hoc properavi vestris apostolicis adesse vestigiis, expetens et deprecans, ut fidei Christianorum periclitanti manum porrigere, etc.*"

"Accede, then, Holy Father! to this request, which I prefer in behalf of all the Orientals, and as a shining lamp, which diffuses over the face of the Universe the light of the Gospel, dispel the shades of heresy." "*Sed sicut luminaria in universo mundo verbum vitæ retinentes, introductas extinguite tenebras hæresum.*"

A memorial to the Pope, drawn up by thirty-seven Archimandrites, Priests, Deacons, and Monks, in the name of all the Orientals, reëchoed the views expressed by Stephen. The dispositions which dictated this document, may be judged from its own words: "We pray, implore, and conjure the Apostolic See, to pronounce upon this matter." "*Petimus, interpellamus, et conjuramus Apostolicam sedem.*" *

* Hard. iii, 711.

On the same occasion, Sergius, the Bishop of Cyprus, wrote to the Pope: "According to the declaration of Eternal Truth, you are Peter, and upon the ground-work of your faith the columns of the Church are erected." "*Tu enim sicut divinum veraciter pronuntiat verbum, Petrus, et super fundamentum tuum Ecclesiæ columnæ confirmatæ sunt.*" "You keep the keys of the Kingdom of Heaven; you have the power of binding and loosing, both in Heaven and on Earth; you are the censor of pernicious errors and the teacher of indefectible faith." "*Tu princeps et doctor immaculatæ fidei.*"

The African Bishops of Numidia, Mauritania and Byzantium, emulating the example of their brethren, likewise presented an address, in which they discoursed, in the following terms, upon the prerogatives of the Pope: "There can be no doubt, that, like a pure and inexhaustible spring, the Apostolic See pours its waters, in a constant stream, over the whole Christian world. Accordingly, the Fathers have ruled, that in the remotest provinces nothing should be done or undertaken, before being referred to the consideration of the Holy See, by whose approval every proceeding is stamped with the sanction of authority." "*Ut quidquid, quamvis in remotis ageretur regionibus, non prius tractandum vel accipiendum sit, nisi ad notitiam almæ sedis vestræ fuerit deductum, et hujus auctoritate justa quæ fuisset pronuntiatio firmaretur."*

They declare that, from Rome and the Holy See, the other Churches have derived the right of preaching the word of God.

We would fain invite the attention of our readers not only to the marked uniformity of belief, with which the North and South, the East and West recognized the doctrinal Infallibility of the Roman Pontiff, but also to the marvelous similarity of language in which they conveyed their meaning. Even the most superficial observer must be struck by the perfect unity of belief, reflected alike in the unclassic sentences of the austere African and the rounded periods of the polished Greek, in the grotesque imagery of the vivacious Oriental and the sober reality of the phlegmatic Saxon.

The striking unanimity with which the whole Christian world, in the first ages, declared itself in favor of the Infallibility of Christ's representative, and, in particular, the unfeigned submission with which it received the condemnation of Monothelism, were among the most powerful motives that led the illustrious Doctor Newman into the pale of the Church. They taught him that the doctrine of the primitive Church harmonizes in

TESTIMONY OF THE HOLY FATHERS. 65

this, as in every other particular, with that of modern Catholics. His logical mind did not shrink from drawing the inevitable inference, nor his iron will from conforming his life to his belief. Henceforth, he not only subscribed, in theory, to all the tenets of the Catholic creed, but practically did homage to the principle of unity, by recognizing in the Pope the infallible vicegerent of Christ.

Let us now listen to the testimony of St. Maximus, whose versatile genius and wonderful erudition won for him the reputation of an eminent theologian, philosopher, and statesman, and qualified him to be the master of the great Anastasius. He, at first, held the post of imperial secretary, in the cabinet of Constantinople, but, on witnessing the intrigues practiced by the court, he retired from public life and buried himself in the seclusion of a monastery, near Chalcedon. From this holy retreat, in which contemplation only quickened the vigor of his intellect, he wrote a letter, which thus animadverts upon the duplicity of Pyrrhus: "If Pyrrhus wishes to clear himself of the charge of heresy, let him justify his conduct publicly. Let him prove his innocence to the Pope of the Roman Church, that is, to the Apostolic See, which possesses, to the fullest extent, the power of binding and loosing." "*In omnibus et per omnia.*" "Because it is the Eternal Word Himself, who, from the highest Heaven, binds and loosens in the person of the Roman Bishop, His Vicar upon earth. If, then, Pyrrhus justifies himself before prelates of an inferior rank in the Church, instead of making out his cause before the Sovereign Pontiff himself, he resembles a man who, when arraigned for murder or other misdemeanor, would evade the action of the law by establishing his innocence before unauthorized persons, and not before a judge, who has the right of acquitting or condemning him."

Anastasius, faithful to the precepts of his master, always evinced the same reverence toward the Holy See, which, in a letter to the monks of Cagliari, in Sardinia, he designates "as the inexhaustible source of true faith." At this epoch, the faith began to diffuse its light over the north of Europe, and history bears witness to the eagerness with which the first apostles of that vast territory turned to Rome for direction in their doubts, and for counsel in their perplexities. The Holy City witnessed the arrival of a Willibrord, and a Hubert, who quitted the sea-bound shores of the North to visit the Father of the faithful. It witnessed the arrival of a ST. BONIFACE, who received from Pope Gregory II the mission of bearing the tidings of the Gospel to the distant tribes of Germany, with an order to follow the instructions given him, and to address himself, in every difficulty, to the Holy See. When invested with the Episcopal character, Boniface solemnly engaged to maintain inviolably the unity and purity of the Roman Church, aware, as the Pontiff suggested on the occasion, that the Apostle St. Peter is the head both of the Apostolate and the Episcopate. *"Quia B. Petrus Apostolus et Apostolatus et Episcopatus principium existit."*

After replying to an inquiry of the holy Apostle, Gregory remarked: "We answer not thus of ourselves—*non ex nobis, quasi ex nobis*—but in virtue of our Apostolical authority."

How happy would Germany be, and how united in faith, if, in after years, her sons had not forgotten the lessons taught them by their first Apostle, but had ever faithfully reproduced in themselves the example of their sturdy ancestors, whose devotion to the chair of St. Peter merited, from the pen of Boniface himself, the following encomium: "They looked for the doctrine of primitive Christianity in the living oracles of Christ's representative, rather than in the sacred pages, or the traditions of our ancestors in the faith." Because both Holy Writ and tradition are liable to misconstruction and falsification, and can not be known to be the unadulterated Word of God, unless recognized as such, and interpreted under the guidance of a divinely-commissioned teacher, who is the Pope. "*Et antiquam christianæ religionis institutionem magis ab ore prædecessoris ejus quam a sacris paginis et paternis traditionibus expetunt—illius velle—illius nolle tantum expetunt.*"

How is it, children of St. Boniface, that now so many of you are guided by other maxims than those of your first Apostles? Holy faith can not change, because Christ, its author, is always the same, "to-day, yesterday, and forever." You must, then, yourselves, have changed, and by changing, have forfeited the inheritance of the faith. Ah, yes! sadly have you strayed from the way of your forefathers. However, your losses are not irreparable; you may yet be reinstated in your birthright, if you will return and listen, as your ancestors did, to the voice of the Roman Pontiff, the successor of St. Peter, whose disciples were the first heralds of salvation among you.

At the epoch to which the foregoing remarks apply, two luminaries, of the first magnitude, destined to light up, with their effulgence, the West as well as the East, just began to peer above the horizon of the Church. One of these was the profound scholar BEDE, whom St. Boniface himself styled the torch of the Church; while Walafried, Strabo, and William of Malmesbury,* struck at his varied acquirements, declare that he can never be praised as much as he is admired. Even those who are loath to do justice to the superior attainments of the schoolmen, and who affect to sneer at the monkish authors, are forced to pay an unwilling tribute to his learning. It is, then, with great satisfaction that we refer our readers to this complete Encyclopedia of sacred science. Hear how he descants upon the subject in question: "Together with full judicial power on all controverted points of doctrine, Peter received the keys of Heaven, as a sign to all the children of the Church, that if they separate themselves from the one faith, which he teaches, they surrender all hope of being acquitted of their guilt and of entering the eternal portals." †

The same authority writes of king Oswio: "This Saxon recognized the Roman Church as Catholic and Apostolic, because her Sovereign Pontiffs have succeeded each other, in an unbroken line, from St. Peter down." From these

---

* De gest. Angl. III, 3. † Hom. de S. S. Pet. et Paul.

premises he naturally inferred that she is the first, and, therefore, the true Church of Christ.

And here we would remark, in passing, that the validity of this argument, which seemed so conclusive to the Saxon monarch, can not be fairly disputed by professing Christians. For, as the founder of the New Covenant has promised, that His Church, built on the rock, Peter, shall never give way to the assaults of hell, all religious controversy, among the several Christian denominations, must finally resolve itself into the historic question of priority, in point of time. Now, the uninterrupted succession of the Popes, back to the Prince of the Apostles, proves, beyond a doubt, that the Catholic Church is the primitive Church, and therefore the Church of Christ.

The faith of this intelligent Saxon was also that of the Synod held at Calchut. Witness the statutes sent to Rome for approval, and signed by the bishops, abbots, kings, and princes of England, who all unite in doing homage to the Holy See, and express their readiness to believe and do, whatever the Vicar of Christ may see fit to prescribe. The other illustrious luminary, who, at that time attracted the admiration of the Catholic world, was St. John Damascene. He had fallen upon an unhappy age; for heresy stalked over the provinces of the East, and with a spoiler's hand, ravaged and desecrated the sanctuaries of the true faith. Saddened by the outrages daily committed by impiety, which was crowned in the person of Leo, the Iconoclast, the intrepid champion of the faith, exclaims: "Hear, ye peoples and nations of every tongue. Hear, ye young and old. Depart not from the doctrine of the Apostolical Church, even though an angel should come and teach you otherwise." "*Licet angelus evangelizet vobis præter id.*"*

The celebrated Abbot, STEPHAN, expresses himself in a similar manner. About this epoch, Copronymus, the Iconoclast, held a conventicle, which was designated as the Seventh General Council, and afterward dispatched emissaries to notify him of its proceedings. Supported by the highest patronage in the land, these minions of an earthly power approached the illustrious Abbot, who was confined in prison by the Emperor, and, with characteristic arrogance, delivered themselves of their commission, somewhat in this form: "The Seventh General Council decides." Undismayed by the solemn formality of pretentious words, the Confessor of Christ replied with a smile: "How can a Council convene and legislate, without the authority and consent of

* Serm. de Transfiguratione.

the Apostolical See?" His firm attitude silenced these creatures of a heretical court, and foiled all their schemes of intimidation. "We are vanquished," said the imperial commissary, Callistus, to the Emperor; "it is impossible to resist the learning and reasoning of that man."*

In connection with this subject, we can not forbear inserting the declaration of the three Patriarchs who, at that time, governed the Churches of Jerusalem, Alexandria, and Antioch. After informing the Emperor that, in consequence of the irruption of the Saracens, they would be prevented from attending the Synod, they remarked, that their absence would by no means invalidate its decrees, provided the Sovereign Pontiff approved of its convocation, and, through his legates, presided at its meetings and confirmed its actions. In support of their assertion, they cite the Sixth General Council, whose decisions were received by the Church, though the same three provinces were unrepresented.

These circumstances may be built up into a powerful argument. For, if these Patriarchs, with all their suffragans, considered their absence from a General Council as quite immaterial, provided the Pope would exercise the authority vested in

---

* Butler xvii, p. 358.

his person, they evidently did not suppose that the right of imparting validity to a dogmatic decision ultimately resides in the body of the assembled Episcopate, but in the Apostolical Holy See. Why should they deem their presence less necessary than that of others? What was true of them, held with equal force of the other dignitaries of the Church.

The latter half of this century admired the wonderful erudition of ALCUIN, whom Charlemagne associated to himself in the glorious work of literary restoration in France and Germany. This preceptor and friend of one of the most illustrious sovereigns that ever swayed the destinies of Europe, has left a book, entitled "*De Divinis Officiis*," wherein he speaks of the Holy See as the head from which the gifts of grace are diffused through the whole body of the Church. In the same spirit, he wrote to the newly elected Pope, Adrian: "As I acknowledge you for the successor of St. Peter, so I also recognize you as the heir of his wonderful authority." "*Ita et mirificæ potestatis hæredem confiteor.*" "I, therefore, surrender myself entirely to you. Blessed be the tongue of your mouth, which speaks the saving words of life, and at whose bidding the portals of Heaven are opened to the believer." "*O beatissima lingua oris vestri in qua est æterna medicina salutis, per quam cœli aperiuntur credentibus.*"

In a letter to Pope Leo III, he seems at a loss for words to express his profound veneration for the head of the Church. "In you," writes he, "faith is resplendent. Under your pastoral care, the flock of the Lord increases. You are the consolation of the afflicted, the help of the oppressed, the hope of them that call on you, the light of life, the ornament of religion."* These words, addressed to Leo III, well-nigh a thousand years ago, apply, with equal propriety, to the Pontiff now reigning. Is not faith eminently resplendent in Pius IX? Is he not our consolation, our hope, our help, and our protection? To the skeptical ears of reformed Germany these expressions, dictated by the ardent faith of her Alcuin, sound like the uncouth jargon of a barbarous age, but to the faithful they are familiar household words, all the sweeter because they come to us repeated by the distant echoes of a thousand years.

Extracts like the above do not represent the wild fancies of a solitary enthusiast. Agilram, Bishop of Metz, writes to Charlemagne: "Every one knows that the Pope, wielding the power of St. Peter, is authorized to pass sentence on all

---

* Baron. ad annum 772.

the Churches, and is not amenable to another tribunal." *"Utpote quæ (sedes) de omnibus Ecclesiis fas habeat judicandi, neque cuiquam licet de ejus judicare judicio."*

The so-called Carolingian books—*"libri Carolini"*—likewise testify to this common faith of all France and Germany. In allusion to the sedulous care with which Rome watches over the religious instruction of the faithful, these venerable chronicles remind us, that the Holy See presents to all the Churches of the world the chalice of her sublime doctrine. *"Mellifluæ prædicationis pocula Catholicis per orbem ministrat Ecclesiis."* Hence the duty of seeking, in matters of faith, for help from her, who has neither "stain nor wrinkle," and who, while crushing the dragon-head of heresy, strengthens, in the truth, the mind of the believer. *"Ut ab ea post Christum ad muniendam fidem adjutorium petant, quæ non habet maculam, neque rugam et portentosa hæresum capita calcat et fidelium mentes in fide corroborat."* France and Germany owe their confirmation in the faith to the Apostolical See of Rome. *"Inde semper suscepit fidei Chrismata."**

The same convictions are expressed by Aga-

---
* Lib. i, c, 6.

bond, in his letter to Louis the Pious, and by Jonas of Orleans, in a treatise entitled "*De institutione regia.*"

Jesse, Bishop of Amiens (†836), exhorts his clergy to cling to the doctrine of the Holy See, lest the door-keeper of Heaven close the portals against them, should he see them dissent from his teaching.

The religious history of France, at this period, is particularly interesting. Synods met successively at Soissons (867), at Douzi (871), at Pontigny (876), at Troyes (878), at Tribur (895), and in their acts emphatically declared for unquestioning submission to the decisions of the Holy See.

Æneas, of Paris, wrote a book, in which it was his object to prove, by historical documents from the time of Ignatius to that of Photius, that the Pope is not indebted, for his supreme judicial power, to any Council or Synod, but only to Christ, from whom he received it in the person of St. Peter.*

Even in the East, which was now on the eve of a lamentable schism, we see the sun of faith still lingering upon the horizon, and gilding, with its departing glories, the mountain heights of learning. In an address to Leo III, the

---

* Specil. D'Achory, 143, 148.

celebrated Theodore Studita styles the Roman Pontiff the "head of all heads," "*omnium capitum caput*," "τῶν ὅλων κεφαλῶν κεφαλὴν," and strenuously contends, with all the energy of conscious truth, that every novelty broached by those who have strayed away from the right path, falls, of necessity, under the ban of Peter and his successors. "*Ad Petrum utique vel ejus successorem quidquid in ecclesia catholica innovatur per eos, qui aberrant a veritate, necesse est referri.*" Alluding to the example of Leo the Great, he writes: "Imitate, we beseech you, the illustrious Pontiff, who bore the same name as yourself, and who sprang up, like a lion, when the Eutychian heresy broke out." "*Æmulare, præcamur cognominum tibi papam, atque ut ille, pullulante tum hæresi Eutychiana, leonum in morem experrectus est,*" etc.

"The Holy Spirit himself," pursues our author, "directs and guides the head of the Church." "*Ejus est, de cætero, quæ Deo sunt placita, facere Spiritus Sancti ductu, a quo, ut in aliis, sic in hoc quoque regitur et gubernatur.*" * Of those who, by their obstinate disobedience, rend the unity of the Church, he remarks: "I solemnly declare before God and man, that they are sundered

---

* Bar. ad ann., 809; Bero. vlii, 142.

from the body of Christ and from that chief See to which the keys of faith have been committed, and against which, according to the promise of the Eternal Truth, the gates of hell never have prevailed in past ages, nor shall prevail unto the consummation of time." " *Deum hominesque contestor, sejunxerunt se a corpore Christi, a coryphœa sede, in qua Christus posuit fidei claves, adversus quam non prœvaluerunt per omne sœculum, nec prœvalebunt portœ inferi, sicut promisit ille, qui non mentitur.*"*

In his letter to Pope Paschal, he writes: "You are Peter; you fill and adorn his See." "*Petrus enim tu; Petri sedem coronans et gubernans.*" "Confirm, then, your brethren; this is the proper time. Come from the West and stretch out your saving hand to the East."

There is little doubt that many a well meaning Greek of that period shared the views of Theodore. But it strikes us as somewhat curious that the schismatic Greek and Russian Churches should have clipped from his writings so startling a condemnation of their errors as the following passage, which they have placed among the pious lessons read on the eleventh of November: "Stretch out thy hand to help the

* Hard. ix, 605.

Church of Constantinople, and prove thyself the successor of the first Leo. Listen favorably to our petition, because thou art Peter, to whom Christ has said, 'Confirm thy brethren.'"*

Is it not surprising that, up to this very day, these fallen Churches should continue to publish the memorial of their own apostasy, and despite the reflections that it is likely to call up, should persist in their schism? How incomprehensible are the ways of Providence, which makes even enemies subserve the interests of the Church! The unaccountable conduct of these sectaries is far from being a solitary instance. Even Photius unwillingly contributes his mite to the truth when he tells us that the Manicheans styled themselves Christians, while they denominated real Christians ROMANS. How re-assuring to the Catholic, who at the present day so often hears himself assailed as a Papist and Romanist. These appellations, though meant to be opprobrious epithets, are, in reality, highly expressive of the character of genuine Christianity, and ally the true believer to those who, in the earlier days of the Church, fought the battles of the Lord.

In the West, the celebrated HINCMAR, of

* De Maistre, Du Pape, p. 90.

Rheims, who flourished about this time (882), made his profession of faith before the Council of Douzi: "The Roman See, the teacher of all the Churches in the world." "*Omnium Ecclesiarum in toto orbe magistra.*" Nay, according to the testimony of Flodoard, Hincmar affirmed, in the most explicit manner, that all controversies, once brought before the tribunal of the Apostolical See, are terminated by its irrevocable sentence. In a letter to his nephew, he calls the Holy See "the source of religion, and of all ecclesiastical discipline and jurisdiction." "*A quo rivus religionis et omnis ecclesiasticæ ordinationis atque canonicæ jurisdictionis profluxit.*" No theologian will fail to perceive the weight of this testimony; for Hincmar is distinguished as the most zealous advocate of every shadow of episcopal right.*

RATRAMNUS, of Corbey, and Paulinus, of Aquileia, both contemporaries of Hincmar, profess the same faith. Ratramnus teaches: "All ecclesiastical decisions must be submitted to the judgment of the Pope, that he may ratify what is proper and amend what is amiss. "*Ad ejus judicium pendeat, quidquid in ecclesiasticis negotiis disponitur, ut ex ejus arbitrio vel maneat constitutum, vel corrigatur erratum.*" †

* Hist. Rem. iii, 13.   † Nat. Alex. xii.

Paulinus, contrasting the tranquillity that reigned in the West with the troubles that agitated the East, ascribes the difference to the significant fact, that the former remained firm in its allegiance to the Holy See, while the latter plunged headlong into a fatal schism. The same explanation accounts satisfactorily, in our days, for the endless divisions of the Eastern schismatics, and for the uninterrupted unity of the Catholic Communion. *"Nos intra terminos Apostolicæ doctrinæ et S. Romanæ Ecclesiæ firmiter stamus, illorum probatissimam auctoritatem sequentes et sanctissimis inhærentes doctrinis."*

Let us now listen to the celebrated RABANUS MAURUS († 856), who, from Abbot of his monastery, became Bishop of Mayence, and who was so great a patron of learning that he may be deservedly styled the Mecænas of the ninth century. He possessed the happy art of blending the love of literature with that of religion, as we may see from a poem, in which he consecrates the graces of the muse to the service of the Holy See. We quote the following verses on Pope Gregory IV, who then governed the Church of Christ :

> *Sedis apostolicæ lux aurea Romæ*
> *Et decus, et doctor plebis, et almus amor.*
> . . . .

*Vestra valet cælum reserare et claudere lingua
Principi apostolico Petro conjunctus in ævum,
In terra vicem cujus et ipse gerit.*

The voice of Catholicity speaks to Pius IX, in the same strain.

Lupus, of Ferriers († 862), who lived on terms of intimacy with Rabanus and Hincmar, and who took an active part in the administration of the empire, under Charles the Bald, sums up, in a few comprehensive words, all that has been said or sung on the prerogative of the Holy See. "She neither deceived herself, nor was she ever deceived by another," is the laconism which tells us his belief as well as the most elaborate treatise could have done. "*Nec se fefellit, nec ab aliquo falli potuit.*"

Toward the close of the same century, HATTO, Archbishop of Mayence, united with the Bishops of Bavaria, and THEOTMAR, acting under instructions from the prelates of Juvavia, drew up written communications, which were forwarded to Pope John IX, with the view that, if any thing should have been said or done amiss, it might be rectified by his authority. "*Ut vestra potentia ad rectitudinis lineam perducatur.*"

We now enter upon the tenth century. Political intrigues and party spirit sometimes obtruded into the chair of St. Peter candidates whose personal character was not wholly above reproach. Yet, compared with the long list of saintly pontiffs who preceded and followed them, these unworthy representatives of Christ are very few in number. The celebrated Protestant historian HERDER, frankly avows that no lineage of kings or princes, or, indeed, of any order of society, bears so stainless a reputation. He goes so far as to admit, that even those held up, by narrow-minded malevolence, to the derision of posterity, committed sins which, in worldly sovereigns, would have been passed over as the veriest foibles, without so much as eliciting a comment from the annalist. However, as it is not our province to write an apology for the failings of individuals, we shall willingly concede that some did disgrace the sacred character which they bore. Such an admission can only tend to strengthen our position; for, as Baronius notices, none of those Popes who are most open to censure ever decided erroneously on ecclesiastical questions, and still less on doctrinal points. Moreover, as the same writer bids us remark, the devotion toward the Holy See never showed itself so strikingly, in all parts of the Christian world, as under those very Popes whose morality was of a doubtful kind. The faithful did not regard the merits of those who sat on the chair of Peter, but the privileges attached thereto. *"Non merita sedentium, sed jura sedis considerantes."* Hence, the learned historian very ingeniously applies to the Holy See of that time the words of the Canticles: "I am black, but beautiful." *"Nigra sum, sed formosa"*—black, owing to vices of those who occupy me; beautiful, on account of the privileges annexed to me.

These remarks are corroborated by the writings of the most learned and holy men living at that epoch. Thus the Fathers of the Council of Troslei (909), unanimously declared that Christ had founded His Church upon Peter, and that Gaul was indebted to the zeal of the Roman Pontiffs for her unshaken steadfastness in the faith. *"Sed ab eo, ejusque successoribus etiam edocta firmitatem fidei, quam primo accepit, hactenus inconcussam servare studuit."*

St. Odo, of Clugni († 942), whose learning and holiness made him the ornament of his time, hesitated not to affirm that, even in those evil days, all the good that was done in Church matters was due to him, who had received from the Lord the injunction of confirming his brethren.

Otto, of Vercelli, in his work *"De pressuris ecclesiasticis,"* and Pilgrim, Bishop of Passau, in his address to Benedict VII, express themselves in a similar manner.

Even NICHOLAS, Patriarch of Constantinople, anxious to heal the wounds of the Greek Church, invoked the authority of the Holy See, and warned the Prince of the Bulgarians that it is a heinous crime not to recognize it.*

RATHERUS, of Verona, introduced into his Itinerarium the following sententious remark, which discovers at once his fondness for classic brevity and his thorough Catholicity: "Never was that valid which Rome rejected, nor that invalid which Rome approved." "*Nunquam ratum quod illic irritum, et nunquam irritum quod ibi ratum fuerit visum.*" In his appeal to the Pope, whom he styles the Father of the whole world— "*universo orbi Pater*"—his feeling heart pours itself out in the following touching entreaty: "I conjure you for the love of the Almighty to fly to our assistance in the place of Him whose chair you occupy for *this purpose*, that you may prevent the gates of hell from ever prevailing against the Church." "*In Omnipotentis amore precor, ejusque vice succurratis, cujus ideo sedem obtinetis, ne portæ inferi prævalere adversum Ecclesiam non sinatis.*"

The celebrated Abbot FLEURY († 999), charged with several commissions from the Pope to King

---

* Baron. ad ann., 983. Hard vi, 695-739.

Robert, gives an account of his embassy in a document which bears the following inscription: "To the Venerable Pontiff who fills the See of Rome, and who is, therefore, the teacher of the whole Church." *"Domino semper venerabili Papæ Romanæ et Apostolicæ sedis præsidi, et ideo universalis Ecclesiæ Doctori."* In a book containing a collection of canons for the guidance of King Hugo and the crown-prince Robert, the same author reasons thus upon the Gospel text, which so frequently recurs in our pages: "Christ said to his apostle, 'Thou art Peter, and upon this rock I will build my Church.' Mark the words, '*my* Church,' not thine. If the Church is not Peter's, whose is she? If we feel not the peculiar force of this expression, nor model our conduct accordingly, we neither lead the lives nor understand the language of Catholics." *"Certe carissimi principes, nec Catholice vivimus, nec Catholice loquimur."* How piquant this remark when applied to Protestant sovereigns or the Russian Czar, and how very caustic when referred to Catholic princes following in their footsteps?

Almost at the dawn of the eleventh century we meet with equally historic evidence, the same expressions in a letter written to the Pope by FULBERT of Chartres (†1029), concerning the excommunicated Count Falco of Anjou; again, in an allocution of the Archbishop of Burges before the Council of Limoges; and, finally, in a collection of Canons, compiled by Bernard of Worms, the preceptor of the Emperor Conrad.

Ten years later we see the earnest convictions of the age yet more clearly exemplified, in the conduct of Abbot ODILO (†1039). A number of Polish embassadors, one day, presented themselves at the doors of the monastery to reclaim Prince Casimir, who had exchanged the court for the cloister. The Abbot declared himself unable to accord their request, because it involved a dispensation which exceeded the limits of his powers. He dismissed them, therefore, with the words, "That they must apply to the highest tribunal on earth, namely, the Apostolical See of Rome, the Vicar of Christ." "*Proinde supremum in terris tribunal, supremamque potestatem, sedem videlicet Apostolicam Romanam, et Vicarium Christi adirent.*" *

In the Synod of Milan, ST. PETER DAMIAN, renowned for the Apostolic freedom with which he maintained the truth before Kings and Popes, designated the Church of Rome as the holy teacher—"*sanctam magistram.*" In the same spirit of child-like submission, he speaks of the

* Baron. ad ann. 1047.

Holy See as the teaching guardianship of Peter, according to whose righteousness all, that has been disfigured, should be remodeled.

And here remark, in passing, how our Saint's ideas on ecclesiastical reform differ from those of the modern Reformers. According to him, the Church is manifestly a self-preserving organization, whose principle of regeneration lies in the Holy See.

In one of his letters, the same writer compares the decisions of the Roman See to a keen-edged blade, with which Peter cuts off the head of every obstinate error, in order to strengthen all the children of the Church in the unity of the faith. "*Evangelico mucrone veritati resistentium cervicem obtruncat, et ad invictissime dimicandum, totam Christi militiam in unius caritatis et fidei unitate confirmat.*"

The precise meaning attached by the saint to the words *Apostolical See* and *Roman Church*, is evident from the bearing of the whole passage. Still they may derive additional light, by being collated with expressions in another letter, in which the writer himself defines his meaning, when he says: "You are the *Apostolical See;* you are the *Roman Church.*" "*Vos estis Apostolica Sedes, vos Romana estis Ecclesia.*" "Whithersoever Peter leads you, there also is the new

Rome of Christianity."—"*Quo vos Petrus vobiscum fugiens attrahit, illic Romana est Ecclesia.*"* Catholics of our day are, without doubt, sustained by the same abiding faith. Thence that inward assurance, which can smile with placid serenity, while the heel of the spoiler is on the sacred soil of Rome, and an armed band of outlaws threatens destruction to the temporal power. Even though Providence, in its inscrutable designs, should permit Pius IX to be again exiled from the Eternal City, the faith of Peter would remain as unshaken, as it has been for eighteen hundred years. The presence of the Holy Father would transform also a barren island of the sea into a new Rome, into a new Capitol of the Christian world, from which he would rule his spiritual kingdom, and, with the power of Christ, hurl his denunciations against the high-handed injustice of his oppressors.

William of Poitiers, in his history of King William, calls the Pope the teacher of all the prelates of the Church. ARNULPH and VENERUS of Milan, both partisans of the emperor and enemies of the Pope, subscribe unhesitatingly to the dogmatical infallibility of the Sovereign Pontiff. "Never," remarks Venerus, "never did

---

* Baron. ad ann., 1049–1064. Butler iii, 194.

the See of Rome deceive the world by an iniquitous decree, nor could she herself ever be deceived by heretical fallacies." "*Quæ aliquo pravo dogmate nec aliquando fefellit, nec aliqua hæresi unquam falli potuit.*"

Arnulph repeats the same, in his history of Milan.* "Though often violently assailed," writes Anselm of Lucca, "the successor of St. Peter has always stood unmoved." "*Licet pulsatus, licet concussus, tamen stetit immobilis.*" "Because heaven and earth shall pass away, but not the words of Him who said, 'Thou art Peter, and upon this rock I will build my Church.'" †

About the same time, Siegfried of Mayence and the Bishops of the province of Rheims, pronounced, with no less decision, upon this prerogative of the Roman Pontiff.‡ Even in the East, in which the chorus of unity was hushed by the oppression of the schismatics, an occasional voice was heard, reëchoing the strains of other lands. Theophylact († 1096), the Archbishop of Bulgaria, declares in his Commentaries on the Gospels: "To Peter the Church has been committed for instruction in the faith." "*Petro Ecclesia in fide erudienda traditur.*" § "For this reason the Lord has sowed, in the heart of Peter and of his suc-

---

* Hist. Mil., chapt. 13. † Opusc. cont. Guibert.
‡ Thomass. i, 441. § Com. in Evang. Sti. Lucæ.

cessors, the seed of faith." "*Habes recondita fidei semina.*"

Euthymius, the Patriarch of Constantinople, who lived during the reign of Alexius Comnenus, indorses the same views, in his Commentaries on the Gospels, when he calls the Holy Father "the teacher appointed by Christ to read to the whole world lessons of infallible wisdom." "*Orbis magistrum.*"

We have now traced the testimonies of ecclesiastical antiquity, from the birth of Christianity, up to the Pontificate of Gregory VII. The political Constitution of Europe had, meanwhile, been radically changed, by a series of convulsions, which had completely overturned the fabric of the oldest States. England had but lately emerged from the bloody tide of a barbarous war. Yet here, as elsewhere, the faith felt not the throes that convulsed the civil world. Indeed, learning and sanctity never paid a nobler tribute to the Holy See, than they did through the illustrious Archbishops LANFRANC and ANSELM, who, about this time, filled the See of Canterbury. The former (†1089), calls an unbounded docility and submission to the Holy See, the "CONSCIENCE OF CHRISTIANITY," and affirms that, through the course of the Christian era, no dogma was ever so solemnly proclaimed or so generally acknowledged, as this very dogma of the apostolical authority of the Pope. The knowledge thereof is infused, according to him, into the *consciences* of all the faithful. "*Etenim omnium Christianorum conscientiæ inditum est.*"*

The remarks of the learned prelate are applicable to our own day. Now, as formerly, Catholics are moved, by a certain instinctive perception, to accept the doctrine of Papal Infallibility, even without the borrowed evidence of argument. Now, as formerly, the Church is guided by the same "*conscience*," which can not grow callous without serious danger to Christianity itself. Millions and millions, led by the dictates of this "*conscience*" alone, submit with alacrity to the decisions of the Holy See, though they have never heard explicit proofs, such as we produce in these pages. It was, no doubt, for the same reason that, even in civil matters, both princes and people formerly appealed to the arbitration of the Pope. Struck by the heavenly wisdom, which presided at the counsels of the highest ecclesiastical judiciary, when he pronounced upon religious questions, the Christian community was led to refer to his tribunal also many affairs of

---

* Lanf. Contr. Bereng.

state. And no doubt, as Voltaire himself admits, society at large would be much happier, if the differences, which sometimes occur between sovereigns and their subjects, were adjusted by an appeal to the common father of the faithful, instead of being settled at the point of the sword.

ANSELM, the illustrious successor of Lanfranc in the See of Canterbury, when on his way to invoke the authority of the Holy See against King William the Red, spoke in the following terms to an assembly of Bishops: "I am going to the chief Pastor, to the angel of the great Council, to the successor of St. Peter, on whom the Church is built, and to whom Christ gave the keys of Heaven. Hence you may all know that, in those things which relate to God, I shall ever yield a ready obedience to the Pope." "*Quare cuncti noveritis, quod in his, quæ Dei sunt, vicario Petri obedientiam impendam.*"

The same author dedicates his work against the heretic Rosselin to "the Holy Father, whom the Lord has appointed the guardian of the faith."

Among those of Gregory's contemporaries who used their learning in the defense of the Apostolical authority of the Holy See, special mention is due to Leo of Chartres, Bruno of Asti, Godfried of Vendome, Guido the Carthusian, Otto of Bamberg, Adelbert of Mayence, Humbert, Archbishop of Lyons, and Rupert of Deutz. We shall leave it to the last of these witnesses to interpret the meaning of all, in his book, "*De divino officio,*" which contains this remarkable sentence: "The Roman Church, solidly built upon the rock of Apostolical faith, has remained firm, has silenced the heretics, not of Greece only, but of the whole world, and, with supreme authority, has pronounced its irrevocable sentence from the tribunal of faith." "*Romana Ecclesia, super Apostolicæ fidei petram altius fundata, firmiter stetit, et tam Græciæ quam totius orbis hæreticos semper confutavit, et de excelso fidei tribunali, data sententia, judicavit.*" She is to all the faithful, who have recourse to her, a wall of defense emblazoned with the thousand trophies of her former victories.

We have a still more illustrious witness in the Prussian Bishop, ANSELM of Havelberg, whom the Emperor Lolhau dispatched to Constantinople, to recall the schismatical Bishops to a sense of their duty. The imperial envoy strongly urged his case in an address, in which he said to the erring Greeks: "The Roman Church is privileged beyond all others; for, whilst the Churches of Alexandria, Antioch, Jerusalem, and Constantinople wavered in faith, she alone, that was built on the rock, always stood firm—*illa supra petram fundata semper mansit inconcussa*—because the Lord had prayed for Peter, that his faith might not fail. Hence, the injunction, 'confirm thy brethren,' which, taken in connection with the rest of the text, was evidently designed to mean: Do thou, who hast received the grace of remaining steadfast in the faith, act toward all the others as a shepherd, a teacher, a father, a master, gently rebuking and strengthening them whenever they waver." "*Ac si aperte ei dicat: Tu, qui hanc gratiam accepisti, ut, aliis in fide vacillantibus, semper in fide immobilis permaneas, alios vacillantes confirma et corrige, tamquam omnium pastor, et doctor et pater et magister omnium.*"

Then, reviewing the Annals of the Church, he produced incontestable evidence to prove that all heresies have been suppressed by the authority of the Holy See, which crushed their authors with the rock of faith—"*a petra fidei per Petrum destructos.*" From these data he inferred that the Roman See enjoys two remarkable privileges, namely, untainted purity of faith, and supreme judicial authority over all the faithful. "*Præ omnibus incorruptam puritatem fidei et supra omnes potestatem judicandi.*"

He put his arguments in so pointed a form as

to silence the captious Greeks. Oh, that he could rise from the grave to direct his powerful logic against his own countrymen, of whom the majority have imitated the renegade Greeks in their defection! Full three centuries have already elapsed since the sun of faith set upon the land which gave birth to this ardent champion of the Church. A gradual return to his teachings and maxims looks to us like the harbinger of another dawn, that will dispel the shades of heresy and, once more, bathe those regions of error in the glorious sunlight of faith. May the auspicious moment be no longer delayed!

We shall close this long list of Catholic tradition, embracing a period of a thousand years, with the testimony of St. Bernard. Superior to human respect, that constitutional disease of weak minds, the illustrious Doctor dared to speak as he thought, not only to humble monks and common laymen, but also to mitred prelates and sceptered princes. His letter to Innocent III shows us how well he could blend an ingenuous freedom with a respectful veneration. "It is but proper," writes he, "to advise the Holy Father of every scandal which disgraces the Church, and of every danger which threatens the faith; because it is natural to look for an antidote, against the fatal poison of heresy, in that

See, whose faith is not liable to defection. Now, this is the special prerogative of the Roman See; for, to whom but Peter was it ever said: 'I have prayed for thee, that thy faith fail not.'" "*Dignum namque arbitror ibi potissimum reparari damna fidei, ubi non possit fides sentire defectum. Hæc quidem prærogativa hujus Sedis; cui enim dictum est alteri: 'rogavi pro te ut non deficiat fides tua.'*" "Thou canst give us no clearer proof that thou art the legitimate successor of St. Peter, whose chair thou fillest, than by using thy authority to strengthen wavering minds in thy faith."

The Holy Doctor uses similar expressions in his 131st letter on Abelard. But nowhere does he define the prerogatives and the true character of the Sovereign Pontiff with so much accuracy, as in his book of Considerations, compiled especially for Pope Eugenius II, who had been his disciple. As if admonishing the Holy Father, the Saint proposes the question: "Who art thou?" Then, with that comprehensiveness of thought which sometimes compresses into the narrow compass of a few sentences, more solid instruction than is scattered through the voluminous tomes of inferior authors, the Saint himself replies: "Thou art the Sovereign Pontiff, the head of the ecclesiastical hierarchy, the prince of

Bishops, the heir of the Apostles. Thou art like Abel in thy primacy, like Noah in thy government, like Abraham in the patriarchate, like Melchisedech in thy priestly character, like Aaron in thy dignity, like Peter in thy power, like Christ in thy unction. The other Bishops are indeed shepherds, each having charge of a particular portion of the fold; but thou art the only one, who feeds the entire fold of Christ." "*Tibi universi crediti uni una.*" "For thou art the Shepherd of the shepherds themselves. To which of the Bishops, or even of the Apostles, has the whole flock been intrusted? What flock? Forsooth the inhabitants of one particular city or district? No, but *all* the children of the Church. Our Lord Himself has said: 'Feed *my* sheep.' James, who was regarded as one of the pillars of the Church, contented himself with the province of Jerusalem and left the universal Church to Peter. If the 'brother of the Lord' thus bowed to higher authority, who will dare to arrogate to himself the prerogatives of Peter?" "*Cedente Domini fratre, quis alter se ingerat Petri prærogativæ?*" "Others possess a partial authority, thou the plenitude of power. The jurisdiction of others is confined within definite limits, thy jurisdiction extends over all. Thine is the indefeasible title acquired by St. Peter when

Christ delivered to him the Keys of Heaven, and intrusted him with the care of His flock." "*Stat ergo inconcussum privilegium tuum, tam in datis clavibus, quam in ovibus commendatis.*"

Though these passages were designed by the Saint to furnish his illustrious disciple with matter for reflection, they read like a summary of all that Christianity, living on through the vicissitudes of times and places, had previously asserted, in the face of friends and foes, of laymen and clerics; and thus we have given a condensed bird's-eye view of the faithful convictions of the Holy Fathers and the eminent writers of the patristic age, during a period of more than *eleven* hundred years.

Indeed, it would be a difficult task, to find a single dogma of Catholic belief, upon which antiquity has pronounced so decisively, as upon the infallible apostolical power of the Sovereign Pontiff, when teaching or defining matters of faith. Lanfranc was right when he styled this belief the *conscience of Christianity*, that is, of the Church.

Let us now see how the Church herself, represented by her Bishops, has recognized, in all her General Councils, this exalted prerogative of the Sovereign Pontiff.

III.

TESTIMONY OF ALL THE GENERAL COUNCILS OF THE EAST AND WEST,

DECLARING THE JUDGMENT OF THE CHAIR OF ST. PETER AT ROME TO BE THE INFALLIBLE RULE OF FAITH.

IF, upon a question of so much interest to the true believer, it is satisfactory to learn the private opinions of individual Fathers, it must be doubly so to know the formal declarations made by the Universal Church in her General Councils. Not unfrequently protected by the secular arm, the Bishops were at full liberty to discuss the question of this prerogative so vitally connected with the integrity of faith. Had they been of opinion, that the right of defining the doctrine of the Church resides in the body of the Episcopacy, no time would have been more favorable for asserting their claims than that of a General Council, when their whole order was gathered together, from all quarters of the globe, and, without fear of intimidation, could canvass the subject in all its bearings. Nay, I will say further, that, upon a point of such importance, it was incumbent on them to resist any encroachment, even though the offender were the Sovereign Pontiff himself. For, if they looked upon themselves as the guardians of the faith, they could not, without a serious dereliction of duty, surrender a principle, which all parties must allow to be of vital importance. Now, the history of the General Councils, far from supporting, directly refutes any such assumption, on the part of the assembled Bishops. First, no General Council was ever considered lawful, unless convoked by the Sovereign Pontiff.

Secondly, the Acts of the General Councils had no binding force, unless confirmed by the authority of the Holy See.

Thirdly, whenever the Popes convened a General Council, with the view of settling a dispute in matters of doctrine, they usually anticipated all action on the part of the Fathers, by a *definition*, which was to control the deliberations of the assembly. If they sought the coöperation of the General Councils, it was solely because, in matters of faith, the dogma promulgated with so much solemnity, before delegates from every portion of the Christian world, was likely to be sooner made known to every member of the fold; while, in matters of discipline, such a convocation of Church dignitaries could not but prove highly salutary to the clergy, as well as to the laymen under their jurisdiction.

Fourthly, no ecclesiastical writer, how enthusiastic soever in his devotion to the Pope, ever pronounced himself more decidedly and clearly in favor of the Infallibility of the Holy See, in matters of faith, than did the Fathers, who composed the General Councils. Even the Greeks, despite that hereditary jealousy which was incessantly contending for the boasted rights of Constantinople, did homage to this prerogative of Rome. Let us, then, carefully study the proceedings and enactments of the General Councils.

THE APOSTOLICAL COUNCIL.

AT JERUSALEM.

Though, strictly speaking, the assembly held at Jerusalem, under the auspices of St. Peter, is not entitled to the name of a General Council, nevertheless, because the manner in which it was convened, is not a little remarkable, and because it has served as the model of the General Councils, it may, with some propriety, find a place in these pages.

We shall not, therefore, apologize to our readers for entertaining them, a few minutes, with the transactions of the early Church.

We know from Holy Scripture, that the question at issue related to the observance of the Mosaic Law by the converted Gentiles; that Peter, Paul, James, and Barnabas, together with a number of elders from the Church of Jerusalem, assembled to deliberate upon the subject; and, finally, that a warm discussion arose among them. And here we may be allowed to remark, in passing, that so long as a question has not yet been decided, the same freedom of debate is still allowed, not merely in a General Council, but also in every Diocesan Synod. Here, then, is a striking resemblance between ancient and modern Councils; but it is not, by any means, the only one nor the most important, as must be evident to every person, who knows any thing about the sequel to the proceedings briefly referred to above. We read in the Acts of the Apostles, that, "when there was much disputing" Peter, rising up, pronounced his judgment, while all "the multitude held their peace." The question was settled; and James, who, as Bishop of Jerusalem, rose next to submit some disciplinary remarks, humbly acquiesced in the decision of Peter.

Thus the very first synod, held under the auspices of the Apostles themselves, foreshadowed the Councils of succeeding ages. Peter still decides, by the mouth of his successors; and all the Bishops, no less than the other children of the Church, submit with the same becoming docility as James, "the brother of the Lord."

I. GENERAL COUNCIL
OF
NICE.

The first General Council at Nice, intended to give greater publicity to the condemnation of Arius, was convoked by Pope Sylvester, under the reign of Constantine the Great, who used his imperial authority to facilitate the meeting of the Fathers.* The Sovereign Pontiff presided by his three legates, one of whom was Osius, Bishop of Cordova. The other two were priests. Osius, whom Athanasius styles the LEADER of the Council, occupied the first place, attended by his two companions. How great the deference here

* See Sozomenus l. i, c. 16. Act. i, Conc. Chalc. et Act. xviii, Conc. Constant. III.

shown to the Papal authority, since the mere reflection of it gave even simple priests the precedence of Bishops, who, on the present occasion, were either Orientals or Greeks, and yet never objected to this conduct of the legates, as implying an undue assumption of power. This fact alone suffices to show, that the prerogatives of the Holy See were then acknowledged all over the Christian world. No one, therefore, will be at all startled by the fact, that, even previous to any measures taken by the Councils, the legates, acting under instructions, condemned the blasphemous doctrines of Arius. The Fathers were guided, in their deliberations, by these instructions, as well as by the symbol of faith prescribed by Sylvester and brought from Rome, together with a number of disciplinary regulations. At the close of the Council all the Acts were sent to Rome for confirmation. This circumstance, in particular, was referred to by Pope Felix III, when he said to the Clergy and Monks of the East: "The three hundred and eighteen Fathers assembled at Nice, mindful of the words of the Lord, 'Thou art Peter'—"*Obsequentes voci Domini, 'tu es Petrus'*—transmitted all the decrees of the Council to the Roman Church for confirmation."

Pope Gelasius, the successor of Felix, reminds

the Bishop of Dardania, that, as every Christian should know, the Acts of a Council do not bind in conscience, unless confirmed by the Holy See. "As that, which the Roman See did not sanction, could not lay the faithful under any obligation, so that, which she judged right, was at once received by the whole Church." "*Sicut quod Romana Sedes non probaverat, stare non potuit; sic, quod illa censuit judicare, tota Ecclesia suscepit.*" The decision lies exclusively in the power of the Apostolic See. Those enactments only, which she has confirmed, hold valid; those, which she has rejected, are without binding force. "*Totum in Sedis Apostolicæ positum est potestate. Hoc, quod confirmavit in Synodo Sedes Apostolica, hoc robur obtinet, quod refutavit, habere non potuit firmitatem.*"

Such were the comments, passed by the Popes, when the proceedings of the Council were still fresh in the memory of all.

The force of the argument taken from the sentiments of the Fathers of the Council of Nice is much increased, when we consider the tenor of the canons, which, in all the eastern collections, are usually placed among the canons of the Council of Nice, and which at least, according to all historians, are considered to contain the regulations of the ecclesiastical discipline of the Church at that time, and expressing the sentiments of its faith.

The thirty-ninth canon reads as follows: "The incumbent of the Roman See, acting as Christ's Vicegerent, in the government of the Church, is the head of the Patriarchs, as well as Peter himself was." "*Ille, qui tenet sedem Romanam, caput est omnium Patriarcharum sicut Petrus, ut qui sit Vicarius Christi super cunctam Ecclesiam.*" The words, "as well as Peter himself," point to the marked difference that exists between the Roman Pontiff, as the successor of St. Peter, and the Bishops, as the successors of the other Apostles. Common Bishops are not identified with the Apostles, whose Apostolate, being vested in their person, was not transmitted to their successors. But the Bishop of Rome is completely identified with Peter, whose prerogatives and primatial dignity, being attached to the office, descend, as if by inheritance, to his last successor. In the other Apostles the dignity of the Apostolate, together with its consequent infallibility, was of a personal character; in Peter it was the inalienable privilege of his office. It is for this reason, that the Roman See alone has been always known as the APOSTOLICAL SEE. Why did not the Episcopal Sees of Antioch, Ephesus, Corinth, Jerusalem, and Alexandria, all of which were founded by Apostles, lay claim to the same title? If, then, the Roman See has a right to the distinctive appellation given her, from the first ages of the Christian era, it must be because the prerogative of Apostolical authority is inseparable from the office of Peter, and, therefore, enjoyed by each successive Pope. Even the arrogant and jealous Patriarchs of Constantinople, never daring to claim this title for their See, render testimony to the right in question.

A parallel train of reasoning, founded upon the name "Vicar of Christ," which the Council of Nice applies to the Holy Father, will lead us to the same results. For this title would be altogether inapplicable to him, could he err when solemnly defining an article of faith. Think of Christ, the infallible founder of the Church, become fallible in the person whom He has chosen to represent Him on earth; think of His unerring oracles converted into doubtful opinions by the organ which He uses to communicate them to men! The inconsistency is apparent. We infer, therefore, that the expressions PETER HIMSELF, APOSTOLICAL SEE, and VICAR OF CHRIST are significant appellations, suggested by the conscience of Christianity, to mark the plenitude of Apostolical authority centered in the Sovereign Pontiff.

Pope Boniface I felt the force of this conclusion when, shortly after the Council of Nice, he remarked to the Bishops of Thessalonica: "The Fathers of the Council did not presume to legislate concerning the Roman See, because they saw that the Lord has conferred the plenitude of power upon her." "*Adeo ut non aliquid ausa sit super eam constituere, cum videret nihil super meritum suum posse conferri. Omnia denique huic noverat Domini sermone concessa.*"

The Pope was, no doubt, warranted in this inference. In fact there could scarcely be any thing more complete or comprehensive than the testimony of the First General Council concerning the prerogatives of the Holy See. It covers the whole question, which we have endeavored to prove in these pages.

II. GENERAL COUNCIL
OF
CONSTANTINOPLE.

This Council was, at first, nothing more than a provincial Synod, and if it now holds a higher rank, that distinction, as the ingenious Gerbert remarks, is altogether due to the authority of the Popes, who confirmed its Canons. It was convened by Damasus, to check more effectually the intrigues of the heretics Sabellius, Macedonius, Eunomius, and Apollinaris, against whom he had already pronounced the censures of the Church.

Bossuet assigns this as the object of the Council, on the authority of Sozomenus, who relates that the controversies then agitating the East appeared to have been settled by the rescript of Damasus. "*Quo facto, utpote judicio Romanæ Ecclesiæ controversia terminata, quievere—et finem accepisse visa est.*"

Yet, as the heresiarchs persisted in troubling the peace of the Church, the Sovereign Pontiff determined to promulgate their condemnation in a more solemn manner. Accordingly the Council met, not to discuss the merits of the subject, but solely to coöperate with him toward the total suppression of this heretical movement.

The same point is proven by Baronius, who cites some very ancient codices, preserved in the Vatican Library and elsewhere.*

The reasons, which moved the Pope to summon the Council, also weighed with the Oriental Bishops. Headed by Basil, the Primate of Cappadocia, they addressed Damasus in a letter, to

---

* Baron. ad ann. 381, N. 19.

which we have had occasion to allude above, and in which they express the desire to see the Papal rescript promulgated in all the Churches of the East. "*Omnibus Orientis Ecclesiis publicari et manifestari petimus.*" Why should they have so strongly urged the Pope to issue a public rescript, if they had not felt, with the Church at large, that it would produce the desired effect? Nor was there a feigned submission, but an earnest conviction, which led to practical results. Even after organizing in Council, they did not regard themselves as a sovereign ecclesiastical tribunal, but as a judicial body amenable to the Vicar of Christ. Hence the deferential language in which they petitioned him to confirm the disciplinary canons which they had made, and to anathematize a certain Timotheus, who had learned heresy in the school of Apollinaris. The Pope, while commending their submission, reminds them that, by acquitting themselves of what was a *strict obligation*, they have but furthered their own interests, since, without the sanction of the Holy See, all their proceedings would remain null and void. "*Quod debitam sedi Apostolicæ reverentiam exhibet caritas vestra vobis ipsis plurimum præstatis.*"

He rejected their disciplinary canons of the Council, which were, accordingly, without force, as we learn from a brief of Gregory the Great to the Patriarchs of Alexandria and Antioch, and to Cyriacus, the Bishop of Constantinople.

After remaining, for a long time, in a state of suspense, they were finally approved, under certain restrictions, by INNOCENT, in the thirteenth century. But those acts, which were not confirmed by the Holy See, were never considered as binding in *foro conscientiæ*, nor reckoned among the decrees of General Councils.

The other petition was doomed to a similar fate. The Pope saw no necessity of issuing a special bull, condemnatory of Timotheus, because, as he remarked, the whole ground was covered by the formulary previously sent, by the Holy See, to the Council. *"Jam enim semel formulam dedimus, ut qui se Christianum profiteatur, illud servet—quid ergo Timothei damnationem denuo a me quæritis?"*

III. GENERAL COUNCIL
OF
EPHESUS.

When Nestorius began to disseminate his heresies, Pope Cœlestin, who then governed the Church, immediately issued a bull of excommunication, which was to take effect ten days after being received. If, within that time, which was allowed him for reflection, he would not sign a public recantation of his errors, he was declared deposed from his See, and Cyril, the Patriarch of Alexandria, was authorized to proceed against him, according to the directions of the Pope. "*Aperte hanc scias nostram sententiam ut nisi . . . . intra decimum diem aperta et scripta confessione damnaveris, ab universalis Ecclesiæ Catholicæ communione te scias dejectum.*"*

Besides the rescript which was passed on Nestorius himself, the Pope sent an official communication to the principal Bishops of the East, as well as a Pastoral to all the Clergy and people of Constantinople. By these measures, the Holy Father virtually declared himself independent of a General Council. And, if he sanctioned the meeting of the Fathers at Ephesus, it was with the view of breaking the obstinacy of the heresiarch, and of counteracting the influence of the Emperor, who was supposed to favor the new errors. That this was the object of Cœlestin is apparent from his instructions to his legates: "We command you," said he to them, "to maintain the dignity of the Apostolical See.

* Hard. i, 1299.

When, therefore, any discussion arises, you shall pass sentence on the opinions advanced, but not enter the lists as disputants." *"Ad disceptionem si ventum fuerit, Vos de eorum sententia judicare debetis, non subire certamen."* At the same time he informed the Fathers of the Council, that he had charged his legates to execute, without adding or retrenching, what he himself had *previously* decided — *"ut quæ a nobis antea statuta sunt exequantur"* — and he forbade the assembly to depart, in ought, from the instruction, which he had given to his representatives.

When the legates had read this communication, the entire Council indorsed the Papal claims, with the words: "From the earliest ages of the Church it has always been held as indubitable, that the prince of the Apostles, the pillar of truth, the foundation-stone of the Catholic Church, Peter, who received the Keys of the Kingdom of Heaven, always lives in his successors and pronounces his judgment by their lips." *"Qui ad hoc usque tempus et semper in suis successoribus vivit et judicium exercet."* Accordingly the Fathers favored and promulgated the condemnation of Nestorius; and, when subsequently they notified the Emperor of the result, they offered, as an explanation of their conduct, that they had acted conformably to the instructions of the Pope, whose previous decision had compelled them to take this course. The Council, therefore, justified its proceedings by the authority of the Pope, while the Pope rested wholly upon the absolute power vested in his own person.

During one of the sessions, Theodore, Bishop of Ancyra, exclaimed, in the name of the Assembly: "The Lord of the Universe has signified, by the letters of Cœlestin, that the sentence of condemnation, promulgated by the Synod, is just." *"Justam esse Synodi sententiam demonstravit universorum Deus, per literas Celestini."*

Finally, in a letter, which the Fathers addressed to the Pope, to ask his confirmation of the Synodical Decrees, they stated that they had followed, with scrupulous fidelity, the instructions which they had received.

It need not surprise us, then, that Genadius, Patriarch of Constantinople, speaks of the resolutions of the Council as "dictated by Cœlestin," while Pope Sixtus, the successor of Cœlestin, writes to John, the Patriarch of Antioch: "You may infer, from the transactions of the Council at Ephesus, what is meant by conforming to the sentiments of the Holy See. St. Peter has transmitted to his successors, the power received from Christ." "*B. Petrus in suis successoribus quod accepit hoc tradidit.*"

The fact is so patent, that, down to our days, the liturgical books of the Russian Church, attribute the extinction of the Nestorian schism to Pope Cœlestin, and not to the Council at Ephesus.*

IV. GENERAL COUNCIL
OF
CHALCEDON.

We have compared the testimony of the General Councils to the light of the rising sun. The Council of Chalcedon furnishes us with a striking illustration, inasmuch as it establishes, more clearly than all the preceding Councils, the authority and prerogatives of the Holy See.

Intelligence having reached Rome concerning the outrages committed by Dioscorus, in the Conventicle of Ephesus, and the machinations resorted to by Eutyches, Leo the Great, acceding to the instances of the Emperor Marcian and of the Empress Pulcheria, convoked the Council of Chalcedon. The motive which induced the Sovereigns to urge their request, is clearly stated by

* See Harduin I, 1299; Nicephorus XIV, 34; Hard. I, 1503; Concil. tom. 3, p. 126; and Maistre du Pape, 1, 91.

the Emperor, in his letter to the Pope. As though he were guarding against all possibility of misconstruction, he makes the remarkable assertion, that when soliciting the convocation of a Council, he would not be understood as asking for a new ordinance or definition, but simply for a more speedy promulgation and enforcement of the one already made by the Pope, whose utterances must be received by the faithful as though he were Peter himself. "*Tanquam ab ipso beatissimo Petro cuperet declarari.*"

The letters of Pulcheria breathe the same spirit of submission. The Pope, yielding to these considerations, at length issued a bull for the convocation of the Council, with the formal salvo, "that the dignity and rights of the See of Peter remain unimpaired." "*Petri Apostoli sedis jure et honore servato.*" Six hundred and thirty Bishops answered the summons. Paschasius, the Papal legate, opened the Council and declared, in the name of the Pope, that Dioscorus, having held a Synod without the sanction of the Holy See, had forfeited his claims to a seat in the assembly. The intruder was accordingly ejected and forbidden a place among the Fathers. The Council entered into session headed by the legate, who strictly enforced the instructions given by the Pope, in his letter on Eutyches.

After some preliminary consultation, a profession of faith was drawn up, which, though not couched in the same terms as the one sent by the Pope to Eutyches, was yet an accurate compendium of Catholic doctrine. After the reading of this symbol, all the Fathers exclaimed, as with one voice: "This formula recommends itself to the Council; this was the faith of our ancestors; anathema be he that believes otherwise." This sudden demonstration on the part of the venerable body, was an evident sign that all favored the adoption of the formula. Yet the Papal legates refused their assent, and asked their dismissory letters, with the view of returning at once to the Pope, in whose formulary they would not allow even a jot to be changed.

This step, on the part of the Papal representatives, reversed the decision of the Fathers, who now exclaimed: "What Leo believes we all believe; anathema be he who believes any thing else. Peter has spoken through Leo." "*Ut Leo credimus; anathema ei, qui non ita credit. Petrus per Leonem locutus est.*"

Acropius, the Bishop of Sebastopol, remarked: "His Holiness, the Pope, has sent us a formula; we are bound to follow it, and to subscribe to its requirements." The Holy Synod, taking up the speaker's words, pursued: "That is what we wanted; no better exposition can be made."

The synodical letter, in which the Fathers petition the Pope to confirm the acts of the Council, acknowledges the same supreme authority in the following passage: "We have a rock of refuge in Peter, who alone possesses the absolute right of deciding, in the place of God; because he alone has the keys of Heaven. All his definitions, therefore, bind as emanating from the Vicegerent of Christ." "*Habemus Petrum petram refugii, et ipsi soli, libera potestate, loco Dei sit jus discernendi, secundum claves a Deo sibi datas, et omnia ab ipso definita teneantur tanquam a Vicario Apostolici throni.*"

The condemnation and deposition of Dioscorus having been published in full Council, was received, by all, with the words: "He that is the *foundation-stone* of the *faith* has divested him of his episcopal dignity. Leo, the Bishop of Rome, has but reëchoed the sentence of the Blessed Peter. Whosoever does not abide by the instructions of his Holiness is a heretic." "*Hic, qui est rectæ fidei fundamentum, nudavit eum episcopali dignitate.*"*

In memory of the illustrious Pontiff who so strenuously guarded the prerogatives of Peter,

* Act. Conc. iv, Sess.

the Russian Church still retains, in its Liturgy, a hymn beginning with the words: "How shall I extol thee, O Leo, heir of the invincible rock?"*

V. GENERAL COUNCIL
OF
CONSTANTINOPLE.

Pope Vigilius, yielding to the solicitations of the Emperor Justinian, who professed a special regard for his august person, had consented to visit the Eastern Capital. Yet the intimacy of hospitality could not make him shrink from the performance of his duty. From the very moment of his arrival he censured the arrogant assumptions of a recent imperial edict, and showed himself determined not to surrender the rights of the Holy See. This resoluteness incensed Justinian, who sought to revenge himself by casting his illustrious guest into prison. Vigilius, unruffled by the occurrence, remarked to the assembled dignitaries of the empire: "Remember that, though you have enchained Vigilius, you can not enchain Peter. The fear of man shall never induce me to prove unfaithful to the duties of my charge." The Vicar of Christ had

* De Maistre i, 9.

not overrated his courage. The civil authorities resorted to violence, and Vigilius, aided by the people, sought refuge in the Church of St. Sophia, at Chalcedon. Yet, even from this asylum, he issued a document on the questions agitated at the time, and, with Apostolic authority, subjoined to every article a solemn *anathema* against all who would dare to teach the errors condemned. Finally, he pronounced null and void whatever might be done in defiance of this ordinance. Evidently Peter had not been enchained in the person of Vigilius.

The Council assembled, and the Emperor, as well as the Fathers, invited the Pope to preside in person. But Vigilius, who wished to show the Eastern Church in particular, that the Sovereign Pontiff, when alone, is invested with the plenitude of Apostolical power, as well as when presiding over the assembled episcopacy, declined making his appearance. However, in order to prevent all treachery on the part of some servile Bishops who might possibly be weak enough to betray the cause of the Church for the favor of the Court, he declared invalid whatever the Synod would enact in opposition to his orders. But so far were the assembled Prelates from setting the Pope's authority at defiance, that they followed, in the minutest particulars, the directions which he had given, and professed that they received his letters upon matters of faith with as much submission as they did the four Gospels. *"Professa est Romani Pontificis quoad fidem epistolas, æque ac quatuor evangelia suscipere."* *

Yet the mere apprehension of resistance threw so much suspicion on the proceedings of the Assembly, that, for a long time, many portions of the Catholic Church did not recognize it as a General Council at all. Until it became generally known, that the Acts of the Council had been confirmed, the faithful acknowledged no other guide on the questions then agitated, than the Constitutions of Vigilius.

No more evident and glorious proof in regard to the Apostolical authority of the Pope over a Council can be thought of, than this deportment of Vigilius, a captive Pontiff, in the presence of an enraged Emperor and of a Council originally composed only of Greek Bishops. Indeed it was a grand spectacle for the whole world, to see the Roman Pontiff standing firm as a rock, amidst the waves of persecution, defying the combined power of the Imperial and Episcopal dignity, and finally, when free, without any thought of revenge, confirming the decrees of the Council,

---

* Greg. Magn. Lib. III, Ep. 37, Facand Lib. II.

because the Fathers acted precisely according to his orders. And then only after this his confirmation, the Council was acknowledged as legitimate, and ranked among the General Councils.

Considering the circumstances under which this Council was convoked, and, in particular, the relations which had hitherto existed between the Pope and the Emperor, the course pursued by the assembled Fathers must be allowed to be a convincing argument in favor of the supreme Apostolical authority of the Pope.

VI. GENERAL COUNCIL
or
CONSTANTINOPLE III.

This Council was convoked by Pope Agatho, at the request of Constantine the Bearded. The Papal legates were charged to allow of no addition, subtraction or alteration in the dogmatical decisions of his Holiness, but to require the Council to promulgate, without reservation, the traditions of the Roman See. "*Nihil profecto præsumant augere, minuere vel mutare, sed traditiones hujus sedis Apostolicæ, ut a prædecessoribus Apostolicis Pontificibus instituta est, sinceriter enarrare.*"

Agatho likewise asserted his Apostolical authority in his letter to the Emperor, whom he reminds that the Church of Rome has never strayed from the path of truth into the by-ways of error, and that her decisions have always been received as a rule of faith, not merely by individuals, but also by the Councils. "*Hæc Apostolica ecclesia nunquam a via veritatis in qualibet erroris parte deflexa est.*" This is the rule of true faith. "*Hæc est veræ fidei regula.*" Alluding to the words, "Confirm thy brethren," the Pontiff remarks that the successors of St. Peter have always strengthened the Church in the truth. Hence he infers that "all bishops, priests and laics, who wish to please the God of truth, must study to conform to the Apostolical rule of the primitive faith, founded on the rock Peter, and preserved by him from error."

In his letter to the Council he alludes to the instructions given to his legates, and cautions the Fathers not to regard the questions brought before them as open to debate. He informs them, that they are required to embrace, in a compendious definition, the several articles which he has already pronounced certain and immutable, and then to promulgate the decision all over the world. "*Non tamen tamquam de incertis contendere, sed ut certa et immutabilia compendiosa definitione proferre, simpliciter observantes, ut hæc eadem ab omnibus prædicari, atque apud omnes obtineri jubeatis."*

Here, then, is an instance of the policy, which, from the earliest times, the Holy See invariably observed toward the Councils of the East. Before the Assembly went into session, the Pope had already pronounced upon the point in question and transmitted his decision as a *rule of faith*, from which no one was allowed to deviate even a hair's breadth. The duty that devolved upon the Council, was not so much to define the truth, as to communicate it, in the most expeditious manner, to the more distant provinces of the Christian world. It was on the present occasion, that the Fathers used the words, to which we had occasion to allude above. "It seemed to us paper and ink; but Peter has spoken by the mouth of Agatho." *"Charta et atramentum videbatur, et per Agathonem Petrus loquebatur."*

Demetrius, Bishop of Persias, gave expression to the sentiments of the Council, in the memorable words: "I receive the instructions of Agatho as dictated under the inspiration of the Holy Ghost, by the Blessed Peter, the prince of the Apostles." *"Tamquam a Spiritu Sancto dictata, per os beatissimi Petri, principis Apostolorum ex digito prædicti beatissimi Papæ Agathonis."* This remark expresses the sentiments of all the Fathers. For, in their address to the Emperor, they spoke of the letters of the Pope as written under an inspiration from heaven; and, in a communication to Agatho himself, they declared that they left the whole matter, under consideration, in the hands of him, who stood unmoved upon the solid rock of faith. "*Itaque tibi, quid gerendum sit, relinquimus stanti supra firmam fidei petram.*"

Finally, they once more declared, that they would abide, in all things, by the decisions of Siricius, which they regarded as "Apostolical and divine oracles" with which they had crushed the growing heresy. "*Quas ut a summo Apostolorum vertice divinitus præscriptas agnovimus, per quas exortam nuper multiplicis erroris hæreticam sectam depulimus.*"

These words of the Fathers were reëchoed by the Emperor himself, who wrote to the Pope: "We all received your dogmatical letters with open arms, and thought that we had, when receiving them, the pleasure of embracing Peter himself, when he confessed the Divinity of Christ."

Sending the Decrees of the Council around through the empire, he did not send them in the name of the Council, but of Agatho, as decisions and decrees of the Apostolical See.

VII. GENERAL COUNCIL
OF
NICÆA II.

This Council having been convoked to oppose an effectual barrier to the outrage of the Iconoclasts by Adrian I, the Pope, following the example of his predecessors, decided previously the dogmatical question. He sent this his decision in two letters to the East. The one directed to the Emperor and the Empress; the other directed to the Patriarch Tarasius.

He required his definitions to be received as a RULE OF FAITH, because he filled the chair of Peter, who transmitted the authority he had received from Christ to all succeeding Popes. "*Quibus auctoritatis potestatem, quemadmodum a Domino ei concessum est, et ipse quoque contulit ac tradidit divino jure successoribus Pontificibus.*"

Hence, he infers that the other Churches are indebted for all sound doctrine to the Holy See, which guards the deposit of faith. "*Ex ea cæteræ ecclesiæ fidei documenta sumpserunt.*"

At the opening of the Council the Papal legates put this simple question: "Does Tarasius, does the Council concur in the decision of his Holiness or not?" "*Dicat nobis Patriarcha*

Tarasius, dicat nobis sancta Synodus, si consentiat literis sanctissimi Papæ senioris Romæ, an non?" They assigned as a cause for this summary proceeding, that "neither reason nor faith would permit the raising of any doubt upon a question that had already been irrevocably decided." *"Quia de irreformabili judicio quæri nec ratio nec fides permittit."* All the Fathers replied: "We follow, accept, and acquiesce." *"Sequimur, admittimus et consentimus."*

The necessity of this, their declaration, is confirmed by their remarkable subscription to the Acts of the Council.

The majority of them subscribed with John of Ephesus, in these words: "With the grace of Christ our Lord, the true God, I believe and profess whatever is contained in the letters of his Holiness the Pope of Rome. My faith is that of Pope Adrian. With this faith I wish to appear before the judgment-seat of Christ."

John, the Bishop of Tauriminia, made his profession in the following words: "Whereas the letters sent by Adrian, are the embodiment of divine truth, I believe and confess." *"Cum velut divinæ orthodoxiæ terminus sunt literæ, quæ ab Hadriano missæ sunt, profiteor."*

Tarasius himself, writing to Adrian in the name of the Council, styles the Papal instructions "Divine oracles"—"*Deiloquas doctrinas*"—and he attributes this sacred character to the Apostolical authority of the Holy See. "*Cathedram Apostoli Petri sortita est Sanctitas Vestra.*"

VIII. GENERAL COUNCIL
OF
CONSTANTINOPLE IV.

This Council, whose object was to check the audacity of the refractory Photius, was convened by Pope Adrian II. He was zealously seconded by the Emperor Basil, who, by request of the Pope, exerted his influence to gather the prelates of the Christian world into the great Eastern Capital. The letter addressed by the Pope to the Emperor was read during the first session of the Council. It required the Fathers, under the severest censures, to consign to the flames, in full Council, all the papers of the cabal held by Photius, and to obliterate so completely every vestige of its infamous proceedings, that not even a letter might remain at the close of the meeting. "*Nec superesse apud quemlibet vel unum jota vel unum apicem, nisi forte quis totius clericatus, imo totius nominis Christiani dignitate carere voluerit.*"

The Pope declared that every one who would refuse to do so would lose at once, "*ipso facto,*" every degree of clerical dignity—nay, even the claim to be called a Christian.

Having faithfully executed the order, all the Fathers exclaimed, as with one voice: " Blessed be the Lord, who has deigned to accept some satisfaction for your Holiness."

Adrian likewise sent to Constantinople a document, entitled "*Libellus,*" which was made the test of orthodoxy. Without subscribing to its teachings, no one who had fallen into the new errors could hope for reconciliation with the Church and the Holy See. This Papal document teaches us that the first requisite for salvation is a strict adherence to the rules of true faith. "*Prima salus est, rectæ fidei regulam custodire.*" What this rule is, the Pope himself informs us when he writes: "Our Lord said to Simon: Thou art Peter, and upon this rock I will build my Church." History furnishes abundant evidence that this promise has not been void, because the faith of the Holy See has never been infected with error. "*Hæc, quæ dicta sunt, rerum probantur effectibus, quia in sede Apostolica immaculata est semper Catholica servata religio et sancta celebrata doctrina.*"

All the Fathers of the Council attested in

writing, that, by following the decrees and decisions of the Holy Pope Adrian, they hoped to abide in the communion of that Church, which is the repository of true Christian faith. The formula of their profession reads thus: "In the presence of the undersigned witnesses, I, N. N., Bishop of N., have affixed my signature to the profession of my faith drawn up by the Blessed Adrian, our Sovereign Pontiff and Pope." "*Ego, N. N., Episcopus N., huic professionis meæ libello, facto a me in beatissimo Hadriano summo Pontifice et universali Papa, subscripsi, et testes qui subscripserunt, rogavi.*"

We consider the subscription of this formula of Pope Adrian, by the Fathers of this General Council, as the clearest and most succinct illustration of the mystical union of the members of the Church, with their Head, through faith. The Fathers confess that they believe not as reposing on a vital element of faith, hidden in their own mind, but as believing by that vital element by which the Head of the Church is believing, and from whose faith the strength and integrity of faith for all the members of the Church emanate.

During the second session all the bishops, who had been implicated in the Photian schism, after subscribing to the formula of Adrian, were again interrogated, whether they had heard the "*Li-*

bellus" read and were ready to submit to its decisions. They all exclaimed: "We accept your judgment as that of the Son of God." *"Judicium vestrum tanquam ex persona filii Dei habemus."*

In the third session a letter was read, written by the Pope to Ignatius, in which the decisions of the Holy See are called irrevocable.

Ignatius himself wrote, in a similar manner, to Pope Nicholas. His letter, which was read during the third session of the Council, contains such expressions as the following: "For the ailments of the body there are many physicians; but for the wounds of the soul there is but one, the Bishop of Rome." *" Unum et singularem præcellentem atque Catholicissimum medicum ipse—solus ex toto magister Deus omnium produxit—videlicet tuam fraternam sanctitatem."* "As the successors of St. Peter have inherited his privileges, they have always signalized themselves by rooting out the tares of heresy." *"Eradicatores et peremptores malorum zizaniorum in exortis hæresibus et prævaricationibus."*

The Fathers of the Council also aver that they consider Nicholas, as well as his successor Adrian, to be the organ of the Holy Ghost." *"Itaque beatissimum Papam Nicolaum, nec non et sanctissimum Hadrianum Papam successorem, organum Spiritus Sancti habentes.*

They, as well as Ignatius and the Emperor, petitioned the Pope to recognize the validity of the orders administered by the intruded Patriarch. But in vain. Adrian briefly replied: "*Non est in nobis: Est et non est.*" "Our decision is irrevocable; we can not contradict ourselves."

Such is the history of the first eight Œcumenical Councils held in the East, such the language, in which they speak of the Supreme and Infallible Authority of the Roman Pontiff and his decisions. The weight drawn from the acts of these first eight Œcumenical Councils can not be overrated. They were Councils held in the East where the Episcopacy was protected by the imperial power. These Councils, moreover, were composed, for the majority, of eastern patriarchs, primates, and bishops, who from the very foundation of Constantinople as the new residence of the emperors of the East, looked upon the Western Church with so great jealousy. Nevertheless they bowed with such unbounded reverence and submission to the decrees and orders of Rome, extolling, in yet more emphatical terms, its authority, than the Popes themselves did. It is truly lamentable that the arrogance and pride, so deeply ingrained in the patriarchs of Constantinople, finally involved this once fairest portion of Christianity in so fatal and fanatical a schism. Still even now, all vestiges of that filial devotion to the Holy See have not yet quite disappeared.

IX. GENERAL COUNCIL
OF
LATERAN I.

This Council was convoked by Calixtus II, for the purpose of setting at rest the vexed question of *Investitures*. The thousand bishops who answered his summons, did not deliberate in public sessions, upon the steps to be taken, but, by fasting and prayer, invoked the light of Heaven upon the Holy Father, who was meanwhile making out his final sentence.

Like the Fathers of the preceding Councils, they considered him the "organ of the Holy Ghost;" so that, when he had once given his decision they regarded the point as settled. Accordingly the agreement, which was entered into between the Emperor and the Sovereign Pontiff, was appropriately called the *"Pactum Calixtinum"*—"Compact of Calixtus"—and not the "Compact of the Lateran Council." The Emperor yielded and took the following oath: "For the love of God, of the Holy Roman

Church, and of the Pope, as well as for the good of my soul, I, Henry, renounce all claim to the right of Investiture."

It may not be amiss to remind our readers, that these occurrences belong to a period, during which the faithful were wont to look up to the Popes, as the arbiters, who decided upon even the temporal destinies of Christian nations.

It does not belong to our thesis to enter upon a discussion, by what right the Popes acted in that manner, but we only remark, that evidently the veneration, with which all the Christian world looked upon the Roman Pontiff as the highest and supreme judge in matters of faith and morals, inclined them almost irresistibly to submit also to his arbitration the temporal affairs of princes and peoples.

X. GENERAL COUNCIL
of
LATERAN II.

This Council, convoked by Innocent II, was attended by about one thousand bishops. Its objects were the extinction of the schism headed by the famous Peter Leo, the condemnation of the heresies broached by Peter of Bruis, and the eradication of divers abuses, which the remissness of some prelates had allowed to creep into the provinces under their jurisdiction.

The Pope, in this Council, exercised his supreme judicial authority over the assembled Episcopacy in, we may say, a palpable manner. Innocent, after calling by name those Archbishops and Bishops whom he considered guilty, first severely rebuked them for their faults, and then, with his own hand, stripped them of their Episcopal insignia.

The Council then was held, but all the Canons enacted in that Council were not promulgated in the name of the Council, but in that of the Pope, as it may be seen from the very preamble. "*Innocentius II in Concilio Lateranensi secundo.*" "Innocent in the Second Council of Lateran." This was also the case in regard to all other General Councils, when the Holy Father was personally presiding over them. This manner of promulgating the Acts, Decrees, and Ordinations of a General Council when the Pope in person presided, shows very powerfully in whose authority the whole legislative character of the Council itself was vested. If the announced General Council takes place next year, we have no doubt, that its enactments also will be promulgated under the heading: Pius IX in the Council of the Vatican.

XI. GENERAL COUNCIL
OF
LATERAN III.

The Eleventh General Council assembled, under an order from Alexander III, to suppress the schism commenced by the apostate Octavian, to quell the disturbances excited by the Albigenses, and to correct sundry abuses, which had found their way into the sanctuary.

The Canons, promulgated by this Council, were all of a disciplinary character. The Fathers did not even consider it advisable to comdemn the heresies of the Albigenses, because, after the decision given by the Sovereign Pontiff previous to the convocation, they regarded any further action as superfluous. Besides, the Pope, in the Council itself, exercised his Apostolical authority as the supreme judge in matters of faith in a most conspicuous manner, because, when Peter Lombard, Archbishop of Paris, was charged with teaching that, as man, Christ was a mere mythical personage, Alexander, without so much as consulting the Fathers upon the measures to be taken, summarily condemned the error, and, in a letter to William, the Archbishop of Sens, directed the Bishops of France how to act.

The submission of the French Church, which regarded these Papal decisions as infallible, found its fullest expression in the memorable words of Walter of St. Victor. "Let those troublesome quibblers, stricken by the thunderbolts of an Apostolical definition, cease croaking." "*Qû'ils cessent de croässer, ces importûns sophistes, atterrés qu'ils sont par le tonnerre d'une définition apostolique.*"

XII. GENERAL COUNCIL
OF
LATERAN IV.

This Council, convoked by order of Innocent III, in the year 1215, gathered together no less than twelve hundred and eighty-five prelates, of whom seventy-one were Archbishops, four hundred and twelve Bishops, and over eight hundred Abbots. The Patriarchs of Jerusalem and Constantinople, as well as the Maronite Archbishop, who had lately been reconciled to the Church, assisted in person, together with a number of embassadors from various European courts. The Patriarchs of Antioch and Alexandria sent their delegates to represent them in the Council, and to ask for reconciliation with the Church of Rome.

The Pope in the Council prescribed the profession of faith. During the proceedings of the Council he censured a work of the Abbot Joachim, but spared its author, who had previously made a written declaration to abide by the decision of the Holy See.

The fifth Canon of the Council pronounced the Church of Rome "the mother and teacher of all other Churches." "*Utpote universorum Christi fidelium mater et magistra.*" All decrees of the Council were promulgated in his name.

XIII. GENERAL COUNCIL
OF
LYONS I.

The XIII General Council, held by order of Innocent IV, in the year 1245, was attended by the Emperor Baldwin himself, as well as by the Patriarch of Constantinople. During it the Pope pronounced judgment against the Emperor Frederic, who had rendered himself guilty of flagrant injustice. We have repeatedly remarked, that the authority formerly exercised in temporal affairs, by the successors of St. Peter, was due to that "Conscience of Christianity," which regarded them as supreme Judges in spiritual matters. The Pope himself, acting in his capacity of Supreme

Judge and Ruler of the Council, pronounced his sentence after hearing the advice of the assembled Fathers. All the Canons of the Council appeared under the heading, "*Innocentius in Concilio Lugdunensi,*" etc. " Innocent, in the Council at Lyons."

XIV. GENERAL COUNCIL
OF
LYONS II.

This Council was assembled by Gregory X, in the year 1274, to solemnize the reunion of the Eastern and Western Churches. The Emperor Michael, of Constantinople, as well as all the other European Sovereigns, were duly represented. Even the Great Khan of Tartary had sent a delegation.

The conditions, on which the schismatical Greeks would be re-admitted to the communion of the Church of Rome, had been previously fixed by Gregory X and Clement IV.

As soon as Michael had been raised to the imperial throne, he dispatched embassadors to Rome, with the view of effecting a reunion between the Greek and Latin Churches. Clement IV, who then filled the chair of St. Peter, and following the footsteps of his predecessors, sent to Constantinople a symbol of faith—"*Libellum professionis fidei"* — to which the Emperor and all those who wished their reconciliation with the Church were required to subscribe. This symbol of faith embodied several articles of belief never before defined, and yet it allowed of no discussion or change. *"Non autem ad prædictæ discussionem vel novam definitionem fidei."*

In thus drawing up a formula for the profession of faith, Gregory and Clement exercised a prerogative, which by itself settles our whole thesis, and which the whole theological school, in common with St. Thomas of Aquin, who was then living, have always recognized in the Vicar of Christ.

The Emperor and all the members of the Greek Clergy signed this symbol and sent embassadors, who stated that they had come to make a public profession of the faith taught by the Roman See, and promised to yield perfect obedience to its decisions.

The Pope declared in his letter to the Emperor, that a General Council should solemnize this act of reunion of the Eastern Churches with the true Church of God, but not to discuss any farther the matters already defined by Him. *"Non autem ad prædictæ discussionem vel novam definitionem fidei."* *

* Conc. tom. ii, p. 946.

In the fourth session the profession of faith, which bore the signatures of the Emperor and of the Principal Oriental Bishops, was publicly read. The ecclesiastical as well as the secular authorities of the Empire thereby acknowledged that the Roman Pontiff has inherited from St. Peter, the Prince of the Apostles, the rights of the primacy together with the plenitude of Apostolical power, and that, therefore, all questions, which touch upon the doctrines of faith, must be settled by the decision of the Holy See. "*Quem primatum se ab ipso Domino in beato Petro Apostolorum principe, sive vertice, cujus Romanus Pontifex est successor, cum plenitudine potestatis recepisse veraciter et humiliter recognovit. Sic et si quæ de fide subortæ fuerint quæstiones, suo debent judicio definiri.*"

At the conclusion of this ceremony of reconciliation, the Pope entoned the "*Te Deum;*" and immediately those present, joined in the swelling chorus, amid tears of joy.*

XV. GENERAL COUNCIL
of
VIENNE.

The XV General Council, which various heretical movements and a relaxation of ecclesias-

* Raynald ad ann. 1212, Conc. tom. ii, p. 957.

tical discipline had rendered very desirable, was convoked, in the year 1311, by Clement V.

In his encyclical, he reminded the faithful of the authority vested in the Roman Pontiff, whom the Lord has intrusted with the government of all the Churches, in order that those who have been regenerated in the baptismal font, may insure their salvation by adhering to the teachings of the Holy See, and guard against the fate of such as stray from the path of sound doctrine. "*Sane Romana Ecclesia, mater alma fidelium, caput est disponente Domino Ecclesiarum omnium et magistra, a qua, velut a fonte primitivo, ad singulas alias ejusdem fidei rivuli derivantur—ad cujus regimen voluit Christi clementia Romanum Pontificem vice sui deputare ministrum, ut institutionem ipsius et doctrinam, eloquio veritatis Evangelicæ traditam, cuncti renati fonte baptismatis teneant et conservent; ut, qui sub hac doctrina cursum vitæ recte peregerint, salvi fiant, qui vero ab ea discesserint, condemnentur.*"*

This formula, which gave the tone to all the proceedings of the Council, may be regarded as a fair index of the disposition with which the Fathers assembled. It need not, then, be a matter of surprise, that all the Decrees of the Council, together with the Ordinations, Decisions, and

* Conc. tom. ii, p. 1539.

Decrees passed by the Pope, before and after the convocation, subsequently appeared in the SAME volume under the head of "CLEMENTINE ENACTMENTS." "CLEMENTINÆ." It was but the application of the principle, that the regulations of the Holy See are equally binding, whether made IN or OUT OF a Council.

In the treatise "On the Holy Trinity and on the Catholic Faith"—"*De Summa Trinitate et fide Catholica*"—this Council explicitly states, that it belongs exclusively to the Apostolical See to pronounce dogmatically upon points of faith. "*Ad quam Apostolicæ considerationis aciem* DUMTAXAT, *hæc declarare pertinent.*"

XVI. GENERAL COUNCIL
OF
CONSTANCE.

This Council assembled in 1414, with the view of suppressing the schism occasioned by the uncertainty, in which the election of the new Pope was, at that time, involved. The whole Western Church was divided into antagonistic parties, that contended, with much ardor, for their respective nominees.

This disagreement, concerning the lawful head

of the Church, introduced an element far too important to be disregarded in this connection. Without due attention to this fact, it is utterly impossible to view, in the proper light, the proceedings of the Council previous to the day, on which Pope Martin V was generally recognized as the representative of Christ.

Those who deny the absolute supremacy of the Pope, and advocate the superior authority of a Council, are wont to point to the Synod of Constance, because it started from the principle that every one, "even though he be a person of Papal dignity"—"*etiamsi Papalis sit dignitatis*"—owes obedience to the representatives of Christendom assembled to deliberate on the interests of the Church. Such persons evidently forget that it was the object of the Council to consider the claims of the Papal pretenders. When once it became known, who was the lawful successor of St. Peter, the Council assumed quite a different tone, and acknowledged the supreme authority of the Holy See, in terms fully as explicit as had ever been used by any previous Council.

The Fathers, having taken up the question concerning the Wickliffites, did not pronounce new ecclesiastic censures against them, but contented themselves with reminding the faithful, that the sect and its infamous doctrines had been previously condemned by the decisions of the Holy See. These decisions are irrefragable, remarks the Council, because it is impossible that the Apostolical See, that is to say, the Pope, should err. "*Impossibile est, quod* TALIS SEDES *aliquid determinet et teneat pro fide Catholica recta, quod non esset fides recta.*" For, if she could err, would she lay claim to the name of MOTHER and TEACHER of all the churches? How could she presume to pronounce judgment upon every body, while no one is allowed to pronounce judgment upon her? How could the Christian, who refuses to abide by her decisions, incur the guilt of infidelity? "*Quomodo valebit omnes judicare, de ea autem nullus judicare permittitur? Quomodo Christianus, qui ei obedire contemnit, peccatum infidelitatis incurrit?*"

That the clause "*etiamsi Papalis sit dignitatis,*" had reference to none but the Papal pretenders, is manifest from the declaration of the Council itself, which ruled, in its fortieth session, that a Pope lawfully elected can not be bound by a Council. "*Papa rite ac canonice electus a Concilio ligari nequit.*" Martin V acted upon this principle, as soon as his authority was recognized. While the Council was still in session, he issued a Decree, which prohibited all appeals from the Holy See to any other tribunal. The

Fathers, so far from taking offense at this conduct of the person, who was indebted to them for his elevation, readily subscribed to the Decree. Allowing the Vicar of Christ to be amenable to the Council, such an assumption on the part of Martin could never have been allowed to pass unrebuked, without convicting the assembled Bishops of extreme meanness and serious dereliction of duty. The words of the bull were too explicit to allow of any misunderstanding. "It is not lawful for any person to appeal from the Roman Pontiff, who is the Supreme Judge and the Vicar of Christ on earth, or, by subterfuge, to elude his judgment in matters of faith." "*Nemini fas est a supremo Judice, seu Apostolica sede, seu Romano Pontifice, Jesu Christi Vicario in terris, appellare, aut illius judicium in causa fidei declinare.*" The Popes, certainly as soon as the Fathers of a General Council attempted to transgress their bounds, placed themselves always straight in their way.

The enemies of Papal Supremacy or Papal Infallibility had, then, better seek for more convincing arguments, than those afforded them by the Council of Constance. Had the Pope refused to confirm the Decrees made by the Fathers, the assembly of Constance would never have had any claim to the name of a General Council.

XVII. GENERAL COUNCIL
OF
FLORENCE.

We now come to the most illustrious and most stringent of all testimony taken from the authority of the General Councils to prove the truth of our thesis.

It is Florence, which once more, and for the last time, saw assembled the Hierarchy of the Eastern and Western Church; and let us now hear how those Greek Fathers, living so many centuries in schism, now uniting with the Fathers of the West, pronounced on the Apostolical authority of the Roman Pontiff as the infallible Teacher of the Church.

Their profession of faith on this point is couched in the most solemn way of a definition. They say: "We define that the Apostolic See, that is, the Roman Pontiff, has the right of Primacy over all the churches of the world; that the Roman Pontiff is the successor of St. Peter; that he is the very Vicar of Christ, the head of the whole Church, the Father and *teacher of all the faithful;* that, in the person of Peter, he was intrusted by our Lord with *full* power to feed, direct, and govern the whole flock of Christ. Such is manifestly the doctrine taught by the

Acts of the General Councils, as well as by the sacred Canons." "*Definimus sanctam Apostolicam sedem et Romanum Pontificem in universum orbem terrarum primatum tenere, et ipsum Romanum Pontificem successorem esse Beati Petri, principis Apostolorum, et verum Christi vicarium, totiusque ecclesiæ caput, et omnium Christianorum patrem et doctorem existere, et ipsi in Beato Petro pascendi, regendi et gubernandi universalem ecclesiam a D. N. J. C. plenam potestatem traditam esse, quemadmodum etiam in gestis œcumenicorum Conciliorum et in sacris Canonibus continetur.*" What a glorious and comprehensive testimony, corroborating with the seal of its authority all that we have thus far said and what we shall or can say in future to vindicate the truth of our thesis.

Almost every word of this definition is pregnant with meaning. In it, the Council declares, that the Pope is a very Peter in authority; that he is the true Vicar of Christ, the *teacher* of all Christians, and consequently also of BISHOPS; that he has received from Christ himself, not merely *some* power, but the *plenitude* of power, for the direction and guidance of the Church; and finally, that the acts of the General Councils, and the canons of the Church prove this sovereign authority to have been always recognized by the faithful, and exercised by the Popes from the very birth of Christianity.

We can not omit to call especially the attention of the reflecting reader to the expression: "*Verum Christi Vicarium.*" "The *true* and *real* Vicar of Christ." The Popes often were called the successors of St. Peter, by General Councils and the representatives of Christ. But here the Pope, with all the enforcing strength of a definition, is called the true Vicar of Christ—the eternal truth! Would this be true, if the Pope could err in matters of faith?

Christ himself promised to send, in his place, the *Holy Ghost* as his Vicar. Defining now, that the Pope is the true Vicar of Christ, the Church implicitly identified the authority of the Pope in the Church, with the ministry of the Holy Ghost in and for the Church, to be in the Church the living "organ of the Holy Ghost," the true "Paraclete," its comforter. Yes, we feel it especially in our times. Or is Pius IX not eminently the "organ of the Holy Ghost," and the "Paraclete" and comforter, at present, for the Church of God?

Joseph, the Patriarch of Constantinople, who died at Florence, before the expiration of the Council, repeated, in his last moments, the above formula, to which he had previously subscribed, and then added, with failing voice, that the Apostolical authority of the Holy See, in questions of doctrine, was designed by the Almighty to serve as the solid ground-work, upon which the faith of the true believer should rest.*

XVIII. GENERAL COUNCIL
of
TRENT.

If ever it was important to gather representatives from every quarter of the Christian world, in order to confront the startling errors of pretended world-reformers with the traditionary teachings of the Church, it certainly was so during the sixteenth century. Protestantism was not the denial or distortion of this or that particular article of Catholic doctrine, but a tissue of almost all the heresies that had hitherto been broached and condemned. It was, therefore, quite natural to expect, that it would seek to strip the Holy See of all authority in matters of faith, and, if possible, to rob Christianity itself of that innate "conscience," which instinctively led the children of the Church to regard as divine the decisions of the Sovereign Pontiff.

---

* Conc. tom. xiii, p. 494.

Under these circumstances, the Pope very wisely allowed great liberty of discussion, in order to give more weight to the decisions of the Council. Yet the world was not ignorant of the influence which Rome brought to bear upon the deliberations of the Fathers. It was so apparent, as to excite the anger of the Protestants, and even the disgust of some so-called Catholic theologians of later times. The frivolous German historian Dannemayer, blasphemously declared that "the Holy Ghost, who inspired the Fathers of the Council, was continually sent by mail from Rome to Trent."

The Council itself, in three several decrees, speaks of Rome as the mother and teacher of all the Churches.* In the twenty-fifth session it ruled, "that each and every decree, in whatsoever form or terms it may be couched, be so understood, that the authority of the Roman See shall remain unimpaired." "*Omnia et singula sub quibuscumque clausulis et verbis, declarat, ita decreta fuisse, ut in his salva semper auctoritas sedis Apostolicæ sit et esse intelligatur.*" Beside all the canons and decrees of the Council, which lasted for so many years, only became binding when approved by the Roman Pontiff.

---

* Sess. 14, In. Doct. de Ext. Unct.; Sess. 22, c. 8; Sess. 25, Decr. 2.

We can not conclude this rapid sketch of the General Councils, without alluding to the illustrious assembly of more than two hundred bishops, who met at Rome in the year 1854, to assist at the solemn definition of the Immaculate Conception. During the last session, after all the theologians had argued the point upon the subject, with great depth of wisdom, all the bishops, as though moved by one and the same spirit, turning toward Pius IX, broke out into the exclamation: "Peter teach us!" *"Petre doce nos!"*

This spontaneous and unanimous acclamation showed that, according to the convictions, grounded on faith, of these two hundred bishops, it was not the reasoning of the Doctors and neither their own theological science and ability, and neither their common view already previously expressed in their writings to the Holy Father, but that it was his sole and own judgment—his faith, which they addressed, in order to hear, through his mouth, as the organ of the Holy Ghost, what they and the whole Church were required to believe, in this matter, to be a "dogma of faith."

IV.

TESTIMONY OF THE POPES THEMSELVES,

ASSERTING THEIR PREROGATIVE AS THE SUPREME AND INFALLIBLE JUDGES IN MATTERS OF FAITH.

Though, at first sight, the testimony of the Popes may appear inadmissible upon this subject, because it constitutes them judges in their own cause—"*judices in propria causa*"—yet, upon reflection, it will be found to be quite as conclusive as any other of a less personal nature.

In the first place, not every testimony in one's own cause is, *ipso facto*, invalid; for, then, nobody could advance an argument to prove his rights. Such a testimony is all the more unexceptionable when given in favor of a prerogative due to no individual merit of ours, but inseparable from the office which we hold; of a prerogative publicly asserted before such as know upon what claims it rests; of a prerogative affecting an entire community, and exercised against enemies who would contest it, were there any prospect of success.

Applying these remarks to the subject in question, we hold that the testimony of the Popes furnishes a conclusive argument in favor of their own Infallibility. For, they claimed this prerogative in virtue of their office; they claimed it in the face of Bishops and Priests, of Kings and Princes, of whom many were deeply interested in the matter; they claimed it, in fine, in defiance of their bitterest enemies, of schismatics and heretics in the East and the West: and they sustained their claim by the authority of Scripture and Tradition.

We have only to recollect those most solemn claims for this their privilege, uttered by the Popes on occasion of the celebration of the First Eight General Councils of the East.

Had the Popes not known themselves to be in possession of an entirely indisputable right, when claiming to be the Supreme Judges in matters of faith, all circumstances of time, places, and persons, would have induced them, in all human prudence, to assume, while facing those Œcumenical

Councils, quite a different stand, and to pursue quite another course of proceeding than they actually did.

Reviewing the history of the Œcumenical Councils, the Popes at every step defied the Fathers of those Councils to do any thing further than acknowledge this sublime privilege of the Holy See of St. Peter at Rome.

We remember the examples of a Leo, Agatho, and the two Adrians. They even did not permit so much as the change of an "iota" in their professions of faith, no matter if even the same truth were expressed. They acted so in the face of the Greeks in the far East, whose prejudices against the Western Church were known to them. They acted so, opposed by mighty adversaries, who often were protected by the whole strength of the Imperial power; and, how remarkable! no one dared even to say a word, which would have called in question the Apostolical authority of the See of Rome as the Supreme Tribunal in matters of faith.

Were there no other utterances on the part of the Popes, than those already mentioned in the testimony of the General Councils, they would afford a very strong and more than sufficient testimony in regard to their consciousness in the successors of St. Peter as to their privilege. But they repeated also, on many other occasions, these their claims. To them we shall now devote our attention.

Such declarations were unnecessary so long as no rebellious spirit arose to resist the right in question. The right itself was exercised, even in the Apostolic age, by Pope Clement, and repeatedly through the course of three hundred years; but the "conscience of Christianity," which was far too correct and enlightened to call it in question, required no particular direction in this matter. It was not until the recreant children of the household, protected by the civil power, raised the standard of revolt, that the Sovereign Pontiff found himself necessitated to contend, in explicit terms, for the prerogatives vested in him. Such an occasion, however, presented itself as soon as the cross began to adorn the crowns of earthly princes. Arius had disseminated doctrines which aimed at the very life of Christianity. His partisans, who daily grew in number, went so far as to hold Councils, and sustained by the protection of the deluded sons of Constantine, expelled St. Athanasius and other orthodox Bishops from their Sees. Pope JULIUS, who saw the dangers that threatened the faith, interfered and wrote to the fallen Bishops of the East: "Do you not know that it is customary to write to us, in order that we may define what is right." "*An ignari estis, hanc consuetudinem esse, ut primum nobis scribatur, ut hinc, quod justum est, definiri possit.*" * These words of the Holy Father contain a latent meaning, which should have told with humiliating effect, upon the parties concerned.

The meaning of this reproach by the Holy Father, is evidently as follows: "We understand that you may have been puzzled and misled in regard to your judgment about the mystery of the Holy Trinity; but how could you be so blind or so rash as not to realize the obligation, known for ages, of waiting for our decision upon all points of doctrine?"

After this censure of their conduct, Julius annulled their enactments and restored the deposed Bishops to their Sees. So intimately was the whole proceeding connected with faith, that not even the heretical Bishops could fail to see, in the acts of the Pope, the condemnation of their errors. Yet they feared to make any opposition, and, crushed by the weight of his authority, reluctantly submitted to his decisions." †

Not long after, Constans, who had resolved to control the influence of the Synod held at Rimini, threatened to send Pope LIBERIUS into exile. The fearless representative of Christ replied:

* Hard. i, 610.   † Ibid.

"Thou canst not diminish the words of faith by my solitude." *"Non diminues tu, solitudine mea, verba fidei."* The import of this pithy little sentence can not be mistaken: "Even when I am exiled and compelled to pine away in weary solitude, I still continue to be the bearer of the deposit of the holy faith of all."

Himerius, Bishop of Spain, had asked Pope Damasus for instructions on ecclesiastical matters of considerable importance; but, Damasus having died, his successor SIRICIUS answered the petition: "Thou hast asked us, as the head of the Church; we answer, then, in the name and with the authority of Peter, who protects the heirs of his spiritual power, and we decide, not merely for thy personal direction, but for that of all the Churches in general." *"Quid ab universis Ecclesiis sequendum sit, quid vitandum, generali pronuntiatione decernimus."* Accompanying the answer was an order to inform the Bishops of Gaul, Spain, and Africa of the decision.

Marca directs attention to the fact, that this Rescript claims for the decisions, which were given by Siricius in private, as much authority as if they had been delivered by him in full Council.

In another letter, addressed to all the Bishops of the world — *"ad universos Episcopos"* — the

Pope emphatically declares: "If any body dares to set aside this ordinance, let him know that he is cut off from our communion, and guilty of the pains of hell." *"Si quis, inflatus mente carnis suæ ab hac canonis ratione voluerit evagari, sciat se a nostra communione exclusum et gehennæ pœnas habiturum."*

Abbot Gerbert concluded, with much reason, that Siricius would never have used these expressions and menaces of everlasting perdition, had he not been conscious of his right to decide upon the point in question and of the opinion entertained concerning this right by the faithful at large.

Pope Zosimus (†418) likewise reminded the African Bishops, that no one dared to call in question the decisions of the Holy See—*"Ut de ejus judicio nemo disceptare audeat"*—and he assigns as reason, that the dignity and power conferred by the Lord upon Peter, descends, without diminution, to every succeeding Pope. Hence he infers, that the decisions of the Holy See are irrevocable, and as firm as the foundations of the Church. Finally, he concludes by appealing to the convictions of the prelates, whom he addresses: "You are fully aware of all this," writes he, "as priests are bound to be." *"Ex ipsa quoque Christi promissione, ut et ligata sol-*

veret, et soluta vinciret, par potestatis data conditio in eos, qui sedis hæreditatem, ipso annuente, meruissent ; nec patitur aliquid privilegii aut aliqua titubare aura sententiæ, cui ipsa sui Nominis firma et nullis hebetata motibus constituit fundamenta. Non latet vos, fratres charissimi, sed nostis, quemadmodum sacerdotes scire debetis.

We know the effect of his decision. St. Augustin with all the Africans exclaimed: " Rome has spoken, the dispute is at an end."

A similar tone pervades the letter of Zosimus, to the Bishops of Gaul and to the Synod of Rimini. The faithful of those days recognized the claims advanced by the Pope; but, long after, the famous Causabon, who had not their religious instincts, took offense at the freedom which he assumed, and scornfully spoke of him as a *premature* HILDEBRAND.*

We agree willingly to the application, because it evidently proves that what Gregory VII claimed, was not usurpation and the fruit of the ignorance of the so-called darkness of the Middle Ages, but the clear consciousness of a right, inherited from his predecessors, since the beginning of the Christian name.

BONIFACE I († 422), the successor of Zosimus, was not less positive than he in vindicating

* Exorcit. xv.

the rights of the Holy See. In a letter to his Vicar, Rufus of Thessalonica, he writes: "Never was it allowed to call up anew any point, on which the Holy See had already pronounced;" while, in a communication to Peregines he declares: "No one ever called in question the decision of this Apostolical tribunal, without laying himself open to its censures." "*Nisi qui de se voluit judicari.*"*

A book entitled "*Præteritorum sedis Apostolicæ Episcoporum Auctoritates,*" and commonly attributed to Pope Cœlestin, contains this remarkable sentence: "We profess nothing, but what the See of Peter has taught and commanded by the mouth of his successors; so that we regard it as not at all Catholic whatever is opposed to its decision." "*Ut prorsus non æstimemus Catholicum, quod apparuerit præfatis sententiis esse contrarium.*"

Pope Xistus the successor of Cœlestin, writing to the Patriarch of Antioch, says: "Thou hast now understood what it means to be of one mind with us." And pointing out the reason of this necessary submission to the doctrinal teaching of the Pope, he writes this very remarkable sentence: "Peter, who continues to

* Ep. 8, 9, 10, 15.

live in his successors, teaches the pure unadulterated faith, which he did not acquire from hearing or reading, but which he received from the Lord himself, and which admits of no controversy or discussion." "*Absolutam et simplicem fidem, et quæ controversiam non habet accepit.*"

This passage of XISTUS means, according to the just interpretation of the learned Constant, that "the authority of the Roman Bishop is not due to his erudition or to the facilities which he enjoys of learning what is of faith, but to the relation in which he stands toward St. Peter, who was put in possession of the treasure of faith, by a direct communication from the Lord himself."*

LEO the Great (†454) urged the same point, in the sermons, which he delivered on the anniversaries of his elevation to the throne of Peter: "Who but Antichrist dares to assail the invincible fortress of truth." "*Quis est nisi Antichristus, qui pulsare audet inexpugnabilem veritatem?*" "The disposition of truth remains, and Blessed Peter, retaining the firmness of a rock, does not abandon the helm of the Church." "*Manet ergo dispositio veritatis, et B. Petrus, in accepta fortitudine, suscepta Ecclesiæ gubernacula non relinquit.*"

* Præf. in epist. Pontific.

SIMPLICIUS (†483), admonishing the Emperor Zeno of his duties, reminds him that he was entitled to do so because the Lord committed to Peter the care of his sheep, and that the teaching of the successors of St. Peter for all time to come was to remain the rule of the very Apostolical doctrine: "*Hæc et eadem Apostolicæ norma doctrinæ.*

FELIX III (†492), uses similar expressions, not only in his letter to the same Emperor, who had become a mere tool in the hand of a faction, but likewise in a letter to Acacius and Peter Fullo. The former was summoned to Rome, to give an account of his doings to PETER, and the latter was informed that he had been condemned by ST. PETER HIMSELF.

On another occasion he writes this beautiful sentence: "No matter what danger may beset the Church, the judgment of Peter never can be impaired. So far from being weakened, it grows yet more powerful under the pressure of persecution." "*Quibuslibet sit vallata Ecclesia periculis, nunquam pondus vigoris sui censura beati Petri amittit; tanto non frangitur, sed potius, erudita divinitus, crescit adversis.*"*

Do we not see these remarks strikingly veri-

* Hard. ii, 118.

fied in the steadfast opposition maintained in our times by our Holy Father to the impugners of his highest prerogatives?

St. Gelasius (†496) expresses himself in the following terms: "Peter blessed the Roman See, that the gates of hell never should prevail against it; but that it should be the harbor, in which all seeking safety there, find eternal rest. But woe to whomsoever will despise it—he may see what kind of excuses he will allege at the day of judgment." *"Quam ipse (Petrus) benedixit, ut a portis inferi nunquam, pro Domini promissione, vincatur, omniumque sit fluctuantium portus, in quo, qui requieverit, beata ac æterna statione gaudebit; qui vero contemnerit, ipse videbit, qualia genera excusationum in die judicii obtendat."*

In his letter to the Emperor Anastasius he calls the Roman See the root of the world—*"mundi radix"*—inasmuch as it communicates to the whole world the life of the true faith. Hence, if faith would be poisoned in the Roman See, Christianity itself would die away. *"Nam si, quod Deus avertat, quod fieri non posse confidimus, tale quid evenerit, unde cuiquam resistere auderemus errori? vel unde correctionem errantibus posceremus?"*

In his *Commonitorium*, addressed to the imperial Prefect Faustus, the same author declares:

"All the faithful are aware that the Holy See has the right to annul whatever is done by any Prelate of the Church, because it has the right to judge the whole Church; but no one has a right to judge it." "*Cuncta per mundum novit Ecclesia, quoniam, quorumlibet sententiis ligata Pontificum, sedes Sti. Petri Apostoli jus habet resolvendi, utpote quæ de omni Ecclesia jus habet judicandi, neque cuiquam liceat de ejus judicare judicio.*" She possesses the plenitude of judicial power—"*summam judicii totius.*" He says that he heard of persons appealing to the "Canons" in order to evade his judgment. He ridicules them, "they may keep their foolishness for themselves." "*Ineptias suas sibi servent.*"

"For evidently they do not know what they are saying, because the words of Christ, constant tradition, and the Canons themselves agree in asserting that the Holy See is empowered to sit in judgment on the whole Church." "*Quapropter non veremur, ne Apostolica sententia resolvatur, quam et vox Christi, et majorum traditio et Canonum autoritas fulcit, ut* TOTAM POTIUS ECCLESIAM IPSA JUDICET."

What an overwhelming argument is contained in these few words!

AGAPETUS (†536) required a similar act of submission from the Emperor Justinian, who accordingly subscribed the formula of profession with his own hand, and then sent the document, with his signature, back to Rome.

PELAGIUS I (†559) asserted his privilege quite as decisively, in a letter to the Bishops of Istria, whom he bids remember, that "truth can not lie, nor the faith of Peter waver or change." "*Considerate quod veritas mentiri non potuit, nec fides Petri in æternum quassari poterit vel mutari.*"

GREGORY the Great wrote to the Bishops of Gaul: "Should any dispute arise about matters of faith, it is incumbent on you to apprise us of it, that, by our decision, we may definitively settle the point in question." "*Si quam vero controversiam—DE FIDEI CAUSA evenire contigit—relatione sua ad nostram studeat perducere notionem, quatenus a nobis valeat congrua sine dubio sententia terminari.*"*

The same firmness appears in the writings of Pope THEODORE, and in those of the captive Pontiff MARTIN. In a letter, condemnatory of the imperial statute entitled the *Typus*, the latter declares the judgment of the Roman Pontiff to be the judgment of Peter himself. In a document on the heretical movements of the time, he

---

* Lib. v. Ep. 53 et 56.

adverts to the power conferred on him in the person of St. Peter, and then he exhorts all the Bishops to be the children of obedience—"*obedientiæ filii.*" In fine, he orders his vicar at Antioch to require from all a written declaration of their adhesion to the teachings of the Apostolic See.

GREGORY II (†731) vindicated the claims of the Apostolic Chair with no less resolution than Martin had done before him. He wrote to the Iconoclast Leo the Isaurian: "In virtue of the authority left to us by St. Peter, we cut you off from the Communion of the Church; for you must know that it is the prerogative of the Pope, and not of the Emperor, to decide upon articles of faith." "*Scias, imperator, Ecclesiæ dogmata non imperatorum esse, sed Pontificum.*"

Pope STEPHEN, conscious of his position in the Church, wrote to Pepin, "in the name of Peter," whom he called the enlightener of the whole world—"*illuminator totius mundi*"—and spoke of the Roman Church as the foundation of the Christian faith. "*Fundamentum fidei Christianæ, Romana Ecclesia.*"

VITALIAN and LEO II manifested the same sentiments, as did likewise ADEODATUS in his letter to the Bishops of Gaul.

NICHOLAS (†867) called the Supreme Judiciary authority of the Holy See "the universal rule of righteousness," and, in a letter addressed to the King and to the Synod of Soissons, concerning the Bishop Rothado, he remarked that the rights and privileges conferred by the Lord on the Holy See were the safeguard of the Church, and its bulwarks against the assaults of iniquity. "*Privilegia sedis Apostolicæ tegmina sunt totius Ecclesiæ Catholicæ, munimina sunt circa omnes impetus pravitatis.*" "You have an instance of it," wrote he, "in Rothado himself, the Bishop of Soissons. He fled to us for refuge, and found it. How do you know that what has happened to this Bishop, so unjustly persecuted, may not happen to you likewise? And, if it should happen, to whom will you have recourse?" "*Quod Rothado hodie contigit, unde scitis, quod cras non cuilibet eveniat vestrum? Quodsi contigerit, ad cujus confugietis auxilium?*"

No one can fail to perceive the appropriateness of this reflection. They certainly could not apply, with any hope of success, to simple Bishops of another country, whose jurisdiction is confined to their own dioceses, but only to the general Vicar of Christ, whose authority is recognized in every part of the world. Hence Rothado declared: "I appeal to that supreme authority which no one can dispute or contradict." "*Summam illam auctoritatem appello, cui nullus potest contradicere.*"

We admit that the incident to which we here allude has no direct reference to our thesis; nevertheless it shows most clearly, how becoming it was, that Christ, for the good and protection of the Church, diffused over the whole globe, has invested its Head with a plenitude of spiritual power, to meet every emergency in every part of the world.

Conscious of this supreme power exercised by the Popes, in matters of faith as well as of discipline, Nicholas also wrote to the Oriental Bishops: "What was ever valid, that was not sanctioned by the See of Peter?" "*Quid ratum, quid prorsus acceptum, nisi quod Sedes beati Petri probavit, ut ipsi scitis?*" He held precisely the same language to the Bishops of the West, where he found it necessary to remind them of their duty. Thus, when he had heard that a Synod, held at Mayence, had sanctioned the divorce of King Lolhan, he annulled the proceedings of the assembly, deposed the Bishops who had taken a part in it, and pronounced the following sentence of excommunication: "If any one makes light of the dogmas, mandates, interdicts, sanctions, and decrees relative to faith or discipline, promulgated by the incumbent of the Apostolic See, let him be anathema." "*Si quis dogmata, mandata, interdicta, sanctiones vel decreta pro fide catholica, et pro ecclesiastica disciplina a sedis Apostolicæ præside promulgata, contempserit, anathema sit.*"

JOHN VIII (†882) uses the following emphatic expression in his letter to Michael of Bulgaria: "You are aware, we presume, that the Roman See has never been accused by other Sees of heresy, but that she has often reproached other Sees, and particularly that of Constantinople, for their defection, and that she freed them from the stain contracted, when they were submissive, but condemned them when they proved refractory."

We must not omit the remarkable words addressed by the same Pope to Peter Comes: "Let the King peruse the Gospel record. There he will find that Christ prayed for nobody else than for Peter, who came to Rome; there he lived; there he died; there he left his own authority for all the time to come.*

STEPHEN VI (†897) solemnly asserts the prerogative of the Papal Apostolical teaching authority, in a letter written to Constantinople, when Photius began to manifest his schismatical

* Hard. vi, 16-18, 50, 56, 59, 98, 102.

tendencies. "The Church of Rome," writes he, "was intended to serve as a model and mirror for all the other Churches. Any point which she has defined, is forever decided and unchangeable." "*Romana Ecclesia velut speculum quoddam et exemplum ecclesiis cæteris proposita est, quæ si quid definierit, id omnibus sæculis firmum inconcussumque manet.*" He cautions the Emperor, who showed himself favorable to the Photian faction, not to interfere in Church matters: "You should confine your solicitude to the duties of your civil administration." "*Rerum tantum sæcularium curam gerere debes.*" "The care of the Church has been intrusted by the Lord to the Roman Pontiff, whose dignity is as far above that of an earthly sovereign, as the stars are above the earth."

The writings of Leo VII (†939), of Agapetus II (†955), of John XIII (†972), of Benedict VI (†974), of Gregory V (†999), of Sylvester II (†1003), and of Benedict VII (†983), breathe all the same consciousness of this their privilege and rights.

Fully aware of it, LEO IX (†1047) addressed the schismatic Greeks of his time in the following emphatical ways: "Christ distinctly affirmed that He had asked for Peter stability of faith; and who is so bereft of reason — '*tantæ am-*

entiæ'—as to harbor the thought that His prayer was not heard? The Lord intimated that a time of trial would come; but He also promised that, like an anchor fixed in the bottom of the sea, the faith of Peter would save the imperiled bark from destruction. The promise was not in vain; for the Roman Pontiffs have invariably dispelled the hallucinations of heretics, and strengthened the brethren in the faith of Peter, which has never yet failed, and which never will fail unto the end." "*Tam per Petrum, quam per successores suos reprobata et expugnata sunt omnium hæreticorum commenta, et fratrum corda in fide Petri, quæ hactenus non defecit, nec usque in finem deficiet, confirmata.*" "You may think of me as a man whatever you please—'*de homine credite homines, quod vultis*'—but never shall we permit that you should dare to impair the Supreme Apostolical authority of the Roman See. He that attacks the Church of Rome, aims at subverting not merely one Church, but all Christianity. Because, how will the distressed children be able to breathe? To whom shall they fly for refuge?" "*Cujus enim sustentatione alterius respirabunt filiæ a quovis oppressæ, illa suffocata matre! cujus refugium appellabunt?*" If Pius were to die, with what anxiety and almost breathlessness would the whole Church look for another head. We regard as especially happy, the use which Leo here makes of the word *respirabunt*—breathe, inhale. For the whole Church, and consequently all its members, owe their life, through faith, to their union with the Supreme Pontiff as the visible head of the mystical body of the Church.

Victor II, Stephen IX, and Nicholas II, all reëcho the views of their illustrious predecessor. Nicholas writes to Gervasius, Bishop of Rheims: "We exercise the ministry of Peter, that we may correct errors." "*Quatenus errata corrigamus.*"

In the Synod of Rome, at which the imperial delegates assisted, Alexander II, remarked: "If the Church of Rome remain firm, all the other Churches will remain firm; but if she, who is the ground-work and basis of the rest, be undermined, all the others will of necessity soon crumble into ruin. "*Hac enim stante, reliquæ stant; sin hæc autem, quæ omnium fundamentum est et basis, obruitur, cæterarum quoque status necesse ut collabatur.*"

We have now come to the illustrious, but much-maligned Gregory VII, whom both friends and foes agree in representing to be the exponent of all the claims ever advanced by the Holy See, in the political as well as in the purely ecclesiastical order. The former, as we have remarked above, is not directly connected with our subject; yet indirectly it is, and this in a most positive and striking way, because the people and Princes seeing the Supreme Pontiffs placed as Judges on the tribunal of eternal and celestial truth, thought it but just to commit to their arbitration temporal affairs.

We would be compelled to transcribe nearly the whole *Bullarium Romanum*, because scarcely a single public document has been issued, which does not, either directly or indirectly, claim for the successors of St. Peter the right of instructing and judging the Church, and of approving or condemning whatever bears upon the dogmas of faith and morals.

Let us now consider, in what manner and to what extent the Popes have exercised the right of deciding questions of doctrine, without the concurrence of a Council. For, even though they had not expressed their views upon that subject, the mere exercise of the Papal prerogative of being the supreme and infallible judges in matters of faith, would furnish us with an evident proof of its existence, and of their determination to vindicate it, in the face of the most violent opposition.

V.

PEREMPTORY AND SOLEMN EXERCISE OF THIS PREROGATIVE.

THE POPES OF ALL CENTURIES, DEFINITIVELY BY THEIR OWN AUTHORITY, CONDEMNING HERESY AND ERRORS.

THE prerogative of the Holy See, as being the Supreme Tribunal in the Church of Christ, was exercised by the Vicar of Christ even during the life-time of St. John the Evangelist. The Corinthians being involved in disputes, which threatened to rend the unity of their infant Church, addressed themselves to Pope CLEMENT at Rome. And why should they apply to him for a definitive solution of their difficulties? Why lay their complaints before a foreign tribunal? Why not address themselves to the aged Disciple, or to the incumbent of some Apostolic Church nearer home?

We see but one plausible explanation; they knew full well that the successor of St. Peter is the ordinary Supreme Judge in matters of faith and discipline. Clement at once gave his decision, and restored peace to the Church. Schmitz calls things by their right name, when he speaks of this occurrence as "a recourse of the Church of Corinth to the Roman See."*

Even the famous "*Centuriators*" of Magdeburg acknowledged that, in this instance, Clement acted as Supreme Judge in matters of faith. Besides it is very providential and remarkable that the record of this event was preserved in the Eastern Church, and sent to the West by Cyril, the Calvinistic Patriarch of Constantinople.†

The judicial prerogative of the Holy See was exercised in a very remarkable manner, during the second century, by Pope HYGINUS. He condemned the errors of Valentinus, Cerdonius and Marcion, without calling a Council; and yet, as Bercastel observes, even the heresiarchs themselves did not appeal to any other tribunal, as they would certainly have done, had there been any possibility of calling in question the authority of the Sovereign Pontiff.‡

---

* Dissert. de pot. legisl. Ecc. Heidelberg, 1792.
† See the German Journal: "Der Katholik," Aug., 1825, p. 149.
‡ Bercastel i, 143.

During the same second century, this prerogative was exercised by ELEUTHERIUS against the Gnostics, and by VICTOR against Ebion, Artemon, and Theodotus of Byzantium, all of whom were condemned and *remained condemned.*

It was exercised in the third century by Pope ZEPHYRINUS, against Praxeas and Proclus, Montanus and Tertullian, who were condemned, and *remained condemned.* Like Valentinus and Cordonius, these heretics tried to deceive Rome; but, like them, they failed. For, as Cyprian already remarked, in point of doctrine, Rome can neither deceive nor be deceived.

The same Pope absolved the repentant heretic Natalius, who approached the chair of Peter in sackcloth and ashes, craving pardon and reconciliation. So well were heretics themselves aware, before what tribunal they had to appear in order to justify themselves, that it was quite unnecessary for Rome to send them a formal summons. As Christians, they could not but know in whom the plenitude of Apostolical power resides.

Pope CORNELIUS exercised this supreme judicial prerogative, in the third century, when he condemned Novatus and Novatianus, who accordingly *remained condemned.*

Pope DYONISIUS exercised it, in condemning

the errors of Sabellius and Paul of Samosata, which *remained condemned.*

By this Apostolical authority SYLVESTER condemned Arius and his heresy, and it *remained condemned.*

Even such as had not embraced the doctrines of Christianity, had heard of the supreme judicial authority recognized by the faithful. Porphyrius, a heathen philosopher, who edited a treatise against the new faith, speaks of Paul reproaching his LORD and MASTER, PETER. The pagan writer mistook the Peter, of whom mention is made in the Acts, for Peter the Apostle. Yet the expression "Lord and Master," though grossly misapplied, furnishes us a convincing proof of the dignity and power conferred on the Prince of the Apostles.

Amianus Marcellinus, also a pagan historian of the third century, adverts, during the course of his remarks on Athanasius and Constantius, to the supreme judiciary authority of the Roman See in matters of faith.

This authority was exercised by Pope DAMASUS, in the fourth century, against Apollinaris, Timotheus, Vitalis, and Priscillianus. This Priscillian, as we learn from the account of Sulpitius Severus, had come to Rome, to clear himself of the charges preferred against him—"*ut objecta purgaret.*" But the Holy Father, suspecting his insincerity and hypocrisy, would not admit him into his presence. "No heretic," remarks Lupus, "ever beheld the countenance of the Pope, before recanting his errors and submitting to the decisions of the Holy See." The pretended reformers of Pistoja experienced the truth of this remark, at a much more recent date.

This right of supreme and infallible judiciary authority in matters of faith was exercised in the same century, by SIRICIUS, the successor of Damasus, against Jovinian, whose errors were condemned, without the concurrence of a Council, and *remained condemned.*

Again, this right was exercised, at this epoch, in a remarkable manner, by Popes INNOCENT and ZOSIMUS, against the Pelagians. When Pelagius and his abettor Cœlestius began to disseminate their errors, the Bishops of Africa assembled in the Councils of Carthage and Melevi, and addressed themselves to the Pope for a *definitive* sentence. Innocent acceded to their wishes and commended them for their submission to the Vicar of Christ. "Their conduct," remarked he, "was a proof, that they understood their obligations to the Holy See." "*Ad nostrum referendum esse approbastis judicium, scientes quid debeatur Apostolicæ Sedi.*"

Innocent is more lengthy and explicit in his answer to the Council of Melevi: "You have followed," wrote he, "what you, as well as I, know to have been the practice of the faithful from the beginning." *Antiquæ scilicet regulæ formam secuti, quam toto semper orbe mecum scitis esse servatam.* "From this Apostolical fountain perennial streams are pouring over all the provinces that thirst for the waters of truth. In matters of faith, especially, all the Bishops should emulate your example, and refer their doubts to no one but Peter, whose authority extends over all the Churches of the world." "*Præsertim quoties fidei ratio ventilatur, arbitror omnes fratres et Episcopos nostros nonnisi ad Petrum, i. e., sui nominis et honoris auctorem referre debere, velut nunc detulit vestra dilectio, quod per totum mundum possit omnibus Ecclesiis in commune prodesse.*"

Even the authority and learning of such men as St. Augustin, who lived at this time, can not overbalance the decisions of the Holy See. As private doctors, they may be entitled to the greatest possible respect; but, like other men, they are still liable to err, and therefore they have no right to make the faithful adopt their own private views as the teachings of the Church. St. Augustin was well aware of this. Innocent and Zosimus certainly did not possess so much genius and learning as he did, but they were invested with a prerogative which he did not enjoy. He could write better books than they on the Pelagian heresy; but he could not, like them, condemn it with infallible authority. He governed the Church of Hippo, which had no claim to the Apostolical prerogative of Infallibility; they filled the See of Rome, which the Lord had promised to preserve from error.

Pelagius and his adherents were condemned by the Holy See, and never called in question the authority of the tribunal, which had pronounced sentence against them. Considering the character of the heresiarch, who was ever ready to subtilize, this silence alone speaks volumes in favor of the veneration then entertained for the dogmatical utterances of the Holy See. Here, especially, the axiom of Gregory of Nazianze has its full application: "$\Pi\rho\tilde{a}\xi\iota\varsigma\ \dot{\epsilon}\pi\dot{\iota}\beta a\sigma\iota\varsigma\ \vartheta\epsilon\omega\rho\dot{\iota}a\varsigma$." He dared not have recourse to fanciful *distinctions*, as the Jansenists in modern times have done, in order to evade the crushing weight of the Apostolical censures hurled against them. On the contrary, he sought to justify himself, as best he might, before the Pope, whom he endeavored to beguile, by a feigned submission to authority. A written explanation of his conduct concludes with these words: "If these our writings should be found to contain any erroneous or rash assertion, we submit it to the correction of him who preserves the faith of Peter." "*Emendari a te cupimus, qui Petri fidem tenes.*" "But if my profession be favorably received by the Apostolical See, no one, who will continue to find fault with me, can fail to be convinced, not that I am a heretic, but that he, be he even an Augustin, is certainly not a Catholic."

St. Augustin himself relates that Cœlestius, the friend of Pelagius, did not dare controvert or impugn the decision of Innocent, but that he resolved on going to Rome and condemning every thing which the Holy See would condemn. Like all heresiarchs, and especially those of the first ages, he did his utmost to pass for a Catholic, and to be recognized as such by the Apostolical Authority of Rome. His journey to the Holy City, though doomed to draw upon him new curses, brought about a temporary delay in the decisions of Zosimus. The forbearance shewn by the Pope at first gave offense to the Africans, who objected that, as Innocent had already condemned the teachings of Pelagius, there was no reason for giving Cœlestius another hearing. Zosimus met their complaints with the reply, that certainly no change could be made in a

* Aug. l. ii: de pecc. orig. cap. vii.

decision given by the Holy See on an article of faith; but that, as Cœlestius had appealed to the Sovereign Pontiff and invited his accusers to come to Rome and prove him guilty of the condemned propositions, and had moreover promised to retract and condemn them, should he be found guilty, it was necessary to avoid all precipitation and leisurely examine the whole matter.

Having satisfied himself of the complicity of Cœlestius, he confirmed the condemnation of the Pelagian heresy, in that remarkable letter from which we have quoted above, and of which St. Augustin said: *"Rescripta venerunt, causa finita est; utinam finiretur et error!"* The dispute is at an end; would to God that the error were also at an end!* It was on this occasion that Prosper remarked: "Zosimus, by his decision, has armed the right hand of the Bishops with the sword of Peter."

Making use of this his prerogative and plenitude of Apostolic Power, CŒLESTIN condemned Nestorius, and he *remained condemned.*

Nothing more illustrious and authoritative can be imagined than the dogmatical letters of this Pope, and of Pope LEO, condemning Eutyches and his errors. And they also *remained condemned.*

* Serm ii, de verb. Apost.

Felix III, in the fifth century, exercised the same prerogative of the Apostolical See, when he condemned the errors of Accacius and of Peter Fullo, both of whom *remained condemned.*

Agapetus exercised it, in the sixth century, against Antinuis; John IV, in the seventh century, against the *ekthesis* of the Emperor Heraclius; Theodore IV against the type of Paul of Constantinople; and Agatho against the Monothelites—all of whom *remained condemned.*

In virtue of this Apostolical prerogative, Adrian I, in the eighth century, pronounced the censures of the Church against the Iconoclasts; Adrian II, in the ninth, against Photius and his followers; Leo IX, in the eleventh, against Michael Cerularius and the errors of the Greek Church; Victor II against Berengarius; Gregory VII against the Henricians; Innocent II against Abelard.

St. Bernard and the Bishops of Soissons had charged Abelard with heresy, but they dared not condemn him. In a letter addressed to the Pope, on the part of all these prelates, the Saint gives expression to their common feeling in these words: "We refer the case to thee, who hast the authority and the power, to defeat every contrary opinion, to frustrate every effort of rebellion against the Lord, and to subject every intellect to the obedience of Christ." "*Et in captivitatem redigendum omnem intellectum ad obsequium Christi.*"

The Pope, fully conscious of the duty that had devolved on him, gave his decision in these forcible words: "Seated on the Chair of Peter, to whom the Lord hath said, 'Confirm thy brethren,' we condemn the propositions of Abelard, and impose on him, as a heretic, perpetual silence." †

In virtue of this prerogative, EUGENIUS III, in the twelfth century, pronounced sentence of condemnation against the errors of Gilbert of Parret; XISTUS IV, in the fifteenth century, against those of Peter Osma; and LEO X, in the sixteenth, against the famous "theses" of Martin Luther.

The arch-reformer did not, at first, dispute the right of the Sovereign Pontiff. On the contrary, he acknowledged it in terms which the majority of Protestants would probably denounce as the profession of some ultramontane Catholic.

As Luther's apostasy from the faith was the gradual result of his unbridled passions, it was not to be expected that he would at once manifest that fiendish hatred and contempt of the

* Ep. 192.   † Conc. tom. 10, p. 1023.

Holy See, for which he and his followers were afterward distinguished beyond all the heretics of earlier times. Hence, it need not surprise us that he wrote to LEO X, "Holy Father!"

"Prostrate at thy feet I offer myself, with all that I am and all that I have. Vivify or destroy, confirm or repeal, sanction or condemn, just as thou pleasest. I will listen to thy voice as to that of Christ, who lives in thee, and speaks by thy mouth." "*Prostratem me, O pater, pedibus tuis, offero cum omnibus quæ sum et habeo: vivifica, occide; voca, revoca; approba, reproba, ut placuerit; vocem tuam vocem Christi in te præsidentis et loquentis agnoscam, etc.*" "I protest," (how different this *protest* from that drawn up, a few years later, by his adherents!) "I protest that, by all my words and actions, present, past and *future*, I mean to render homage and obedience to the Roman Church." The world knows how he kept his promise. "Should I have said any thing which has not this for its object, I will regard it and I desire others to regard it as though it had not been said," etc. *Protestor me colere et sequi Romanam Ecclesiam in omnibus meis dictis et factis, præsentibus, præteritis et futuris. Quodsi quid aliter dictum fuerit, pro non dicto habere et haberi volo.*"

In a book entitled, "Resolutio Propositionum,"

and written in the year 1519, we find this sentence: "The whole world admits that by the words, 'thou art Peter,' the Pope's authority over the Church was established."* What do Protestants think of this assertion?

It was not until Leo had shown himself stern and inexorable, that Luther poured out a torrent of abusive and scurrilous language against the Holy See. The Pope had now become "Antichrist," and Rome the "whore of Babylon." †

Yet, even for many years after, whenever his passions subsided a little, his conscience forced him to make confessions quite incompatible with his own new doctrine, and that of Protestantism in general. Thus, in a work written twelve years after his separation from the Church, against the *Sacraments–Schwœrmer,* that is, *Revellers in regard to the Sacraments,* the apostate monk makes this reflection: "It is an awful and appalling thing to believe and teach a doctrine at variance with that, which the Church has believed and taught for fifteen hundred years. The man who does so, condemns not only the Church, but also Christ, who said 'I am with you all days even unto the consummation of the world,' and the

* Opp. Jenens, tom. v.
† Luth. de Capt. Bab., 1820.

Apostles, who inserted into the Creed the words, 'I believe in *one holy Catholic* Church.'"

It was thus that Luther moralized on the errors of others. But as soon as there was question of his own, he completely changed his tone. No sooner was he condemned than he forgot all his former *protests* and exclaimed: "What do I care whether the Popes cry out, 'The Church! the Church! the Fathers! the Fathers!' The Prophets and Apostles have erred. With the word of God we judge both the Church and Apostles."

He was, at last, so utterly blinded by his passions, as to proclaim his own infallibility: "I do not care for a hundred texts of the Bible," said he, "and if you find that my doctrine is contrary to that of the Church and of the Fathers, you must know that I care not for all that." And whence, think you, did he derive his certainty in matters of faith if he cared not for the Bible, the Church, and the Fathers? "My words," he tells us, are the words of Christ, my tongue is the tongue of Christ—I am *certain* that I can not err."*

What do you say to that, Protestants? Are

---

* See the History of the Life, Works, and Doctrines of Luther, by Audin, 1845.

you prepared to subscribe to the infallibility of the Arch-reformer? You certainly recoil at such a request, and, nevertheless, you can not refuse to do so, if you admit his principles. For, according to them, not only your master but you yourselves are invested with more than papal prerogatives. The genuine Protestant must believe in his own infallibility, or deny all certainty in matters of faith. He claims the right of believing what *he* holds, is the word of God contained in the Bible; and, therefore, he virtually makes his *own* judgment the ultimate criterion of revealed truth, the highest infallible tribunal in matters of faith, because he believes that he will be saved by faith alone. Therefore, every logical Protestant practically has to assert his own infallibility; and still he calls, with contempt, Catholics *Papists*, because they believe in the infallibility of the head of the Church. What inconsistency! This very name of *Papists*, which originated with Protestantism, and which is meant to be an odious appellation, proves that Protestants are aware to what the Catholic Church is indebted for her strength, nay, for her very existence and spiritual life. It is the immovable strength of its Head and foundation, invested in the authority of the Roman See, and Papal prerogative. We, therefore, glory in that name of Papists; for we remember the words of St. Ambrose, "Where Peter is, there is the Church." "*Ubi Petrus, ibi Ecclesia.*" Yet Protestants, cut off from the Head of the Church, adopted soon the well-known axiom, "*Cujus est regio, ejus est religio.*" The Protestants, like the Russians of our day, transferred to crowned heads the prerogatives of the Holy See. Even a woman, who chances to wear the diadem of royalty, thus becomes a very Pope for the deluded partisans of error, who are unwilling to recognize the rights of Christ's lawful representative. What a travesty of genuine Christianity!

Pius V and Gregory XIII exercised the prerogative of the Papal infallible authority against Baius, whose errors were condemned by them, and *remained condemned*. Urban VIII, Innocent X, and Alexander VII, in the seventeenth century, exercised it against the errors of Jansenius, which were condemned and *remained condemned*.

As Jansenism is one of the latest developments of error, it may prove of interest to the reader to give a brief sketch of its origin and progress. Its history furnishes us with another evidence of the strength of truth, which is not afraid to meet its opponents in broad daylight, and of the weakness of error, which never dares to appear under its true colors.

Jansenius himself had declared, before dying, that he submitted all his writings to the judgment of the Apostolical See. Yet, after his death, his errors began to spread with such alarming rapidity, that the Bishops of France found it necessary to refer the case to Rome. In their letter to Pope Innocent X, they remarked that, by appealing to the Holy See, they followed the practice of ages, which the unfailing faith of Peter will never suffer to be abrogated. "*Quem fides Petri nunquam deficiens perpetuo retineri pro jure suo postulat.*" Their appeal was soon answered; for, in the year 1653, on the 9th of June, the Pope condemned the erroneous propositions of Jansenius.

As soon as the Bishops were notified of the Pope's decision, they addressed him a letter of felicitation, in which they remarked that, as, at the request of the African Bishops, Innocent I had condemned the Pelagians, so, at the request of the French Bishops, Innocent X had condemned the Anti-Pelagians, namely, the Jansenists. "The judgment of the Holy See," wrote they, "has a divine authority throughout the whole Church, and every Christian is bound to submit to it, in all sincerity and without reservation." "*Qui omnes Christiani ex officio ipsius mentis obsequium præstare tenentur.*" "Congratulating you, therefore, by whose mouth Peter has spoken, as the Fourth Œcumenical Council declared he had done by the mouth of Leo I, we cheerfully and unhesitatingly add your Decree to the Decrees of the General Councils."

But the Jansenists, with the view of eluding the condemnation, pretended that it was sufficient to submit exteriorly by keeping "an obsequious silence," while interiorly they adhered to the same heretical principles. This, again, was referred to Rome, and, as every Catholic knew beforehand, the answer was soon returned, that this feigned submission by no means satisfied the obligations of the faithful toward the Holy See. "*Obedientiæ fidelium erga hanc sedem debitæ, non satisfieri obsequioso silentio.*" Hence, the formula to which all the Jansenists, desirous of being reconciled, were required to subscribe, was conceived in the following terms: "I, N. N., submit to the decisions of the Roman Pontiffs, and I reject and condemn the five propositions of Jansenius. . . . . . in the sense intended by the author. So I swear, and so help me God, and this His Holy Gospel."

The fatal blow was dealt to Jansenism, which has ever since *remained condemned.*

Clement IX exercised this Apostolical prerogative against Paschasius Quesnell; Innocent XI against Michael Molinos; Pius VI, in the eighteenth century, against the Synod of Pistoja; and in this our own century Pius VII exercised this his supreme judicial and Apostolical authority against the adherents of the so-called petite Eglise; and Gregory XVI against De La Mennais and Hermes.

Finally, Pius IX not only condemned the errors of Guenther and Froschhamer, but, in the full consciousness of his power and of his obligations as the Vicar of Christ and the divinely-commissioned teacher of mankind, censured, in his Syllabus, the false opinions taught by modern pseudo-philosophers; the dangerous theories held by certain naturalists on subjects of science; the unsound views entertained by pretended world-reformers concerning progress and civilization; the extravagant notions carried out in practice by an unchristian liberalism; and the weak concessions of a shallow theology, which panders, through a mistaken policy, to the tendencies of the times. Undismayed by the hostile attitude of empires and nations, he taught those who boasted of being the most profound thinkers of their day, that, before him, the expounder of the eternal truth revealed by God to men, in order to teach them the way of salvation, they are as mere pupils who must follow the directions of an unerring master. Armed with the power of the Most High, he fulminated the thunders of his anathemas against all who dared dispute his decisions.

Apparently the enemies of the truth and of the Church might scorn the threats of the aged Pontiff, but, in the secrecy of their hearts, they marveled at his superhuman courage; and, if they still believed in the revealed word of God, though they might have been dragged along by the current of public opinion, they now began to feel uneasy and troubled in conscience. The living members of the Church, on the other hand, rejoiced and thanked the Lord that they had been preserved amid the anarchical decomposition of thoughts and principles which threatened the destruction of all order; that, while so many fed on the poisonous weeds of error, Peter, ever alive in his Church, nourished them with the wholesome food of unfailing truth.

But the occasion on which Pius exercised his divine right and privilege in a more decisive and conspicuous manner than ever a Pope had done before, was that on which, by his own authority, he defined the dogma of the Immaculate Conception of the B. V. M., mother of God. On the 8th of December, 1854, he arose from the Apostolical throne of Peter, and, surrounded by more than two hundred princes of the Church, proclaimed, without any reference to their opinion or judgment, that the B. V. Mary, mother of Christ, was conceived without stain of original sin. All the Prelates of the Church, absent as well as present, were bound to submit, and did submit, to this authoritative decision; and every one who would have dared to resist, would have, *ipso facto*, become a heretic.

Now, we ask: Was Pius IX, when he proclaimed this revealed truth to be an article of faith, conscious of his infallibility in matters of faith, or was he not? If not, how could he pronounce such anathemas against all non-believers, no matter how exalted their dignity or how great their number. Before he had definitively pronounced upon the subject, fifty of the Bishops thought such a step premature; but as soon as he had spoken, all orders of the clergy throughout the whole world bowed in humble submission, and, by so doing, declared their belief in the infallible authority of the Sovereign Pontiff.

Besides the twelve articles of the Apostle's creed, no dogma had as yet been defined by the Church, unless called for by some particular heresy, that had dared to attack a tenet of Catholic belief. In this respect, therefore, the dogma of the Immaculate Conception might be called the thirteenth article of the Creed. It certainly is as much "of faith" as any article of the Creed, because it was proclaimed in virtue of the same Apostolical authority which has been transmitted by St. Peter to every one of his successors.

There is something strikingly appropriate in the fact—a charming parallelism—that the extraordinary privilege conferred on no one but Mary, was made known to the world in virtue of a privilege, likewise bestowed on but one person, namely St. Peter, who is still living in his successor, the Roman Pontiff.

Considering the unbroken chain of declarations and exercises of their Apostolical authority, nobody who is of a candid character will ever assert that the Popes entered into possession of this their right and prerogative in the darkness of the Middle Ages, but that they asserted and exercised it from the beginning of the Church— not bestowed on them by the Church, but by Christ, through Peter, and that they spoke and acted accordingly in the face of the whole Christian world.

VI.

TESTIMONY OF THE MOST CELEBRATED THEOLOGIANS AND UNIVERSITIES,

SINCE THE TIME OF THOMAS AQUINAS, MAINTAINING THE INFALLIBILITY OF THE POPE, WHEN SPEAKING "EX CATHEDRA."

WITH St. Bernard the age of the Fathers closes; with St. Thomas and St. Bonaventura, that of the Doctors of Divinity opens. The authority of the Doctors is of great weight in determining the doctrine of the Church. For they did not invent new dogmas, but derived all that they taught from Scripture and Tradition. Hence we find that upon the present subject, as well as upon every other, their doctrine reflects in the most perfect manner, that of the earlier ages to which we have already alluded.

We shall begin with St. Thomas of Aquin, commonly known as the Angelic Doctor—*Doctor Angelicus*. None is ignorant of the respect with which the entire school of Divinity is wont to receive the dicta of this prodigy of philosophical and theological learning, who never, perhaps, found his equal among the children of men except in St. Augustin.

Treating in his "Summa Theologiæ" of the right of making a *Symbol of Faith*, he maintains that it is the *exclusive* prerogative of the Pope, the successor of St. Peter, for whom the Lord "prayed that his faith fail not." In support of this assertion, he quotes the text of St. Paul to the Corinthians.*

"It were impossible," argues the holy Doctor, "to comply with this injunction of the Apostle, if, when a difference arises concerning doctrinal matters, the controversy were not settled by him, who was constituted the head of the Church, that so the whole Church might unhesitatingly receive his decisions." *Quod servari non possit, nisi quæstio fidei exorta determinetur per eum, qui toti Ecclesiæ præest, ut sic ejus sententia a tota ecclesia firmiter teneatur.*†

* 1 Cor. i: "I beseech you, brethren, that you all speak the same thing."
† Sum. St. Thom., 2, 2, q. i, ar. 10.

In another part of the Summa he reasons thus:
" The Church can not err, because He that ' was
heard for His own dignity,' said to Peter: ' I have
prayed for thee that thy faith fail not." "*Ecclesia errare non potest, quia ille, qui exauditus est
in omnibus pro sua reverentia, Petro dixit: Ego
rogavi pro te, ut non deficiat fides tua.*"* It is especially deserving of notice, that St. Thomas here
infers the Infallibility of the Church from that
of the Pope, and not the Infallibility of the Pope
from that of the Church.

In a work, "Against the Greeks," in which as
a Doctor of the Latin Church, St. Thomas stu-
died above all to avoid every appearance of ex-
aggeration and rhetorical parade, and to give a
plain and accurate exposition of Catholic doctrine, we find the following passage: " Christ,
who received from the Father the sceptre of the
Church, so that all ranks and conditions must do
Him homage, likewise gave to St. Peter and his
successors the *fullest* power, in the *fullest* manner,
so that He delegated to *no one* else His *full* authority." "*Et Petro et ejus successoribus plenis-
simam potestatem plenissime commisit, ut etiam
nulli alii quam Petro, quod suum est plenum ipsi
dedit.*" Had St. Thomas doubted the Pope's
right to decide authoritatively on questions of

---

* Sum. St. Thom., p. 3, q. 25, art. 2.

doctrine, he certainly would never have allowed himself expressions like these. For if this right was not given to the Pope and is nevertheless possessed by the Church, it must have been given to some one else united to the Pope. But such an hypothesis is at variance with the assertion of the Saint: "He gave to St. Peter and his successors the *fullest* power in the *fullest* manner," and "He delegated to *no one* else His *full* authority."

Let us listen, next, to St. BONAVENTURE, whose appellation of "Seraphic Doctor"—*Doctor Seraphicus*—is sufficient evidence, that, like his contemporary and friend, St. Thomas, he is looked upon as "an Angel in the schools." We read in his "Hexameron:" "Like the sun among the planets, the Pope *alone* has the plenitude of power over all the Churches." "*Solus summus Pontifex universaliter, sicut sol super planetas, habet plenitudinem potestatis super omnes ecclesias.*" Mark the terms of the comparison. St. Bonaventure does not say, "like the sun among the *stars*," but "like the sun among the *planets*." The planets are not self-luminous, but shine with light borrowed from the sun. The application, which every one may easily make for himself, will serve to show that St. Bonaventure, as well as St. Thomas, infers the Infallibility of the Church from that of the Pope.*

* Hexameron, Serm. 21.

In his "Summa Theologiæ," in which he treats this question *ex professo*, he lays it down as incontrovertible that the Pope can not err, provided that he teaches as the Head of the Church, with the intention to oblige the faithful to believe.*
In any other case this special prerogative is not necessary for the Unity of the Church, and, therefore, not necessary at all, because it was not conferred on St. Peter for any personal advantage, but for the benefit of the Church, whose very existence requires the strictest Unity.

These two leaders of the theological school, in the thirteenth century, have been followed by the most eminent theologians down to our time.

In proof of this, in order not to be too diffuse, we can do little more than refer to the works of the principal authors, unless a special reason should make it desirable to quote their words. We, therefore, mention, among others: *John of Paris*, in his work "De Regia Potestate et Papali;" *Augustinus Triumphus*, "Summa de Potestate Ecclesiastica;" *Durandus of Pourçain*, "De Origine Jurisdictionum, seu de Ecclesiastica Jurisdictione;" *Petrus Paludanus*, "De Potestate Ecclesiastica;" *Petrus Bertrandus*, "De Origine et Usu Jurisdictionum, seu de Spirituali et Temporali Jurisdictione;" *Alvarus Pelagius*, Bishop

* Bon. Sum. Theol, I. Art. 3, D. 3.

of Sylves, "De Planctu Ecclesiæ;" *Joannes Turrecremata*, "De Summi Pontificis et Generalis Concilii Potestate," and "De Ecclesia et ejus Auctoritate."

Even in the East of that epoch there were those who adhered to the traditions of the old Greek Church and strove to bring their countrymen back to the faith of their forefathers. Among these we may rank *Bessarion* and *Joseph*, Bishop of Modon, and the Greek monk, *Manuel Calecas*, who remarks in his book "Contra Errores Græcorum:" "There have always been among us men of superior learning, who condemned our separation from the Church of Rome as extremely foolish and at variance with the faith and teaching of our ancestors."*

George Scholarius, in his Apology of the Council of Florence, writes: "The Bishop of Rome is the successor of St. Peter, the Vicar of Christ, the teacher of all Christians. Who can deny it? Our Savior and all the Doctors of the Church proclaim it in accents louder than the thunders of heaven." "*Hæc profecto, quomodo quis inficiari possit, cum apertissime Christus et omnes doctores manifestius, quam si tonitru insonaret, hoc ipsum vociferantur.*"

Similar expressions are made by *Abraham* of

* Contra errores Græcorum, l. 4.

Crete, in his Preface to the translation of the Acts drawn up by the Council of Florence, and by *Philotheus*, Patriarch of Alexandria, in his answer to the "Document of Union," sent to him by the Pope. *George* of Thrapezunt writes: "As Christ gave to Peter the keys of heaven, those, who reject his doctrine and leave his communion, shall in vain exclaim, 'Lord open unto us.'"—"*Domine aperi nobis.*" *John Plusiadenus*, Archpriest of Constantinople, wrote a book bearing the title "Dialogus pro Synodo Florentina," in which he enlarges upon the Papal right of confirming, examining, directing, and correcting whatever bears upon faith. "*Ipse auctoritatem habet confirmandi, examinandi, dirigendi, et corrigendi quæ ad fidem pertinent.*"

The Infallibility of the Holy See was also taught and defended by *Alphonsus Tostatus*, a writer of such ability, that, according to *Wharton*, he wrote more in twenty-two years, than an ordinary man can attentively read during a lifetime. We refer our readers to his commentary on the xvi chapt. of St. Matthew. *St. John of Capistran* most explicitly defends this privilege of the Holy See, in his works, "De Dignitate Ecclesiastica," directed against the Hussites, and "De Papæ et Concilii Dignitate," against the Synod of Basel.

St. Antoninus distinguishes, as we have done, between the Pope's opinions, as a private theologian, and his dogmatic utterances, as the Vicar of Christ. "The Pope," writes he, "may err as a private person; but he can not err, when, in his capacity of Pope, he defines an article of faith." He even goes so far, as to stigmatize with heresy every body, who disputes the Infallibility of the Sovereign Pontiff. "*Dicere quod in hujusmodi Papa erraret, esset hereticum.*"*

The heresy here spoken of must, of course, be understood as interior; because there is no explicit definition, which makes a person exteriorly chargeable with heresy for such an act. The Saint means, that, upon this subject the teaching of the Church is so plain and unmistakable, that no one can maintain the contrary without rendering himself guilty, before God, of a culpable error in faith.

John Nauclerus is the author of a work entitled "De Monarchia," in which he pronounces an appeal from the Pope to an Œcumenical Council simply ridiculous, because there can be no Œcumenical Council without the Pope, whose confirmation is necessary to give validity to its Decrees. To appeal from the Vicar of Christ to

---

* St. Ant., pars iv, lib. 8, o. 3, § 4, and pars iii, lib. 12, o. 8, § 3.

a Council is, moreover, according to him, an act of rebellion, that falls under the censures of the Councils themselves; but to appeal from a Council, however numerous, to the Vicar of Christ, is a privilege always allowed and conformable to the Canons of the Councils.

Cajetan advances the same opinion in his book " De superioritate Papæ super Concilium;" and even *Erasmus*, whose varied learning the Protestants of his times tried, by every means in their power, to secure to the service of error, submitted all his writings to the censure of the Pope, whom he looked upon as the highest exponent of God's authority on earth.*

The prerogative of Infallibility claimed by the Holy See is likewise defended by *Melchior Canus*, in his celebrated work " De locis Theologicis." He, too, is of opinion that those who deny the Infallibility of the Pope in matters of faith, are no less guilty of *interior* heresy than those who deny his right of primacy over the Church.

To this series of celebrated Divines we must add *Bellarmine*, " De Romano Pontifice;" † Car-

---

* See his letters to Bishop Christoph of Basel, to Morus, Beda, Faber, Melanchton, and to the Swiss.

† We were surprised to read, in a book recently published in New York, an article in which the very distinguished author, whilst asserting the Infallibility of the Pope in his de-

dinal *Orosius*, "De irrefragabili Romani Pontificis auctoritate in definiendis fidei controversiis;" *Francis*, Archbishop of Rouen, "Apologia pro Catholicis ad Jacobum Britanniæ regem;" Cardinal *Gotti*, "De vera Ecclesia Jesu Christi;" *Milante*, Bishop of Stabium, "Exerc. 19, supra propos. 29;" *Fenelon*, Archbishop of Cámbray, "Instructio pastoralis;" *Jacob Serry*, "Dissertatio de Romano Pont. falli et fallere nescio;" *St. Francis de Sales*, who treats the subject, as we already observed, in some of his letters, and in a

cisions on matters of faith, limits its sphere in such a manner, that he rather seems to prove his fallibility. But it is quite inconceivable how this respectable author could go so far as to cite Bellarmine in his favor, pretending that this celebrated Doctor of Divinity made the Infallibility of the Pope dependent upon the approval of a General Council. Has the author ever looked for himself into the controversial works of Bellarmine? There he may read the following two propositions, asserted and defended by Bellarmine:

"Summus Pontifex, cum totam Ecclesiam docet, in his, quæ ad fidem pertinent, nullo casu errare potest." Lib. 4, de Potest. Summ. Pontificis, c. 3.

And again: "Summus Pontifex simpliciter absolute est supra Ecclesiam universam, et super Concilium Generale, ita ut nullum in terris supra se Judicem agnoscat." This is the doctrine of Bellarmine. The author must have had before him an entirely corrupted and interpolated edition, when he wrote his remarks concerning the views of this prominent Theologian. All the world knows that Bellarmine is rather considered, by friends and foes, as one of the most valiant champions in defense of our thesis.

manuscript preserved in the Bibliotheca Chigiana.*

This right and privilege of the Holy See is also defended by *Antonius Charlas*, in his " Tractatus de libertatibus Ecclesiæ Gallicanæ ;" by *Cœlestinus Sfrondati*, in his " Regale Sacerdotium ;" by *Chartier*, " De infallibili et suprema auctoritate S.S. Pontificum;" *Bosevinus*, "tom. iv, de Conc.," *Thyrsus Gonzalez*, " De Rom. Pont. Infallibilitate ;" *Troila*, " De Pontifice ;" *Petrus Matthæi*, " Summa Const. ;" *Duval*, " De Suprema Potest. Rom. Pont. ;" *Cabassutius*, " Notitia Conc. ;" *Pitidier*, " Dissertation sur le Concil de Constance." To these series of Doctors we add the illustrious names of *Sotus, Suarez, Nicenus de Lyra, Spondanus, Thomassinus, Ludovicus Bail, Joannes Buteanus, Charmes, Dominicus Bannes, Berti, Mansi,* and *Roncaglia*,† who all unanimously defend our thesis.

Considering the weight of these and innumerable other authorities, at the verge of the eighteenth century, Sardagna reasons thus in his treatise " De inerrantia Rom. Pontificis: " " In theological questions which involve a divine right, we are obliged to follow the oldest and most common opinion. But the opinion which holds the Infallibility of the Pope in matters of

*See De Maistre, Du Pape, li.   † Adn. in Nat. Alex.

faith, is older and more common than the contrary; for, before the Council of Pisa and Constance, there was not a single theologian of any note who would have ever questioned it. Indeed no one could have done so without being at once declared a heretic."

The causes which led some theologians, after the Council of Pisa and Constance, to advance the novel opinion that Infallibility is a privilege peculiar to a General Council, are too obvious to be mistaken. These Synods which assembled at the time of the great Papal Schism, with the view of examining the claims of the different nominees, asserted their superiority over the *pretenders* to the Chair of St. Peter. From this circumstance shallow-minded and partial writers took occasion to impugn the prerogatives of the lawful Vicar of Christ. Their views met with especial favor in France, because they flattered the ambitious Louis XIV, who was resolved on establishing a National Church, and making himself its head. Before long the new doctrine was embodied in the famous "Four Articles," which tended so much to embarrass the action of the Sovereign Pontiff, until they were finally condemned by the Church.

German Febronianism and Josephinism favored these Gallican tendencies, and, with strange inconsistency, represented the Apostolical authority of the Holy See as hostile to the rights of the whole Church assembled in a General Council. How illogical and utterly untenable such an opinion is, will appear from our answers to the objections commonly raised against the Infallibility of the Pope by authors of this class.

Yet the immense majority of theologians worthy of this name, also after the Councils of Constance, and the schismatical convention of the French Bishops in the year 1682, invariably and most learnedly defended this undeniable prerogative of the Apostolical See. The most distinguished of them are *Mamachius*, " Antiq. Christ. et in lib. contra auctorem opusculi: Quid est Papa," (the shameless pamphlet of Eibel); *Zarachia*, " Antifebronius;" the Brothers *Ballerini*, " De vi ac ratione Primatus;" *St. Alphonsus Liguori*, " De Infallibilitate Papæ;" *Devoti*, " Inst. Jur. Ecc. Romæ, 1824;" *De Maistre*, " Du Pape;" *Muzarelli*, " Auct. Rom. Pont., etc.;" *Perrone*, " Prælectiones Theologicæ;" and, finally, Pope GREGORY XVI (Capellari) in his celebrated work," Triomfo della Santa Sede."

Other authors, balancing between human respect and duty, professed to give the arguments *for* and *against* the subject. Yet, even among these, there were no theologians of distinction who have left us at all in doubt concerning their own opinion. Like Tournely and Lieberman, they range on the side of the affirmative.

To this well-nigh unanimous testimony of the theological school we must yet add that of entire Universities. Before the Council of Constance, no diversity of opinion was allowed, upon this matter, in those venerable seats of theological learning. We may easily satisfy ourselves upon this subject by referring to the queen and leader of all the universities, the *Sorbonne* of Paris, whose teaching was the standard, to which all the others at once conformed. Erasmus, who was certainly well acquainted with the customs that obtained among the learned of his day, compares the influence exerted by the Sorbonne over all the Universities, to the authority exercised by the See of Rome over the whole Church. "*Parisiensis Academia semper in re theologica non aliter principem tenuit locum, quam Romana Sedes Christianæ religionis principatum.*" Every one was confident of carrying his point when he could say: "The Sorbonne of Paris teaches this; the Academy of Paris agrees with me," etc.

Let us, then, study the teachings of the Sorbonne, before Louis XIV sought to concentrate in himself all authority in Church and State.

In the year 1320 this celebrated University

condemned the propositions of Marsilius Paduanus, who taught that the Pope could err in matters of faith. In the year 1324, the University, having united with the whole French Church, under Stephen, Archbishop of Paris, declared, "that the Church of Rome is the mother and teacher of all other churches; that she is founded on the unshaken faith of Peter, the Vicar of Christ, who is authorized, as the *universal* judge of Catholic truth, to approve or reject doctrines, to solve doubts, to decide what is to be believed, and to refute errors." "*Romana Ecclesia fidelium omnium mater est et magistra in firmissima Petri Vicarii Christi confessione fundata, ad quam velut ad universalem regulam, Catholicæ veritatis pertinet approbatio et reprobatio doctrinarum, declaratio dubiorum, determinatio tenendorum, et confutatio errorum.*"

Pièrre de Aliaco, who presided over the Sorbonne, under Clement VII, affirmed: "This is the faith which we have been taught by the Catholic Church. Should we have advanced any rash or erroneous opinion, we hope that it will be corrected by thee, who hast inherited the faith and the See of Peter. We are aware, and we firmly believe, that the Apostolical See is the chair of Peter, on which the Church was built, and of which, in the person of Peter, seated on it, it was said: 'Peter,

I have prayed for thee, that thy faith fail not.'"
"*Non ignoramus, sed firmiter tenemus, et nullatenus dubitamus, quod S. Sedes Apostolica est illa Cathedra Petri, supra quam fundata est ecclesia; de qua sede et persona Petri in eadem sedenti dictum est: Petre rogavi pro te, ut non deficiat fides tua."*

In the year 1534 the Sorbonne condemned the propositions of John Morandus and Marcus Antonius de Dominis, who maintained that the Pope is not infallible.† The celebrated Peter De Marca positively affirms that, in the seventeenth century, not only the University of Paris, but all the Universities of the whole world, taught the infallibility of the Pope in matters of faith.‡ The same thing is asserted by Petidier in his treatise, "De Auctoritate et Infallibilitate S. Pont."

In the year 1544, the University of *Louvain* solemnly anathematized the errors of Luther by the following proposition: "We must firmly believe that there is on earth one, true, Catholic, and visible Church of Christ, which was established by the Apostles, which has outlived the vicissitudes of ages, and which subscribes and

---

* See Lib. 4, Hist. Univ. Paris, ad an. 1387.
† See Duval and Nauclerus, p. 4, 1, 8, o. 6.
‡ Stephen Baluzzi in Comp. ejus vitæ libris de Concordia præfixo.

clings to whatever is proposed, or will be proposed, in matters of faith or religion, by the Chair of Peter, on whom she was founded by Christ, that she might not err in what appertains to faith and religion." *"Firma fide credendum est, unam esse in terris veram atque Catholicam Christi Ecclesiam, eamque visibilem, quæ ab Apostolis fundata in hanc usque ætatem perdurans retinet et suscipit, quidquid de fide et religione tradit et traditura est Cathedra Petri, supra quam a Christo est fundata, ut in iis, quæ fidei sunt et religionis, errare non possit."* The University, therefore, held, with St. Thomas and St. Bonaventure, that the infallibility of the Church results from the infallibility of the Pope.

Taperus, chancellor of the theological faculty of Louvain, bears us out in the statement, that no difference of opinion existed in the schools, previous to the Councils of Constance and Basel, the real aim of which was entirely misapprehended by a few weak minds, ready to dogmatize before they understood the point at issue.* Gerson himself concedes that, before the Council of Constance, any one, who would have disputed the infallibility of the Pope, would have been branded as a heretic.†

* Tract. Theol. N. 6 et 7.
† De Potest. Eccles. Consid. li.

The theological faculties of *Cologne* and *Salamanca* solemnly professed the same doctrine, condemning the propositions of M. A. de Dominis, as opposed to the teaching of the Church. Sardagna and even Tournely attest, that during the eighteenth century all the Catholic Universities, with the exception of a few members in some, that had been infected with Gallican principles, were all defending the personal Papal infallibility in matters of faith.

Gallicanism, Febronianism, and Jansenism, combined with those revolting blasphemies of infidelity, which were rife during the time of the French Revolution, and subsequently the secularization of the Church in Germany, and the wars that deluged the face of Europe with blood, all tended to convert into passive tools some of those, whose learning should have raised them above the weakness of vulgar minds. But the mist which hung over the Church, has been rapidly vanishing, since the day on which GREGORY XVI rose up in defense of Clement Augustus, the captive Archbishop of Cologne. At present there is scarcely a single theological faculty, which would tolerate the opinion that the Pope can err when teaching the faithful in His capacity as the Head of the Church. The professor may still lay before his scholars the arguments *pro* and *contra;* practically all difference of opinion has disappeared, because no theologian would, at this day, dare to teach an opinion condemned by the Holy See.

Since the publication of the "Syllabus," quite a number of eminent Theologians have raised their voices in defense of the Papal Infallibility, as extending to the teachings of the Pope communicated to the Church, by such decisions as Pius IX and others of his predecessors made in regard to certain doctrinal propositions. Among them, we notice the celebrated Archbishop of Westminster, Dr. *Manning*, in his work "The Temporal Mission of the Holy Ghost," page 83; Dr. *Murray*, in his "Dogmatical Treatises;" Dr. *Ward*, in his "Controversy with Dr. Ryder," in the Dublin Review of last year and this year; Rev. S. *Schrader*, "De Unitate Romana;" the series of dissertations on the "Syllabus," published by Father *Ries*, and other French Jesuits; the explanations on the "Syllabus" by *Gury*, *Perrone*, and Dr. *Torsi;* finally, the articles in the "*Civilta Catolica*," published in Rome itself. Meanwhile not a single theologian rose up to teach that the Pope can err in matters of faith.

The most illustrious document, expressing the sentiments of the learned Hierarchy of our days, is that of the five hundred Bishops who flocked to the celebration of the jubilee of St. Peter. They assert, "that the Chair of St. Peter stands like a sacred Pharos within the tempestuous sea of life, directing the path of mortals, and showing to them, by its light, the way to the harbor of salvation." *"Stat Cathedra Petri velut sacra Pharos in procelloso vitæ æquore mortalium iter dirigens, et portum salutis luce sua demonstrans."*

" We seek nothing more anxiously," they continue, "than to believe and teach what Thou believest and teachest, and to reject those errors which Thou dost reject. Under thy leadership we shall unanimously walk the way of the Lord. We follow thee."

"There is no power against God," says St. Paul; and we may add: "There is no power against truth, and therefore not against faith." A truth of faith may be for a time obscured by a mass of jarring opinions; but, like the sun peering from behind the clouds, it will soon shine with increased luster, and wrap the world in a blaze of light. Such has been and is the case with the privilege of the Holy See for which we contend.

VII.

THE TESTIMONY OF PRINCES AND PEOPLES,

ACKNOWLEDGING THE AUTHORITY OF THE ROMAN SEE TO BE THE HIGHEST TRIBUNAL ON EARTH, AND THE ROMAN PONTIFF THE INFALLIBLE JUDGE IN MATTERS OF FAITH.

THE testimony which we here adduce in further support of our thesis is not lightly to be passed over as of little weight in the balance of argument. The living faith which actuated princes and peoples of all nations, and in all the ages of Christianity, in their veneration of the Supreme Pontiff, and their recognition of his privilege as Supreme Arbiter in matters of faith, carries along with it a whole world of witnesses. The princes, on their part, had no undue personal inducement toward such a recognition, inasmuch as they were taught by experience, that the Pope was ever ready on occasion to use his right against themselves, and, if they had consulted a narrow and selfish interest, they would rather have been led to over-exalt the power of bishops who depended purely upon themselves, than of one who owed them nothing, and had less reason to fear their influence and power. Nevertheless, we shall see how many were found, who, with undiminished reverence and obedience, submitted themselves to the decisions of the Roman Pontiff, as the successor of St. Peter, whose faith could not fail, and the Vicar of Christ, the eternal truth.

The very first instance that we adduce to usher in the long line of princely witnesses, is all the more striking, inasmuch as it is one of the still heathen Emperors of Rome, Aurelius. While he was at Antioch, a Synod assembled to judge the heretical Paulus, whom they deposed, substituting in his place a certain Domnus. The condemned but contumacious Paulus refused to submit, and would not give up to Domnus the church and episcopal residence to which he had no longer a right. Aurelius was appealed to, and gave for decision that the church and residence should be made over to him whom the Bishop of Rome should designate. This decision should suffice to show us how universally the rights of the Roman Pontiff must even then have been known and acknowledged, since a Roman and heathen Emperor was acquainted with, and enforced them. Seventy Bishops appeal to him in the same city where the scandal occurs, and yet he does not decide for himself, nor refer the case to them, nor to the Bishops of the country, but orders them to inform the Bishop of Rome and abide by his decision.

So great and imposing is the weight of this fact, that there were Bishops among the schismatical Greeks, who endeavored to find therein the first rise of that Primacy which was afterward recognized throughout the world. Of such was Leo of Acrida, but any one can detect the *post hoc ergo propter hoc* of this inversion.* No, it was not an invention of Aurelius, who would have known that a blunder in this matter would not have settled the difficulty; he evidently wished to terminate the dissensions among the Christians by appealing to an authority which they were bound to acknowledge. As Bossuet† justly observes, he was a true Roman and loved justice, and liked to see Christians, as Christians, judged by their own usages—*praxis*. It was

---

* Lupus. Scholia viii, 103.
† Discours sur l' Histoire Universelle.

this widely-known *praxis Christianorum* which was the inspirer of his decision.

When we find a heathen emperor rendering such a decision, we need not be astonished that Constantine the Great, the first Christian Emperor, should have called the decision of the Roman Pontiff "a heavenly judgment," "*cœleste judicium*," and have cried out against the lamentable blindness of heretics appealing to him (the Emperor) against a decision, which he himself was obliged to obey as a "*cœleste judicium.*"

It has been justly remarked that one of the most illustrious testimonies to the superiority and supremacy of the Spiritual Majesty and Authority of the Pope over even imperial dignity, is in the remarkable resolution of the same Constantine, on becoming a Christian, in abandoning Rome to its Pontiff, and building for himself a new imperial city, Constantinople. He felt the inconvenience of living in the same place with one, whose power eclipsed his own, and the impropriety of the Head of the Church residing in a city, of which he did not possess the sole control. In this, Constantine showed himself a true Christian, and gave a lesson to all princes of the love and respect which they should pay to the Pontiff of Rome. His successors in the West continued to give the same wonderful proof of

Christian sentiment. For, although they continued to claim sovereignty in Rome, where the Senate held its sittings, they themselves resided at Milan, Ravenna, or in other cities, even farther distant, as Trier in Germany.

Gratian, in the year 383, to maintain the Supremacy of the Popes, in matters of faith, issued a decree by which he obliged his people to live in communion with the Holy See.* The rule by which he judged the orthodoxy of any one was the answer to the question whether he held the same faith with Damasus—*complectere doctrinam Damasi*. He rebuked the heretical aspirant to the See of Constantinople to his face, saying: "I am astonished at thy shamelessness in resisting the truth, since thou knowest the teaching of Damasus." "*Miror te tam impudenter resistere veritati, nam probe scias Damasum*," etc.†

The same testimony was given by the Emperor Theodosius in his treatment of Flavian and Nectarius. The Emperor Honorius, writing to the Emperor Arcadius, furnishes the same evidence. That of Valentinian in his letter to Theodosius, the younger, is yet more remarkable: "Since the Bishop of the blessed City of Rome, on whom antiquity confers the supremacy of the Priesthood, has the office and faculty of judging the

---

* Cod. Theod. xvi, l. 1, c. 2.   † Butler xviii.

faith, and the priesthood." "*Quatenus beatæ Romanæ civitatis Episcopus, cui principatum Sacerdotii super omnes antiquitas contulit, locum habeat et facultatem de fide et sacerdotibus judicare.*"* Therefore, it is, he says, that the Patriarch of Constantinople has addressed himself to the Pope concerning the controversy that has arisen relating to the faith. "*Propter contentionem, quæ orta est de fide.*" He did even more; he wrote to the Prefect of Gaul, that all the decisions of the Bishop of Rome were to be regarded and obeyed in the Courts of that Province and elsewhere in his dominions, as if they were imperial laws. "*Sed illis, omnibusque pro lege sit, quidquid dixerit vel sanxerit Apostolicæ Sedis Auctoritas.*" He gives for reason, that since the time of Constantine, all the Christian Emperors had considered themselves the protectors of the Holy See. What a beautiful and striking example for our own times, and, alas, what a difference between princes! He explains, that while he loves to sanction the Apostolical decisions, it is not with a view of adding to the authority, which they have in all fullness from the Pope, but only that he may the more efficaciously bring the refractory to their duty. "*Sed nostram quoque præceptionem hæc ratio provoca-*

* Baron. ad an. 407.

vit, ne ulterius unquam alteri liceat præceptis Romani Pontificis obviare." Those Emperors of old had not as yet dreamed of a *"placitum regium!"* Most pertinent and confirmatory is that assertion of Valentinian in this same Edict: "Peace would reign throughout the Church, if all would acknowledge but the one ruler." *"Tunc enim omnium Ecclesiarum pax ubique servaretur, si rectorem unum agnoscat."*

Yes, that is the reason why the Right and Privilege in question was conferred on ONE, so that unity and peace might be preserved for all. In this the Emperor agrees with St. Cyprian, who had said: "All the trouble of sects and schisms arises from the sole fact, that heretics and schismatics do not submit to the one Judge, holding the place of Christ."

How plainly and decidedly this privilege was recognized by Marcian and by the accomplished Empress Pulcheria, we have already pointed out when treating of the Œcumenical Council of Chalcedon.

Justin, writing to the Pope by the hand of his Minister and successor Justinian, says: "This we hold to be the Catholic truth, what, namely, thy answer shall make known to us." *"Hoc enim credimus esse Catholicum, quod Vestro responso nobis fuerit intimatum."*

This was the faith and the language of Emperors living before the time of Gregory the Great, in those ages, namely, when Protestants concede the Church to have been free from error. The same sentiments were held by the Eastern Emperors, who stood in no need of temporal help from the Pope, and who, had they liked, could have used to their advantage the jealousy, more or less prevalent, of the Patriarchs of Constantinople, or of the "New Rome," as it was called. Justinian himself, when Emperor, wrote to Hormidas, Pope: "The unity of the Churches is based upon the doctrine and authority of your Apostolate."* "*Unitas Ecclesiarum per doctrinam et auctoritatem Apostolatus Vestri provenit.*"

To the Patriarch Mennas he says: "All must be referred to the Apostolic See, and the more especially, because, when heresies have arisen, they have been extinguished by the sentence and judgment of that Venerable See." † "*Eo maxime, quod, quoties hæretici pullularunt, et sententia et judicio illius Venerabilis Sedis, coërciti sunt.*"

Writing to Pope John II, he says, that he had abandoned to him every thing relating to the Church, and he received in return the praise of the Pope, because in that he had done his *duty.*"

---

* Ballerini de Vi ac Ratione Prim., p. 208.
† Cod. de Summ. Trinit., l.

Later, it is true, when giving away to passion, we find him behaving with shameful violence toward Pope Vigil, but at the same time, as we before mentioned, we did not believe that he could act validly without his sanction, even though supported as he thought he was by the Bishops of the Fifth Œcumenical Council.

The acknowledgment of this Right and Prerogative of the Pope, as made by Phocas the Emperor, was so clear and explicit, that Luther with the Centuriators of Magdeburg, have endeavored to ascribe to this Emperor the rise of this doctrine in the Church. It was in the same spirit, and with the same lack of judgment, that Leo of Acrida ascribed its origin to the answer of Aurelius.

King Childebert of France in his embassy to Pope Vigil, and King Athelbert of England in his legation to Pope Boniface IV, recognized the Supremacy of the Holy See in matters of faith and discipline. To the latter the Pope answers in the strongest manner: " If any King succeeding, or any Bishop, Clergyman, or laic, shall essay to infringe the decrees of the Popes, he should incur the anathema of Peter and of all his successors." *"Quæ ea decreta, si quis successorum regum, sive episcoporum, sive clericorum, sive laicorum irrita facere tentaverit, a Principe Aposto-*

lorum Petro et a cunctis successoribus suis anathematis gladio subjaceat." Englishmen of our days may see here, how ancient is the language which Popes use to declare their rights, and on the other hand, how different the obedience which is paid to them since the days of Henry VIII. Is it not manifest that their forefathers must have professed a far different faith, and that it is they themselves, not the Popes who have changed? A solemn acknowledgment was made of this supremacy by Oswin, of Northumberland, and Egbert, King of Kent, in their delegation of Wighard, elected by themselves and the whole Episcopacy and Clergy of England, to refer to the Pope the question of the Paschal celebration, in which, although they maintained that their practice was derived from St. John, the Apostle, they submitted themselves to the decrees of Rome. Soon after this date, we find Ceadivalla, Kenred, and Offa making pilgrimages to Rome to pay personal homage to the Vicar of Christ and receive his immediate instructions. King Knulph, Offa's successor, imitated in his day the example of the royal pilgrim, his predecessor.

When speaking of the Sixth Œcumenical

* Hard., tom. iii, p. 644.

Council, we made mention of the testimony of Constantine Pogonatus, and we now join to him the record of Anastasius, who sent his profession of faith to Rome, as to the surest and highest tribunal of truth; so, too, the Empress Irene and her son and heir, as we have already observed, when treating of the Seventh General Council.

Pepin's devotion and submission are so well known that we need only allude to the fact. Scarcely less devoted were the sentiments of Charlemagne, as exhibited in his "Capitularia," and in the so-called "Caroline books,"* where he makes open and explicit profession of his faith in the Holy See as the Supreme Tribunal of faith on earth.

Louis the Pious, son of Charlemagne, walked in the footsteps of his illustrious father, as we may easily gather from his Constitution: *Ego Ludovicus et*, etc., and from his address to the Bishops of Thionville, and from his Capitular of the year 823. He even referred the division of his empire to the Pope's confirmation, and from that time it became the usage and practice that the Franco-Roman and German Emperors became such only with the consent of the Roman Pontiff and on being crowned by him. Nor was this

---

* L. 56, vii, 364, c. 6.

the case with the Emperors of the West alone, for the kings of England, Poland, Hungary, Croatia, Sweden, and Denmark loved to receive their crowns at his hands, and to place their dominions under the especial guarantee and protection of the Holy See.

We avoid, here, all question of political right, convention, or compromise. We merely point out the historical fact as evidence in what estimation the peoples and princes of those days held the Roman Pontiff, and with what veneration they looked upon him as the Vicar of Christ and the Supreme Arbiter of all on earth, according to the saying, "He who is competent to the greater, is also competent to the less." Enlightened by faith, they saw an order established on earth by Divine Providence, on such a basis and with such an extent of power, that if peoples and princes were but willing to submit to it, they would find eternal peace and the settlement of every controversy in the decision of the common Father of all the Faithful, the Successor of St. Peter, the Bishop of Rome, Supreme Pastor and Head of the Church.

This ideal of Christian order, of which *De Maistre* speaks so beautifully in his work, "Du Pape," is so truly attractive that even a *Voltaire*, forgetting himself for awhile, can not refrain from paying to it a tribute of praise and homage. In his "Essai sur les Mœurs," he proves by many historical examples, that not only the kings of Denmark, but all other Christian princes, were in common in considering the Pope to be a Judge between them and their people; and in his "Essai sur l' Histoire Générale," he has these remarkable words, by which he acknowledges the salutary advantages of such a tribunal: "The interests of mankind demand a bridle by which princes may be restrained, and the people saved. This bridle might by common consent be placed in the hands of the Roman Pontiffs. Such a High Priest, mingling in worldly conflicts only to silence them, admonishing alike the sovereign and his people of their duties, condemning their crimes, and visiting his excommunication on great wrongs, would be looked upon as the living representative and likeness of God upon the earth."

How deeply that feeling of submission of princes and peoples in temporal things was rooted in the veneration which, as Christians, they had for the Pontiff in spiritual matters, is made strikingly evident in the letter of David, Emperor of Ethiopia, converted to the true faith in the sixteenth century. He writes to Pope Clement VII as follows: "Why, O Holy Father, do you not make all Christian princes, who are thy sons, lay down their arms and live in peace, as becomes those who are brethren, since they are thy sheep, and thou art their shepherd?" Why? The fault is their own. They listen no more to the voice of Christian feeling.

As for himself, the Emperor makes the following beautiful profession of faith: "As thou art the Head of all the Bishops, and the Teacher of the faith, I obey thee with reverence; and as thou art the peace of all, it is but just that all should obey thee." "*Pater Sancte, qui es caput Pontificum omnium, magister fidei, ego tibi reverenter obedio, cum sis pax omnium, ita œquum est, ut omnes tibi obedientiam præstent.*" Is it not lamentable that the princes of our own so-called civilization seem not to perceive the logic of that Christian feeling which made the Ethiopian Emperor give utterance to such sentiments?

To return to our chronological series, Basilius, the Emperor, evidently acknowledged this prerogative of the Roman Pontiff when he referred to him for decision the case of Photius and the clergy ordained by him. Charles the Bald expresses the same belief and sentiments in his Chapters.* So, too, King Ethelwulf and his son Alfred the Great, of England, especially in his

* Lupus viii, 81.

letters to the Pope asking the confirmation of his University at Oxford. Otto, King of the Germans, and Louis of France give expression to the same belief at the Synod of Ingelheim.

Hugh Capet, King of France, with all the Bishops of his kingdom, addressing the Pope in relation to Arnulph of Rheims, says: "Be pleased to order, thou who holdest the place of the Apostles, what we have to do with the new Judas, and prescribe to us a form of judgment." The Bishops joined their supplications to that of the King and wrote: "Help the falling Church; may we experience in thee another Peter, the defender and confirmer of Christian faith." "*Adesto, Pater, ruenti Ecclesiæ, sentiamus in vobis alterum Petrum, defensorem et corroboratorem Christianæ fidei.*" *

The same prerogative was acknowledged in the Roman See by his successors Robert and Otto II, as may be seen in the "Memorandum" of the Abbe of Fleury.

Still more to the point is the document in which Henry II confirmed the right to the territorial possessions of the Holy See. An interesting incident of his life occurs to us in this connection. Being at Rome, he noticed that the *Credo* was not sung there. On asking the rea-

* Hard. vi, 730.

son, he received for answer that the Roman Church had never deviated from the path of truth, but had remained unshaken in the faith of St. Peter.* *"Quod Romana Ecclesia . . . non fuisset aliquando ulla hæresi infecta, sed secundum Petri doctrinam in soliditate Catholicæ fidei permaneret inconcussa."*

As regards the Kings of Poland, every historian is aware with what unshaken fidelity, after the elevation of Casimir to the throne, they adhered to the Roman See.

This prerogative was solemnly acknowledged by Henry II of France in the case of Bruno, Bishop of Orleans; and not less so by Henry III, and by Ferdinand, King of Spain, to VICTOR II; as also by Edward, King of England, to LEO IX and NICOLAS II. The attestations and letters of the Kings Heisa, Salomon, and Ladislas of Hungary, of Suenos and Erich of Denmark, Wratislas of Bohemia, the Czar Demetrius of Russia, King Anzir of Mauritania, Demetrius, Duke of Croatia, Michael, King of Sclavonia, and of Philip of France, we merely mention to refer the reader for fuller detail to the pages of the general historian.†

Even during the protracted struggle between the Roman Pontiffs and the Emperors of Ger-

* Baronius ad an. 1114.   † Hard. vi. Baron. in 12 smo.

many, this privilege in matters of faith was never disputed even by the Pope's most embittered enemies. This is made evident by no less testimony than that of Veneri of Vercelli, the fierce partisan of Henry IV.

When one of the faction of this same Henry attempted to impugn this spiritual prerogative of the Pope, during the Synod of Quedlinburg, he was at once condemned by the Synod. Henry himself, when attending to the voice of his conscience, deprecated before the Pope the crime of his own disobedience. His son Henry V, as we are told by Conrad of Arsberg, condemned the errors of his father and professed unlimited submission to the decisions of the Holy See.

Objections may be taken, as is sometimes done, from the right of interference, claimed by the Emperors in the Papal election. The only principle, in such cases, capable of defense, is the propriety of a mutual concord and assistance of the two powers, spiritual and temporal, in so universally important an action. When, however, as in the election of Alexander II, we hear the Imperial Commissioner asserting that, without the consent of the Emperor, no Pope could be legitimately elected, we find the assertion rebutted by the question: What part had the Emperor in the election of Pope STEPHEN, SIXTUS, CORNElius, Damasus, Colestin, Boniface? etc., and the simple question suffices to silence the Imperial Commissioner.

The real answer to such an objection is to be found in that of Louis VII, King of France, to the Emperor Frederick. The latter had set up an anti-Pope, and had written to the French monarch to solicit his adherence, and to engage him to urge that of the Bishops of his kingdom. Louis answered the Imperial Embassadors that, "he wondered that the Emperor could speak so foolishly. Was he ignorant that Christ had committed his whole flock to Peter? Are Emperors or Kings excepted in the Gospel, or do my Bishops not belong to the flock of Peter?"

However much Kings and Emperors may have desired for awhile, being led away by selfish and political ambition, to set themselves up against the privileged decisions of the Roman Pontiff, they were obliged, soon or late, as in the case of Henry II of England, the murderer of St. Thomas of Canterbury, to confess their error, and, prostrate before his throne, to profess submission to his ordinances.*

History tells us how even a Frederick Barbarossa, the incarnation of bold resistance to

---

* Berc. xii, Baron. ad an. 1154.

Papal authority, was finally led, by the heavy hand of God, to bow his head and sue for pardon. The same penitent submission, though doubtless, with greater sincerity, is to be witnessed in his son Henry VI.

In contrast to these last sovereigns, let us consider the Christian example of the Queen mother of Richard the Lion-hearted, who wrote to the Pope: "Did not the Lord confer Plenitude of Power on Peter, and on you through him? Blessed be the Lord who gave such power to men, that no king, no emperor, no duke can withdraw himself from its jurisdiction. The Prince of the Apostles still governs in his See, and a judicial power is constituted in our midst. Draw, then, the sword of Peter. The Cross of Christ takes precedence of the Imperial Eagles, and the sword of Peter goes before that of Constantine. Has not God spoken to you in the person of Peter, '*Whatsoever thou shalt bind?*'" etc. "*Nonne Petro Apostolo et in eo vobis a Deo omnis potestas committitur? Benedictus Deus, qui talem dedit hominibus potestatem! non rex, non imperator, non dux a jugo vestræ jurisdictionis eximitur. Princeps Apostolorum adhuc in Apostolica Sede regnat et in medio constitutus est judiciarius rigor. Restat ut exeratis gladium Petri. Christi crux antecellit Cæsaris aquilas, gladius Petri gladio Con-*

stantini. Nonne Deus Deorum locutus est vobis in Petro Apostolo, dicens: Quidquid ligaveris," etc.* Hear ye kings of modern times, the lesson of this Queen, *"Et nunc reges intelligite."*

The Emperor Baldwin confesses the same rights in his edict, *"Ad omnes ubique Christianos,"* as also the King of the Bulgarians in his embassy to the Pope. The Emperor Philip, in a letter to the Pope, along with another letter from the other princes of Germany, writes: "As Rome was once the center of superstition, so now, by Divine Providence, it has become the center of salvation." Peter of Arragon, in his coronation oath to King John of England, in a special epistle to the Pope, Philip II of France, and King Henry of Norway, in the year 1241, express the very same doctrine and sentiments.†

The conscience of Christendom, to which Lanfranc alluded, manifests itself most remarkably in the celebrated Synopsis of Laws for the Southern States of Germany, called the "*Schwabenspiegel*," and in that for the Northern States, called the "*Sachsenspiegel*." In both, mention is made of two swords, the one temporal, in the hands of political power, the other, spiritual, in the hands of the Pope, the Head of the Church.

* Natal. Alex. xiii, Baron. ad an. 1189, Hard. v.
† Spond. ad an. 1213, Bero. xiii.

Frederick II, himself, in his apology, speaking of the harmony in which these two powers should act for the welfare of the human race, compares them to the sun and moon, which, in perfect harmony, illumine and preserve the life of Nature. In developing this comparison, he points out their mutual relation and subordination, in a way which is not a little remarkable in such a one, as we know him to have been. "*In exordio nascentis mundi Dei providentia in firmamento cœli duo statuit luminaria, majus et minus . . . . quæ duo sic ad officia propria offeruntur, ut unum alterum non offendat; imo, quod superius est, inferiori suam communicat claritatem. A simili æterna provisione duo voluit esse regimina, sacerdotium, scilicet, et imperium, unum ad cautelam; alterum, ut homo duobus retinaculis frœnaretur et sic fieret pax orbis.*"

This prerogative was acknowledged also by St. Louis of France, by his son Philip the Bold, and by the Kings of Sclavonia, Servia, and the Princes of Bosnia, by the Embassies which they sent to Rome in the fourteenth century, as any one may see for himself by reading the Annals of Spondanus.

The Emperor Paleologus I, personally at Rome, and Paleologus II, personally also at the Council of Florence, made this same confession of faith in the prerogatives of the Roman Pontiff. Similar to the decision of Aurelian is the testimony offered by the Sultan of Egypt, in the name, which he gives to the Pope of "the tongue of Christians and the Judge of the Christian people." "*Universalis loquela Christianorum, judex populi Christiani.*"*

Abul Feda, Prince of Havana, in his Arabian book of history, gives the same testimony to the general faith of Christendom, which we have been extracting from its own records. Such testimony from men of talent, who are not Catholic nor even pretend to be Christians, has singular weight, since they can not be suspected of partisanship or prejudice, and speak simply in the character of close and accurate observers.

It is in our power also to adduce the testimony of entire nations, as made known by their delegates to the Apostolic See.

Thus Abbot Andreas, Delegate of the Christians of Egypt and Ethiopia, addressing the Pope in public audience says, in the name of the nations whose representative he was: "Thou art Christ and His Vicar; thou art the successor of St. Peter, the head and teacher of the Universal Church to whom the Keys of Heaven have been intrusted; thou art the Sovereign of Kings and

* Raynald. ad an. 1307, Natal. Alex. xv, 39.

the greatest of all teachers." *"Tu es Christus et ejus Vicarius. Es Petri successor, pater, caput, et doctor Ecclesiæ Universalis, cui data sunt claves claudendi et reserandi paradisum. Tu princeps regum, et maximus es magistrorum."*

Those Churches which have separated themselves from their first foundation, their Mother and Teacher, Rome, have become through a just judgment of God, objects of contempt in the eyes of the nations.

Even Englishmen are obliged to confess the contempt and ridicule into which their Church has fallen.

Let us listen to the Delegates of the Syrians, Chaldeans, and Maronites in the fifteenth century. They tell the Pope: "How great the reverence is, which our people preserve for the Holy See, may be seen in the way in which they receive and welcome its Legates. Old and young throw themselves at their feet, kiss them, and strive to obtain relics of their vestments. The whole world knows that they, who separate themselves from Rome, must perish. Therefore the Emperor of Ethiopia has nothing more at heart than to be reconciled with the See of Rome. So great among us is the Roman name and the Latin faith."

The Abbot Nicodemus, on the occasion of the

reconciliation of Ethiopia to the Church, expressed his joy in these words: "Therefore," said he to the Pope, "art thou placed over the See of Peter, that thou mayest feed the sheep of Christ. Strive, then, that all they who are dispersed may return to unity, and that the faith of all may become one." "*Ut sit omnium fides, una.*"

Even from the Japanese, before the breaking out of the last and most cruel persecution, there came delegations to Rome, as in 1585, to testify to the fidelity and submission of that newly converted nation toward the common Father and Teacher of Christendom.

In the West, Louis XI, King of France, rejected and overthrew, at the request of Pius II, the so-called "Pragmatic Sanction," because it contained things not easily reconcilable with the plenitude of the Apostolic power of the Holy See. He answers the request of the Holy Father in words becoming a Christian King: "According to your direction we entirely reject, cast away, and annul the pragmatic sanction." "*Itaque sicut mandasti, pragmaticum ipsum pellimus, dejicimus, stirpitusque abrogamus.*"

In the year 1474, we find the Christian King of Denmark at the feet of the reigning Pontiff, paying him the homage and veneration due to the Supreme Head of the Church. The same was done by Charles VIII of France, and by Henry VII of England, who derived his royal dignity from a Bull of Innocent VIII.

God so ordered it, that even Henry VIII of England, who, carried away by lust and passion, together with his illegitimate daughter Elizabeth, seduced England from her allegiance and forced her into heresy and schism, should first give to the princes and peoples a strong and energetic profession of faith.

Every one knows how, on the rise of Luther, and when Protestantism first threatened to invade England, he wrote a book in which he denounced the heresiarch, and dedicated it to the Pope, as the supreme judge in matters of faith. This work, for which he gained the title still impudently borne by his successors, *defensor fidei*, he sent to the Emperor of Germany, and to all the Kings and Princes of Europe. In it, in the article on Indulgences, he addresses Luther in these terms: "No enemy of the Pope can deny the submission which has been paid to him, by the Christian world, in all times and places. Now, if the Pope did not acquire this privilege by divine right, let Luther point out when and how he became possessed of it. The origin of such power can not be lost in obscurity, especially since it is within the reach of human memory." "*Dicat Lutherus, quando in tantæ ditionis irrupit possessionem. Non potest obscurum initium esse tam immensæ potentiæ, præsertim si intra hominum memoriam nata est.*" He then adjures all Christians to close their ears to the dangerous words of Luther, and to remain faithful to the Holy See. The wretched man, on the day of judgment, must hear addressed to him the words of our Lord: "*Ex ore tuo te judico, serve nequam.*" "From thy own mouth I judge thee, wicked servant." But if Henry could safely challenge the world to point out the time, when the Supremacy and Infallibility of the Pope first arose, the world, in return, can easily fix the date, in which the Sovereigns of England first arrogated their usurped power over the Church, if that should be called a Church which yields them spiritual allegiance.

A martyr under this same brutal persecutor, Thomas More, confirms by his testimony, what we have proved of the faith of Englishmen up to this period. Cited before the tribunal of his iniquitous judges, he said: " Having noticed the intention of the King to disobey the Pope, for the last seven years, I have thoroughly examined the question, to ascertain whence the authority of the Pope originated, and I have found it clearly proven to be of divine right." To the question, how he dared in this to oppose the opinion of so many learned clergymen and laity; he answered: "For one Bishop whom you can cite on your side, I can name a hundred in opposition, and against one kingdom I oppose the voice of all Christendom for the space of over one thousand years. If I alone had to stand up against the Parliament, it would be a difficult task; but with me I have the whole Catholic Church, that great Parliament of Christianity."

Mary, Queen of England, and Mary of Scotland, remained faithful to the truth, and England for a time was able to discern and follow the faith of her fathers, until Elizabeth ascended the throne and forced the nation into the false path in which it has hitherto walked, and where it is kept by disobedience to the voice of him, who is the Head of the true and only Church of Christ. In these our days, we rejoice in the prospect of a better time for that once isle of saints, now that so many of her purest and best, most illustrious and learned, are commencing to search for themselves, and to listen to the powerful voice of old traditions, and, led by the love of truth, are finding their way back to the arms of their Mother—of that Church whose Head welcomes them, as his saintly predecessor, GREGORY the Great, called them to the faith.

ACKNOWLEDGING THIS PREROGATIVE. 245

In the commencement of the Reformation, Maximilian I wrote to the Pope: "Nobody can judge these perilous doctrines but your Holiness, and as you alone can, so you ought to do it." "*Quo sola ut potest, ita debet.*" Of Luther, whom he had learned to know intimately, this Emperor said: "When I am dead, this monk will cause much trouble and misery in the Empire." "*Me mortuo, monachus iste calamitates et miserias gravissimas in imperio excitabit.*"*

Charles V acknowledges this privilege of the Holy See in what is called the "Interim," and, so soon as Henry IV of France returned to the Church, he sent embassadors to the Pope to signify his entire submission to him and to his decisions, as, he says, was the practice of French monarchs. The same was done by Louis XIII, his son, and even by Louis XIV. This proud and self-willed Sovereign, notwithstanding his schismatical tendencies, was finally compelled, by conscience, to retract the four articles of Gallicanism, which he had extorted from a servile episcopacy, and which he again foreswore in his last will and testament.

The devotion and submission of the Maximilians and Ferdinands who succeeded Charles V on the imperial throne, are too well known to

* Spond. an. 1517.

need exposition here. Besides these the Kings of Spain, Portugal, Naples, and others continued in the path traced out to them by their predecessors. Napoleon the Great was not the man to undervalue or ignore the authority and influence of the Pontiff upon the Universal Church, and hence his persistent effort to make him his willing and submissive subject. But his power disappeared in the fogs of St. Helena; that of the Pope remains resplendent on the rock of Peter, in the midst of all the cataclysms that agitate our age. The unrelenting animosity of the enemies of the Church is not so much against Pius IX, as against the faith that he defends and the Church of which he is the Head; promising themselves that, in spite of its more than thousand Bishops, they will easily triumph, if they can but break or weaken the prerogative and privilege of its Ruler and Teacher, the Roman Pontiff, successor of St. Peter, Vicar of Christ. Little do they foresee or seem to know that, even though they were to succeed in banishing him from Rome, they would be no nearer to success, since his authority goes with him, and where he is, there is Rome, the rock of Peter.

No doubt, the "conscience" of Christianity is yet awake. Wherever the Pope may be, the true sheep of the flock of Christ will listen to his voice as to that of Peter. Even a *Renan* is conscious of this faithful sentiment of Christianity, as we may understand from the words of his last work, "Meditations Contemporaires," published last year in Paris, where he says: "The Pope knows better than his adversaries what it means to be a Catholic. He published his Syllabus, well aware that it would not do for a Catholic to brave the teaching of a Pope." Yes, the Catholic world at large, without any difference of nationality, hemisphere, or zone, acknowledges also in our times, by an interior conviction of faith, the Apostolical See as the highest tribunal on earth in matters of faith, and the Roman Pontiff to be the infallible teacher of the faithful peoples on the globe.

VIII.

THE "RATIO THEOLOGICA,"

OR THE EVIDENCE OF THE TRUTH OF OUR THESIS BY THE FORCE OF LOGICAL CONSEQUENCES.

By the "Ratio Theologica" we understand the deductions which right reason, logically exercised, acquires by its own light from that which faith has taught. "*Ex datis et concessis.*" Therefore, though reason can not invent new articles of faith, it has its due weight in arguments concerning faith, more particularly when the arguments are approved and sustained by the two sources of faith, the authority of Scripture and tradition, as taught and understood by the Church their legitimate interpreter. We have only to look into the works of St. Thomas, in order to perceive how justly and highly the weight of reason, and the force of logical consequences, were always appreciated by the Doctors of the Church. Let us, then, hear what calm and sober reason has to tell us touching our proposition.

Reason, then, on considering the words of Christ as contained in Holy Writ, holds the following language:

According to what Christ promised to Peter, He had to grant to him and to his successors the privilege of Supreme and Infallible authority in matters of faith. It was certainly in His power to grant it, and the way in which He introduced and established it in the world, made it eminently *convenient* and *necessary* that He should confer this right and privilege on the Head of the Church—therefore, He did in fact confer it. *Promisit, potuit, dedit.* He promised it, he could, it was proper that He should, therefore, He *did* give it. This is briefly what we have to say and to prove, in order that we may perceive the logical strength of this deduction or theological conclusion.

FIRST. We remark that Reason dictates, that if any one promises a thing as infallibly certain, and that promise draws with it necessarily the fulfillment of another condition, without which the former promise can not be kept, then if he sincerely promises the first, he as certainly includes the second. Such, in point of fact, were the promises made to Peter and to his successors for the good of the Church, necessarily involving the right and privilege of which we are treating; hence, as Christ did certainly promise and sincerely promise the former, he as certainly conferred the latter. As to the words of *promise* we proved them, when treating the testimony of Sacred Writ, and as to the conditional necessity of the prerogative, we hold that no candid man can doubt it; so, therefore, the consequence necessarily follows. Hear the proof of our consequence:

There can be no doubt, we repeat, that having constituted Peter and his successors the foundation of His Church, and having *promised* that the gates of hell should never prevail against her, it follows of necessity that he must so strengthen that foundation, that it can never fail.

Having imposed on Peter and his successors the office of confirming their brethren, it became a necessity that He should so strengthen their faith that they should be able to fulfill the office, that is, that they should never fall into error in that, which they had to confirm.

Having imposed on Peter and his successors the care of feeding both the lambs and the sheep, and hence upon the flock the obligation of following them as leaders, it necessarily follows that he must have rendered it impossible that Peter or his successors should ever lead them astray into the path of error. To deny any of these three premises, with their common consequence, forming, as they do, one and the same argument, would be as much as to say that either Christ did not know what He was promising, or could not fulfill what He promised. The former would be blasphemy—the latter no less.

SECOND. We say that Christ *could* do it. To deny the possibility, would be to limit the power of the Almighty, or to deny the Divinity of Christ. Moreover, according to our opponents, He had it in His power to do so for the whole Church, since they claim infallibility for it, and will they tell us that what He could do for the many, He could not do for one? Each one of the many whom they would collectively invest with this privilege, is after all but one; what incongruity or impossibility is there in the single Head of the Church enjoying what they suppose to have been granted to a body of single individuals?

THIRD. We said it was *convenient* or proper, that He should do it. We would not be understood to determine *a priori* what Christ must or must not do, in order to make His Church infallible; a thousand ways were open to Him, no doubt, of which we can know nothing. For instance, He could have sent for every fresh emergency an Angel from heaven to teach or direct the faithful. We do not attempt, therefore, to prescribe or dictate what He had to choose or do; but we have a right to use the reason which He himself gave us, and say if the manner in which He established His Church, is such, as of itself to require that He should have invested its head with such a prerogative in matters of faith, then His own infinite wisdom compelled Him to have done so. Now such is precisely the case, and thus it is that we say that it was convenient and proper that He should do so.

Does the manner in which He constituted His Church so compel Him? This is all that we have to prove, for that once granted, it is plain that our consequence must follow.

He constituted that Church, the kingdom of truth, a visible Church, to be set on the top of a mountain, and to be acknowledged as such by all who are of good will. Now, how can that Church be a kingdom of truth of which the Head may be the mouthpiece of error, or how can it be visible to all, that is, be a beacon for their wandering steps, if its summit be lost in the mists of ignorance or willful falsehood, and thus cease to direct them? Where, and how should the children of men look for the truth, save in the visible head of the one true Church, the kingdom of truth? When there is only *one* to attend to, the search is possible, but not in the supposition of our adversaries, when it would be necessary to consult the majority of the Bishops, dispersed throughout the world or assembled in Council. Both these suppositions, considering the manner in which the Church exists, can be easily shown to be *impracticable*, as means to arrive at the object of man's search, the true faith. Not the General or Œcumenical Council can be the common and ordinary tribunal of faith, and so established by Christ, since, by the ordinary circumstances of time and place, it is subjected to so many impediments that its use is for centuries made impossible.

History has proved this beyond the possibility of contradiction.

Three hundred years elapsed after the birth of Christianity, many heresies had arisen, and no General Council had been possible on account of the exterior difficulties. In the meantime the Papal decisions were found sufficient to grapple with and destroy the growing errors. Moreover, since the Council of Nice, in sixteen hundred years, only seventeen General Councils have been held; and from the celebration of the last to our own time, three hundred years have elapsed. Alas for the Church, if, during the intervals, all that agitated her had to remain in suspense, and undecided until the convocation of a future Council, of which no one could be certain that it would ever be held! Especially is this verified in the case of the last Council, that of Trent, held three hundred years ago. Can any one pretend that it was more convenient and proper that Christ should have instituted for His Church, that might any day stand in need of most important decisions concerning the faith, a tribunal that could only meet in spite of great difficulties?

And at the time when a Council is convened, what number of Bishops will our adversaries assign as requisite for such a Council to be admitted as representing the *whole* Church? How will they vindicate such a claim when nearly an equal number of Bishops is arrayed on both sides, as happened at the outbreak of the Greek schism? Nay, there are Councils, as the I and V of Constantinople, at which only a small minority of Bishops assembled. In such a case, how ought we to ascertain the sentiments of the rest of the Episcopacy? The whole difficulty returns to the so-called authority of the assent of "the Church dispersed."

But even on the supposition that the entire Episcopacy can be convened, or that it has actually been convened, our adversaries can not hold their ground. They themselves admit, that though all the Bishops of the whole Catholic world were assembled in council, their decisions in matters of faith could lay no claim to infallibility before being confirmed by the Pope. Consequently, their decisions, so long as they are not confirmed by the Pope, can not oblige the faithful under pain of heresy. But the same thing can not be said of the Papal decisions in matters of faith. History furnishes us with conclusive evidence that such Papal decisions were always regarded as *final* and as *binding* in conscience, even before the other Bishops gave their assent, and, therefore, that they were considered as emanating from an authority of *itself* infallible.

Gallicanism, of course, attacks our premises. Even in our own days there are some theologians, of a so-called "*juste milieu,*" who do indeed admit the Pope's superiority over the Bishops, even when assembled in Council, but deny his personal infallibility, except when the other Bishops concur in his decisions.

But such an assumption can not be reconciled with the teachings of Holy Scripture and Tradition.

According to gospel, Christ solemnly declared that he prayed for Peter that his faith should never fail, and that he imposed on him *alone* the office of confirming his brethren. The Pope, in the supposition of our opponents, would not possess this privilege, but would have been left by Christ under the necessity of being *himself* confirmed by the assent of his brethren.

It is Peter *alone* whom Christ made the Pastor, to feed and to lead His whole flock—the lambs and the sheep—not that they, in any case, should lead Him.

It is Peter *alone* whom Christ made the immovable rock, so that His *faith* should sustain the whole Church, whether united in Council or not.

The assumption is likewise also contradicted by Tradition, or rather is crushed entirely by its weight. In proof of it, we have only to remember the numberless testimonies alleged in this book.

We only refer here to the acts of the Popes concerning the first eight Œcumenical Councils of the East, and to the acts of those Councils themselves.

The Popes, as we have shown, almost always previously decided the agitated question before those Councils met, often without leaving any opportunity for further discussion—asking sometimes the Fathers to subscribe their definitions, even before they were allowed to take a seat in the Council, and not permitting even the least liberty to change a single word. We heard the Legates of Adrian I, in the VII Council, giving the reasons for such absolute orders: Because, they said, to discuss a matter already decided by an irrevocable judgment, neither faith nor reason permits. *"Quia de irreformabili judicio quæri, nec ratio nec fides permittit."*

How could the Popes, in the face of a General Council in the East, dare to behave and to speak in such a manner? and how could those Councils submit to such a usurpation if the infallible teaching Authority would have been intrusted by Christ not to *one*, but to *two* exponents—the Pope and the Episcopacy?

How could they solemnly define the Pope to be their *Teacher?* Is it the assent of the disciple, which makes the sentence of the Teacher true?

If the assent of both of them, according to Christ's command, constitutes the only *final* tribunal of faith in the Church, why should have been condemned the appeal from the Pope to a General Council, as it actually was *condemned* by Martin V in the Council of Constance?

But the force of logical consequences pushes our adversaries even much further, because what tribunal of faith would Christ have left for his Church, if the two exponents of the teaching authority were in opposition, as in the case of Rimini?

Moreover, the Church, admitting the opinion of our adversaries, would not be *absolutely*, and *at all times* infallible, but only *occasionally*, namely, when the Episcopacy agrees with the Pope. The Pope himself would stand no degree higher as regards infallibility than any other Bishop, and consequently, the very idea of the Primacy, as the guarantee of unity for an infallible Church, would pass away, with the impugned dilemma, and the infallible tribunal of the Church sink into a mere mockery, as we engage to prove.

The celebration of a General Council not being within the reach of the Church sometimes even for centuries, we ask by what other criterion shall the faithful learn the agreement of the Episcopacy with its Head, the Pope?

Our adversaries have no other alternative than to appeal to the consent of the so-called "*Ecclesia dispersa*"—the Church spread all over the globe.

Of course we admit that the Church, taken as the one mystical body united with its Head, can never err in matters of faith; but we deny that this "consent" was intended by Christ to be for the faithful the tribunal of the infallible teaching of the Church, and assert that to assume it, as taking place of the Papal authority, involves all the consequences which we have mentioned.

Here are our proofs:

1. The appeal to the consent of the "*Ecclesia dispersa,*" as to the supreme tribunal of faith, contradicts the same promise and command of Christ, which we have just quoted. For if we suppose that the assent of the Church dispersed is the last and highest test of infallible teaching, then we say again, it is not Peter who confirms his brethren, but rather his brethren confirm him. Until that consent is infallibly ascertained, the Pope must necessarily remain in suspense, if not in doubt.

He would not be sure to lead his flock on an unerring path, and the foundation of the Church would be in danger of giving away. In our thesis, the words of the Lord are verified.

II. It contradicts the declarations of the Holy Fathers, whose testimony we have before cited. They do not predicate the orthodoxy of the Roman See on its agreement with the teaching of the other Churches, but just the contrary. Their Canon of Orthodoxy for the other Churches is the agreement of their teaching with the faith of Rome, and this, too, as a final and absolute condition, absolving them from any further proof of their agreeing with the faith or teaching of any other Apostolic Church. To agree with Rome is to be orthodox, nothing more is needed. To agree with other Churches would be nothing for or against, since they too must conform to the same rule, and agree with Rome, with which, in the words of St. Irenæus, "*necesse est convenire omnem aliam Ecclesiam,*" because it was founded on Peter and inherits his faith through its Bishop, the successor of Peter.

In the same way the most learned St. Jerome exclaimed: "Let others think and say what they please; I say, he that holds with you, agrees with me." "*Siquis Cathedræ Petri jungitur, meus est.*" And why? "Because on this rock the Church was built." That, and not the consent previously obtained from the dispersed Church, is the reason of the unconditional submission paid by the Fathers to the Roman See. They urge it upon others, because, with St. Augustin, they hold it *a crime* to contradict the decisions of Rome; with the Fathers of Chalcedon, and others, that it is not the Church dispersed, but Peter who speaks through the mouth of the

Bishop of Rome. *Per os Leonis et Agathonis, Petrus locutus est.*

In reasoning thus, as we must do in view of the declarations of the Holy Fathers and of our Lord Himself, we do not, of course, pretend that the universal teaching of the Church on any point is not also an infallible sign of truth, according to the widely celebrated canon of St. Vincent Lerens, "that which was, ever, everywhere and by all believed." "*Quod semper, ubique et ab omnibus creditum est.*" However great the weight justly due to this canon, it can not be laid down as a principle whereby to establish a tribunal of faith, that is, a rule whereby a truth known of faith is definitively promulgated by the Church of Christ, and which so entails the obligation of belief, that any one refusing to give it interior and exterior consent, becomes a heretic and ceases to be a member of the Church.

In this respect we affirm that the canon of orthodoxy is that given by St. Jerome: "I hold with him who adheres to the Church of Rome; that is Catholic which is Roman." "*Hoc Catholicum, quod Romanum.*" The consent of the Church, *dispersa*, can never be substituted for such an ultimate tribunal, because:

III. Such consent is destitute of the qualities necessary to form the tribunal in question.

Those qualities are *visibility, distinctiveness*, and *applicability*.

By the first, *visibility*, we mean the moral facility and possibility of arriving at a knowledge of the fact of its decision. Now this is not the case in regard to the consent of the Church dispersed throughout the world. To arrive at the knowledge of such consent, an amount of learning is required which few persons possess, together with opportunities of scrutinizing various documents, historical, critical, and scientific, beyond the reach of the vast majority of the faithful. No one who does not live in an imaginary world, instead of the world as it is, can question the truth of this assertion.

In respect to a decision by the Roman Pontiff there is no such difficulty, and if any one doubted the nature of that decision he could at least consult the Holy Father himself. This, as we have seen, was done in all ages. Persons traveled from the far East, from the South of Africa and the North of Europe, as from the extreme isles of the West, for the sake of a personal audience with the Holy Father, and to receive from his own lips an answer to their doubts or difficulties. We have seen it done even by peasants, as in the case of some Tyrolian pietists. And now, more than ever before, is such access open to all, whether by visit or by word of writing.

By *distinctiveness*, we mean its excluding all want of precision and doubt as to its meaning, and every possibility of misinterpretation. This quality is necessary to a tribunal which compels an act of *faith*, and, we need hardly add, is not attached to a consent of the Church dispersed throughout the world, since it presupposes an infallible certainty in judging of the existence of that consent. A moral conviction that some truth is universally or generally held throughout the Church, can justify it as a Catholic opinion, but can not impose the obligation of exciting an act of faith, under the penalty of being otherwise accounted a heretic. Such a consent of the Church can never claim the prerogative of being a tribunal of faith, or rule of faith, even though it were a Thomas of Aquinas who applied himself to the task of verifying the fact of its existence.

This we witnessed at the time of the definition of the Immaculate Conception. Six hundred Bishops had already given their answers by letter; two hundred were assembled together at Rome, and yet had not PIUS IX raised his voice, and proclaimed that truth to be an article of faith, no one could to-day assert with the infallible certainty of faith, the Immaculate Conception of the Blessed Virgin Mary. But from the moment that Pius IX proclaimed his definition, not only every Catholic could, but was obliged to believe it to be an article of faith, whether he had ascertained the general consent of the Church or not. Take the very subject of our present discussion. What a number of documents have we not cited in its favor, and yet the truth which we defend is not held as an article of faith, and will not be, until it has been made the subject of a precise definition.

Moreover, what if a great part of the Church dispersed, amounting apparently to a majority, should seem to favor error, as in the time when St. Jerome exclaimed, "The whole world was astonished to find itself Arian?" Such occasions might possibly occur again. At least, it will always be in the power of obstinate heretics to pretend that the consent of the Church has not been expressed with sufficient unanimity or clearness, with the advantage on their side of counting themselves among the judges of the common tribunal, and thus lessening, in a very obvious way, the distinctiveness or preciseness of the judgment.

The third quality which we denied to this

method, and which is also necessary to such a tribunal of faith, is *applicability*, or its general fitness for use. For the majority of men, we may say that it is simply impossible to consult or to decide upon the general consent of the Church in reference to any question; and as nobody, not even the most learned, can hope to arrive at absolute certainty in this matter, it would follow that Christ, if He had constituted this the regular and ordinary tribunal of faith, would, in fact, considering the state of mankind and the Church's position in its midst, have provided no tribunal at all, and have thus left His children no distinctive and decided help or certainty in matters of faith. We say, therefore:

IV. The assertion that the consent of the Church dispersed must be considered the last and highest tribunal in matters of faith, is about on a par with that which Protestants make with regard to the Bible alone as interpreted by individuals. What Catholics answer to their pretensions might equally well be brought forward against this theory of the "*Ecclesia dispersa.*"

Indeed, what are the principal Catholic arguments on this point? Are they not:

1. That the question of the canonicity of each and all the parts of that sacred volume is a fact

that has to be settled elsewhere and not from the book itself.

2. The Bible is not sufficiently clear and decisive in itself alone, to be considered as the rule of faith or its highest tribunal.

3. The Bible itself contradicts the supposition, and points out another and different rule of faith.

4. If, indeed, the Bible be the sole rule of faith, then, taking it as it is, it can only be such for a few very learned men; but Christ came for all, and all need the rule of faith, especially the poor and ignorant, the many.

5. The private interpretation of the Bible, in the actual order of God's Providence, necessarily remains private and human, whereas the rule of faith must be divine, and be the same for all.

Now these same reasons obtain, and with even greater weight, against the theory that we are refuting.

1. The existence of a consent of the Church dispersed, is a fact which has to be proved elsewhere than from the consent itself, that is, by the evidences of the consent. To ascertain this fact is a yet more difficult task than to establish, that one or other book of Sacred Scripture has been authoritatively accepted in the Church as canonical. Strictly and severely speaking, the fact itself of the consent would, in that case, be the ob-

ject of another approved consent of the Church—and, so far, an endless round.

The objection can not be retorted against us, where there is but one question to be asked and answered: "Did the Pope, addressing the faithful, teach or define it or not?" If there should be place for doubt, that doubt can be easily solved by recurring to the Pope himself.

2. The consent, as we have shown, is not and can not be sufficiently *clear* and *definitive* to be a rule of faith. The Pope's definitions, on the other hand, are in precise and positive terms and immediate answers, word for word, to the questions proposed.

3. The general consent of the Church, as we have seen, is, as far as it can be ascertained, *adverse* to the supposition, and points very significantly to our own as the correct thesis.

4. The investigation necessary to prove the existence of this consent, would be for the *few* and the *learned*, not for the poor and the multitude. The same reasons, therefore, founded on historical, critical, and scientific, not to mention literary difficulties, militate against this investigation equally, as against the fair and correct interpretation of Holy Writ.

5. Finally, as in Biblical interpretation so in this case, the judgment could not ascend higher

than its premises, and would remain private and human, not divine, and therefore not free from liability to error. Have we not, time and again, seen the most learned Theologians of the Church bringing up authorities, which, no doubt, they believed to settle the question, and, after all was said on both sides, it remained still at variance with the general consent of the Church concerning the point in dispute? Do not St. Thomas Aquinas and St. Bonaventure sometimes disagree, though both would have been unwilling to differ from what they knew to be the general consent of the Church? Not only individual Doctors, but whole Universities, Religious Orders, Provincial Churches, have been found to disagree in their interpretation of what was the doctrine on certain points of the *Ecclesia dispersa*. Now, this can not be said of any decision by the Roman Pontiff; it has always been sufficiently explicit to carry its meaning with it, and the only dispute was the unwillingness on the part of some to acknowledge, that they had held the error which he condemned. The consent of the Church dispersed, would be of little avail to silence a discussion or controversy, whilst, to use the language of the Fathers, a Papal decision is a sword in the hands of the Pastors, with which to cleave away the hydra-heads of heresy.

But let us here say a few words concerning the chief reason which influences our opponents in their resistance to our thesis. They are loath to acknowledge that a single individual, in other things liable to error, should be even in any way held infallible. They fail to grasp the distinction between the personal and the official action, and to understand, how this infallibility is restricted to the Pope defining or teaching the universal Church, in which there is no such cause of apprehension, as they seem to entertain, and no contradiction or repugnance to the Providence of our Lord over His Church.

It is not for himself or for his personal advantage that such a claim is made, but for the good of the Church, when he addresses it as its Head and Chief Pastor.

The prerogative, if it has been granted at all, as we claim, has been granted by One who can as easily confer it on a single individual as on the whole Church.

Reason, moreover, can recognize in such a provision of Almighty God, that which commends itself as *becoming* and *adapted* to the circumstances of the Church, which He designs to protect, and the usual method pursued by Him in the supernatural sphere. For, as we have said before, so here we repeat, that it is fit that the

Church, as a visible kingdom, should have a visible head, and that the head of it should possess the great privilege which characterizes and sets apart that Kingdom of Truth from every possibility of being subverted by error.

Reason expects that since Christ has promised the end—the preservation of His Church from error—so, too, He has promised and provided the means to the end; and among all those that are discussed, we can not find any better adapted in itself, more consonant to His promises and more easily recognizable in actual history than that which our thesis defends.

Reason discerns no advantage, which is gained by attributing infallibility to many, taken collectively, rather than to one placed at their head. The influencing of the many by Divine Power would seem, humanly speaking, a greater exercise of Omnipotence than the direction of a single individual. Observation of the ways of Divine Providence shows what we may call a *divine parsimony* of force, in equalizing the means to the end, but not in wasting it or effecting in a complex and circuitous manner what is as well done by a simpler way. The analogy of nature to grace leads reason, then, to expect a similar disposition in the higher order, and prepares her to hear that one person has been invested with infallibility, when, as she must acknowledge, the investing of that one is just as effective and useful, to say the least, as would be the endowment of the many. It is such a train of argument as the scholastics embody in their axioms: "*Dei Sapientia non operatur superflua*"—God's wisdom acts not uselessly; and, "*Entia non sunt multiplicanda*"—beings or agents are not to be multiplied without necessity. Now, the infallibility of the many, in our opponents' theories, always involves the infallibility of the one confirming or rejecting; to what purpose, then, was their infallibility?

There is still another analogy to which we may appeal. God, in His divine Providence, loves to make use of creatures as He made them, and to allow the coöperation of human endeavors and efforts even in the order of grace. He employs human prudence, exertion, and ability, and comes in to complete and carry to perfection the work which they fail of themselves, when alone, to accomplish. He connects even His miraculous operations with human action. Thus He appoints Moses, educated as an Egyptian prince, the leader and lawgiver of His chosen people; He selects a St. Paul, versed in the science of his age, as an Apostle to the Gentiles, and a teacher in the Areopagus. So, too, the position of the Roman Pontiff, according to our adversaries' admission, as Primate, the center of communication, surrounded by the chief Doctors and Theologians of the Church, preëminently suggests the design of making him the investigator of doctrine, the expounder of truth, and the judge of controversy. In thus making him the final arbiter in matters of faith, Divine Providence actually makes another and beautiful application of the words: "*Pertingens a fine usque in finem, et disponens omnia fortiter, suaviterque.*" How much more powerfully and sweetly, through *one* the end is obtained, than in a collective infallibility, which is hardly compatible with human frailty, as is shown by the common proverb: "*Quot capita tot sententiæ;*"—"So many minds, so many opinions." This power and gentle force of action we have had occasion to witness in our historical evidence, where we have seen it repeatedly victorious, as in the case of Berengarius, Fenelon, and others of our own times, while on the other hand we have found the massive strength and momentum of a Council for the most only efficient to crush or destroy error, not to save the erring, and the silent and passive protest of the Church dispersed altogether inefficient and unheeded. Therefore, we may say in the words of St. Paul, "*Invisibilia ipsius per ea, quæ facta sunt, intellecta conspiciuntur.*"* " His invisible things are seen, being understoood by the things that are created." The acknowledgment of this one Power, Right, or Privilege of the Holy See averts all possibility of disunion in faith. Here especially to err in one is to fail in all; to mistake the organ of infallibility is to expose one's self to the danger of a lapse in the faith. The Greek schismatical Church is a noted and lamentable case in point. They believe in the infallibility of the Universal Church, but having refused to hearken to the voice of Peter, and having refused to recognize his prerogative, they are a withered, dying remnant, instead of enjoying the strong and active life of the Spouse of Christ. "Thence," to apply the words of St. Cyprian, "come all heresy and schism, because the one Judge in the place of Christ, the judgment of the High Priest, the Head of the Church is not respected as it ought to be." Let all acknowledge to-day this one Prerogative, there would be to-morrow but the one united Church, in North, South, East, and West.

For a philosophical and theological mind the last reflection should have great weight, since

---

* Ep. Rom. i, 20.

the unity of the Church, its greatest, most glorious mark is thus best shown and guarded in the unfailing faith and authority of Peter and his successors.

Even the *essential Character* of the Church on earth, and the very *Name* consecrated by Catholic tradition to the See of St. Peter in Rome, serve to corroborate our thesis.

We say, first, the essential character of the Church on earth corroborates it; because the Church on earth is called the "militant Church." This is her essential character; because, according to Christ's own words, she is exposed at every moment, at every time in every place on the globe, to the attacks of the powers of hell. Now, the common sense of all nations, at all times, barbarous or civilized, finds it wise and best, at the time of an impending battle, to place at the head of the army *one* leading General invested with absolute power. Even in our own struggle, in the civil war, it was proclaimed by the highest authority of the Republic, "Better to have *one* bad general in command, than *two* good ones." If men generally understand the convenience of such an arrangement in time of war, and agree to the principle of concentrating all power in the hands of one Commander-in-chief, why should not reason find it expedient that

Christ having left His Church on the battle-field, exposed day and night, and over the whole world to the attacks of its enemies, should place at the head of it *one* individual in command—the Roman Pontiff, the Successor of St. Peter—endowed with absolute and unerring authority in matters of faith, to guarantee forever in the simplest and most efficacious way the victory to this His Church.

Considering the character of the Church, also, out of the battle-field, in her normal state, in regard to her own constitution and spiritual life, St. Paul compares her to the constitution of the human body.* The Church is a visible, but mystical body. St. Paul does not hesitate to follow this comparison in its consequences. Now, the body, in its actions in regard to *rational* life, depends on the influence of the head. The light by which man is guided, in the actions of rational life, is *reason*, which resides in the head, and even in a single and individual head.

What reason is for man as to his rational life, *faith* is in regard to his *supernatural* life. Well then, following closely the analogical parallel given by St. Paul, reason finds it very appropriate that the strength and influence of faith

---

* 1 Cor. c. 6 et 10; ad Eph. c. 4; ad Col. 2.

should have been placed by Christ in the visible Head of the Church, which is the Roman Pontiff, as the successor of St. Peter, for whose faith alone He prayed. And reason approves the fact, that this Head of the mystical body of the Church is a single and individual one; because, pursuing the parallel given by St. Paul, a collective Head would appear rather to be a monstrosity.

We said, second, that the very *Name* consecrated by Catholic tradition to the See of Rome likewise corroborates our thesis. The See of Rome is preëminently called the *Apostolic See*, and what else could that mean than Apostolic Right, Power, and, therefore, Authority; but this is *Infallibility* in matters of faith. Or, are you prepared to say, that the Apostles, when teaching the faithful in matters of faith and morals, could have erred? Suppose St. Paul had written the "Syllabus," and had sent it to the churches, would you then doubt of its infallible character? Therefore, were the Apostles called Apostles because specially selected and sent to preach infallibly the Gospel of Christ, inspired in this and enlightened by the Holy Ghost. "*Go teach all nations, whatsoever I have said unto you.*" This was the mission, the authority that justified their dispersing themselves throughout the world without apprehending a diversity of teaching or a severance of unity. What was extraordinary in the others remained in Peter and his successors as the ordinary foundation of unity and divinity of faith. Hence his See remains the Apostolic See, involving in the name, unless it be mere irony, the same Apostolic Infallibility. Our thesis is true, or the whole Church, in giving this name, but repeats a falsehood, or inflicts a sneer. We would not so blaspheme the Spouse of Christ; and, accepting the name she gives, we acknowledge its significance and truth, and confess that Peter still lives and speaks in Rome when Rome's Bishop, his successor, warns, exhorts, controls, directs the flock of Christ.

Finally—and this is the most stringent argument of all, drawn from the evidence of reason—we say:

The very *nature* of the *Primacy*, as instituted by Christ, brings along with it, as a "*conditio sine qua non,*" its *infallibility* in matters of faith. All agree that Christ gave to his Church a visible head in St. Peter and his successors, to preserve her unity. Now, this unity refers altogether to her interior union of faith. A fallible Pope could never be the guarantee of an imperishable unity in faith. The Primacy, divested of this infallibility, would be naught else to the Church at large than a higher position in point of disciplinary jurisdiction and authority, and not the link of unity in faith. Wherefore, reason clearly tells us, that if we deny the infallibility of the Pope, we likewise refuse to the Church one of her most necessary and distinguishing marks—her unity.

Hence, an attack on the infallibility which Christ gave to Simon Bar-Jona—Peter—the immovable rock, in his successors is a direct attack made upon the Church herself.

As in the Universe, the law of gravitation is the principle of its unity and stability, so that if this universal law would be impaired in the present economy of nature, not only the admirable harmony among the heavenly bodies would be destroyed, but the world itself, by the centrifugal power, scattered; so in the Church, the Papal teaching authority is to be considered as the center of gravitation for the guarantee of its unity and indestructibility, so that impairing it, not only the wonderful harmony and unity of the Church over the whole globe would cease, but the Church itself scattered into numberless sects, as may be witnessed in all the Christian denominations which have withdrawn themselves from that teaching authority of the Holy See.

OBJECTIONS REFUTED

There is no truth, however evident, which has not been the subject of objections, arising either from misunderstanding, prejudice, ignorance, or the intentional malice of men whose interest it was to impugn the truth. This is especially the case in matters of faith. This assertion is amply proved by the history of heresy. Were it not a matter of record, we could scarcely credit with what a mass of misrepresentation, sophistry, and distortion, heretics in different ages have attacked the several articles of divinely-revealed truth. It is not precisely with such antagonists that we now pretend to treat, since it would be almost useless to contend with those who willfully close their eyes that they may not see. We prefer to address ourselves to those who sincerely believe their objections to be well founded and destructive of our thesis. We propose to consider their difficulties, and, in our answers, to give them entire satisfaction.

OBJECTION I.

" There would be no use for a General Council, if the Pope can define the truth by himself alone. But General Councils have been convoked by the Popes themselves, for the suppression of heresy; consequently they themselves did not consider their own decisions infallible, and did not think others possessed of that belief."

ANSWER.—The convocation and action of General Councils in latter times are no more in contradiction with our thesis than the convocation and action of the first Council at Jerusalem, where there was question of matters of faith, and in which St. Peter, St. Paul, and the other Apostles took part. Such Councils have been convoked for the purpose of acting more powerfully in the suppression of heresy, and more completely depriving it of its mask of orthodoxy; and especially in order that, by the departure of their Bishops, the several flocks may have their attention more vividly excited, and, on their return, they may be more easily and efficaciously instructed concerning the decision and the sentence there passed upon the heresy or its originator. Moreover, it has happened more than once, that, in such Councils, others were found to have participated in the error who were, till then, undiscovered, and who, had they not been unmasked and removed from their Sees, might have continued to prove wolves for the destruction of the flock committed to their care.

General Councils offer this additional advantage, that they unite the talents, zeal, and experience of so many illustrious pastors of the Church, for the preservation of the faith and the extirpation of errors, which, by spreading, would endanger its purity and its very existence, and, in addition, to offer an opportunity, by counsel, advice, and wise regulations, to contribute to the better discipline of the faithful, and enable them to advance more easily and securely in the path of Christian perfection.

What we have said in a preceding chapter, on the history and proceedings of General Councils, confirms our present reasoning, so clearly illustrated by the action of the Apostolical Council at Jerusalem.

St. Paul had condemned Cerinth for attempting to Judaise the Gentile converts, and so certain was he of the truth of his decision, that he dared to say that even an angel from Heaven, preaching another Gospel from his own, should be anathematized. Nevertheless, seeing the obstinacy of his opponent and the virulence of the converts from Judaism, he went to Jerusalem. The Council assembled, St. Peter spoke and decided the question, and St. James, after having assented to his decision, proposed an ordinance to enforce the proper discipline, and so the error was fully suppressed, more quickly and efficaciously than it could have been by the authority of St. Paul, infallible as it surely was in matter of faith.

This reënforcement of infallible authority by a Council is pointed out by St. Leo the Great, when speaking of the Œcumenical Council of Chalcedon: "Truth is more vividly seen, and more tenaciously held, when that which *God has defined by our ministry* has been confirmed by the consent of our brethren."* How far Leo was from considering this consent, as a necessary condition of the truths of the faith there inculcated, is manifest from the previous expressions, in which he says that faith had already spoken through the Pope, and that God Himself had defined it through his ministry. This relation between a Papal definition and the judg-

* See his Epist. ad Theod.

ment of a General Council is made still more evident by what Leo did, agreeing in this with all his predecessors and successors, in positively prohibiting discussion, in the Council, as to matters of faith previously defined by the Supreme Pontiff.* And, as we have proved when treating of the General Councils, this was always the case when, as in this instance, a Papal definition had preceded the Council. Moreover, as we have previously shown, there never was an Œcumenical Council which would have ventured to dispute this right, to disregard his veto, or to give the slightest sign of overturning his decision. Nay, so conscious have these great Popes shown themselves of this right, that, in the presence of the whole Episcopacy united in General Council, they would not tolerate decrees or declarations which embodied the same doctrine, but in words different from those by which they themselves had defined the truth. Such was the course of Popes like Leo, whom the Greeks have held in honor even to our own times. "*Either use the words of Leo, or we return to Rome,*" said the Legates, in accordance with the instructions which they had received from that Pontiff. Such, too, was the course pursued on all other occasions when the Pontiff had once delivered

* Leo, Ep. 82, c. 1, 2; Ep. 90, c. 2; Ep. 93 et 94.

his decision, whether he had to do with the Church at large or in Council assembled.

In later times, especially for the Councils held at the Lateran, when there were no errors of sufficient importance or prominence to be condemned, the Bulls of Convocation assigned, as the principal reason of their being convoked, the wish to promote fervor by the enactment and execution of disciplinary regulations. The utility of a General Council in such cases is beyond a doubt—affording the many Bishops and Prelates the advantage of mutual counsel and communication, without, however, impairing or questioning the authority of the Pontiff in matters of faith. In the particular instance of the Third Lateran Council, the Prelates occupied themselves exclusively with matters of discipline, leaving all questions concerning the faith to the action of the Supreme Pontiff, then Alexander III, in case he deemed proper to act, as in fact he did, by condemning the errors of Peter the Lombard, Bishop of Paris, and this, too, independently, without consulting the members of the Council then assembled around him.

Finally, such General Councils afford the most opportune and efficacious means of controlling the orthodoxy of the Bishops themselves, as the history of General Councils bears witness.

The approaching General Council is a confirmation of all that we have said. The resolution of Pius IX summoning it, so he should not intend the definition of a dogma, would prove to be wise and timely, and have the beneficial influence of strengthening the faithful, uniting them into one army to confront the enemy on the battle-field. The very outcry of those enemies in regard to the approaching Council proves that they are afraid of the combined action of the Church. Therefore the objection drawn from the holding of General Councils against the infallibility of the Popes is void of all force. The head of the Church may pray, think, and take counsel. Divine Wisdom is not opposed to human coöperation, and the Pope, by being infallible, does not become a mere Apollo of Delphos.

The sun, indeed, is not afraid of clouds, the power of its light dissolves them, and it then shines with more brilliancy than ever. Such is the effect of truth in regard to objections.

OBJECTION II.

"If these things be true, the Bishops of the Council are not sitting or acting as Judges, but simply as the Heralds of the Pope's definition. Now, not the latter, but the former is the case, since they DEFINE, *as is proven by the usual subscriptions,* 'definiens subscripsi.'"

ANSWER.—It is true that the Bishops do examine, as Judges, the matter brought before them in Council, and their subscription is rightly called a definition, but neither their judicial character, nor their subscription, can be proved to be in conflict or contradiction with the supreme rights and privileges of the Pope, or the infallibility of his decisions.

A definition is rightly called such, even though it do not pretend to infallibility, and a Judge may be really a judge, without being the last and supreme expounder of the law. Doctors of divinity make many a definition, for which they would be the first to disclaim infallibility. In all governments there are judges, in the strictest sense of the term, who pronounce judgments in accordance with their interpretation of the law, but without pretending that their decision is final, and without disputing the right of the Supreme Justice to review, confirm, amend, or revoke their sentence.

A Judge has a rule before him, the law of the country, and he must strive to decide according to its dictates. For the Bishops, that rule is the teaching of the Church grounded on the authority of the Holy Scripture and tradition. By their *"definiens subscripsi"* the Bishops declare, that the definition of the Council to which they subscribe, in their conviction, is in accordance with the faith based upon the Holy Scripture and tradition. When it is confirmed by the Papal approbation, the Divine Law is more clearly expressed by the definition, and the Bishops, acting as Judges, declare it to be their faith also, and by their subscription, announce its accordance with the normal rule of faith. We would recall in this connection what we before mentioned concerning the subscription of the Bishops to the acts of the Eighth General Council: "I, N. N., Bishop of N., have subscribed the profession of faith made *by me* in the person of his Holiness, Pope Adrian, Supreme Pontiff."

By such a declaration, they affirm with St. Jerome, that they believe with the faith of the Head of the Church; that his faith is their faith; that that is an article of faith which he, as the Head of the Church, pronounces to be such, and their *"definiens subscripsi"* is to show that they were aware of what they did, and intended it, and it was to be the evidence that such faith was the faith of the whole Church. In farther illustration of this explanation, we would allude to that jurisdiction which each Bishop certainly has and exercises in his own diocese. This jurisdiction, with the sentences which he pronounces in exercising it, does not detract from, still less deny that general and superior jurisdiction which the Head of the Church possesses over him and the whole Church. The Bishops are Judges established by Christ over their respective dioceses, to guard the faith and discipline, but still they are subordinate judges.

Has not Christ assured us that the Apostles will judge the world on the last day? But surely their judicial dignity will not impair that of Christ, who is to judge them and the whole world. Neither then does a subordinate judicial authority impair that of the Supreme Pontiff judging in the last resort. If it were pretended that the definition of a Bishop in a General Council had any other than this subordinate value, it would follow that such a subscription would be valid by itself alone, and would not need the confirmation of the Head of the Church. But this is clear nonsense; because it would, if it proves any thing, prove the infallibility of each Bishop; an absurdity which never yet entered the head of any body. Once more, then, Bishops in General Council assembled, have a judicial character, but their *"definiens subscripsi"* does not finally settle a matter of faith.

OBJECTION III.

"The Popes themselves have declared that they could not depart from the decisions of General Councils. If they had thought themselves superior to the Council, they could not have made such a declaration."

ANSWER.—When the decisions of such Councils set forth matters of faith, it is evident that the Pope can not depart from them; for, confirmed, as is supposed, by the Pope, they give us the truth, the Divine law, and no Pope claims or can claim to be superior to that. The supposition that he could, or would do so, is simply absurd, since he would thereby deny the infallible authority of the Church, and debar himself from asserting it for his own decisions, with the consequent obligation of the flock's assenting thereunto. The logical consequence of the Pope's infallibility presupposes that he will not, and can not reverse the decision of his predecessors in matters of faith.

As regards disciplinary decrees and ordinations of General Councils confirmed by the Pope, the case is different. But even so, the Pontiff, notwithstanding his power to modify or abrogate such ecclesiastical provisions, might still use such a form of words, in view of his conscientious obligation, not to act in such things in an arbitrary manner. Such resolutions and decrees of General Councils are made with the utmost care, prudence, and wisdom, by the advice, and with the counsel of learned and pious prelates of the Church. They are not then to be lightly disregarded, changed, or revoked, otherwise there would be a manifest abuse of power to which might be justly applied the reproach of St. Bernard: "You do it, because you have the power to do so; but whether you should do it, is another question." "*Facitis quia potestis, sed utrum etiam debeatis, quæstio est.*"

The power which the Pope has received to rule the Church is not given for destruction, but for edification, as St. Paul affirmed of the Apostolical power given to himself — "*non in destructionem, sed in ædificationem.*" This is the reason of the Pontiffs regarding with so much respect the decrees of Œcumenical Councils, confirmed by his predecessors. And for the same reason they have always looked with reverence and respect upon the ordinances of the Popes, their predecessors. They have often declared that they intended in nowise to recede from such ordinances, and have even called them unchangeable and irreformable, as did Adrian II, in regard to the decrees and ordinances of Nicholas. Could any one thence infer that the Papal authority of Nicholas was superior to that of Adrian II, or that of Pius VI to that of Pius VII, or of Gregory XVI to that of Pius IX?

* But notwithstanding this reverence for the disciplinary enactments of Councils and of their predecessors, the Popes have ever been conscious of that plenitude of Apostolic power attached to their office and dignity as Head of the Church, whereby they could, and, on occasion, would restrict, change, or abolish ecclesiastical regulations, no matter by what ecclesiastical authority introduced, just so soon as they thought it better for the Church in their age. No Catholic will ever dispute this power to the Supreme Pontiff, as Pope Benedict justly asserts in his work, "*De Synodo Diocesana*," where he says: "That the Pope has received from Christ our Lord the power of his own authority, to relax or abrogate any merely ecclesiastical law, no Catholic doubts." "*Pontificem habere a Christo Domino concessam potestatem omnem legem ecclesiasticam propria auctoritate relaxandi, vel penitus abrogandi, a nemine Catholicorum in dubium avocatur.*"* Of this we have evident proof, and that, too, in a Pontiff especially distinguished for his modesty, Gregory the Great. He, who had declared that he accepted the first four General Councils of the Church as he did the Gospels, nevertheless, in favor of the English nation, abrogated the law of the Church, in respect to marriages among kindred of the seventh degree.

There was an axiom among the scholastic Doctors, affirming: "He that distinguishes well, can teach well." "*Qui bene distinguit, bene docet.*" In regard to the present objection, and all those to which we shall yet reply, it will be seen that the difficulties are only apparent, originating from mistatement, confusion of ideas, and want of careful discrimination.

* De Synod Dioces., l. 2, c. 8. num. 3.

OBJECTION IV.

"Did not the General Council of Constance and that of Basel solemnly declare that all persons, even though of Papal dignity, had to submit to its ordinances? How is this consistent with the Apostolic plenitude of the Papal power?"

ANSWER.—This objection we have already partially answered, when speaking of the Council of Constance in a preceding chapter. The Council was not treating of the authority of one who was undoubtedly Pope, but of aspirants who were doubtful claimants of the Papacy. The very expression, "*etiamsi Papalis dignitatis existat,*" is a proof of the intention of the Council. This is evident from the motive of its convocation, viz.: to suppress the then existing and deplorable Papal schism, when there was more than one claimant to the Papacy—each one strenuously urging the validity of his election and denying that of the others. And this, too, the Council itself declared, by a decree in its fortieth session, in these words: "*Papa rite et canonice electus, a Concilio ligari non potest.*" "A Pope, rightly and canonically elected, can not be fettered by a Council."

This is the only sense in which the decree cited against us can be interpreted, since otherwise it would be plainly heretical in fixing the Primacy, not on the successor of Peter, but on the Episcopacy separated from its Head, and declaring the decrees of such Councils valid without the approbation and confirmation of the Pope, since the decree speaks of obedience to the Council being the duty of the Pope, "*debitam obedientiam.*" It would, therefore, establish the whole source of Infallibility in the Episcopacy separated from their Head, thus serving only the cause of our common adversaries, "*nimis probans,*" and would fall under the condemnation of the many Councils that preceded or followed the Council of Constance, and more especially the Council of Florence.

Let it be taken, however, in whatever sense it may, it can not be urged against us as a decree of a General Council, since it was never approved by Martin V or by any other Pope, and has, consequently, no Ecclesiastical authority.

Martin confirmed only those decrees of the Council of Constance, which were canonically made and promulgated, which was by no means the case with this decree. It was made by a part only of the Fathers of the Council, not by all, by those alone, who supported John XXIII, and against his protest. Those also who supported Gregory XII and Benedict XIII protested against it.

Moreover, it was not carried in a regular session, but in a meeting of those Bishops of the clergy in general, and even by the laity, in what might be almost called a tumultuous assembly, as appears from the protest of the French Embassador, read in the Twenty-Eighth Session, and from the letters of John XXIII to Ladislas, King of Poland, and to the Duke of Bourges, read in the Sorbonne. Peter of Ailly, one of the Fathers of the Council, gives this testimony, and he was an eye-witness, and all the historians confirm it, especially Spondanus, Mansi, and Emmanuel Schelstrade.*

Finally, the decree, taken in the sense of our adversaries, would be in direct opposition to the decree of Martin V, who, in a Bull addressed to the King of Poland, condemned, as heretical, the opinion that an appeal could be taken from the Pope to a General Council. It would likewise be in direct opposition to the declaration made by the Fathers of that same Council, in

* Ailly: de Auctoritate Eccles. et Cardin. Mansi: In Animadvers. in Decr. s. 4 et 5 Con. Const. Tom. II Natalis. Spondanus: ad ann. 1418. Emm. Schelstrade Dissert. de Sess. 4 et 5 Conc. Const.

the Eighth Session, against the Wickliffites, in which they deny the possibility of the Roman See falling into error in matters of faith, since such a supposition would be in open contradiction to the character of that See, and to the power and rights with which it has been divinely invested, "to be the Mother, the Teacher, the head of all the Churches, which judges all, and can not be judged by any body, so that every one contradicting its teaching, is to be considered heretical."

So speak the Fathers of this Council in a Decree solemnly published against the followers of Wickliffe, and it becomes manifest, therefore, how vain it is to attach any other meaning to the Decree cited above, wherewith to justify any attack upon the privileges and rights of the Apostolic See in matters of faith.

As for the Council of Basel, we would not need to make any answer, were it not that our adversaries still persist in quoting it, as though they were not aware that there is really no weight to be attached to its decrees opposing the supremacy of the Pontiff over the Council, and his infallibility as Supreme Judge in matters of faith. They should know that all the propositions of that Council which favor their opinion were explicitly condemned, in the Council of

Florence, by Eugene IV, with the consent of the General Council then assembled, and in these words: "All these propositions, taken in the perverse sense of the Council of Basel, we condemn and reject as contrary to the Holy Scripture, to the Holy Fathers, and even to the Fathers of the Council of Constance, and as scandalous and godless."

Besides, every real theologian should know with what scorn and contempt the decrees of that Council are considered by men such as St. Antoninus and St. Capistran, inasmuch as, shortly after its convocation, it betrayed a schismatical tendency by opposing the transference of the Council to Florence. By their obstinacy, the Bishops remaining at Basel had no longer a claim to be considered a Council, much less a General Council. It was not a Council, but a cabal, or, according to St. Antoninus, "a synagogue of the Devil."* *"Conciliabulum viribus cassum, et synagogam Satanæ,"* and, according to St. John of Capistran, "a profane and excommunicated Synod, and a den of serpents."† *"Synodum profanam et excommunicatam, et Basiliscorum speluncam."* Our adversaries should seek for better authorities than this so-called Council of Basel.

* St. Antoninus, p. 3, tit. 22.   † De Papæ et Com. auct., p. 3.

OBJECTION VI.

To the authority of the Holy Fathers and the practice of the Church, our adversaries would oppose the authority and example of St. Cyprian, in his resistance to the ordinances and decisions of Pope Stephen.

ANSWER.—It is curious how frequently the good St. Cyprian is brought forward to help the enemies of the Holy See in their attacks upon its supremacy. We would pity him, but that we remember how St. Augustin is made to preach Jansenism, and how St. Paul is wrested to the defense of Protestantism.

Let us review the argument which our adversaries essay to build upon the authority of this Holy Father. It is this: St. Stephen decided that baptism should not be re-administered to heretics on their conversion and admission into communion with the Church. St. Cyprian, nevertheless, insisted on the contrary practice, and would not yield to the authority of a Papal decision, and therefore did not believe that the Popes were invested with that Supremacy in matters of Faith which we claim for them.

We answer: First—Supposing, for the sake

of argument, that St. Cyprian was not of our opinion, can the authority of one Father outweigh that of so many others whose testimony we have already quoted?

If, instead of St. Cyprian only, we had arrayed against us the testimony of a whole province, it would not diminish the authority which follows the teaching of the universal Church. Individual Fathers and provincial Churches can err, and have erred, without impairing that authority, as has been witnessed in the Eastern schisms. Therefore we should still say with St. Augustin, "I do not, by any means, regard the letters of Cyprian as canonical; but I rather judge them according to the canons; and what I find in them in accordance with the teaching of the Holy Scripture, I receive with praise, and what does not so agree, I, in peace with him, reject."

Second—We say with St. Augustin, what St. Cyprian believed and held concerning the Papal authority in matters of faith, is not to be determined from that, which he said or did in excitement or passion, but from those assertions which he penned when calm and disinterested. At least the harshness of some expressions should be compared and reconciled with other declarations, given at other times and in different circumstances, since no author of reputation and honor is to be held willing to stand in contradiction with himself.

Now no sincere adversary can deny that St. Cyprian, on other occasions, most publicly and solemnly recognized and asserted the same Papal prerogative and rights which we have been defending, as we have shown when quoting his testimony among those of the other Holy Fathers. He positively declares and confesses that the Roman Pontiff is the Supreme Judge, *in the place of Christ;* that is, as His representative—that all have to obey him—and that if all would but do as they should do, submit to his decisions, there would be no room for heresy or schism. He most explicitly calls the Roman Church the root and mold of the other Churches." "*Ecclesiam radicem et matricem.*"

In his book on the "Unity of the Church," he strongly asserts: that every one who separates himself from the See of St. Peter, on which the Church is built, separates himself from the Church. He laughs at those who traveled to Rome to essay an impossible justification of themselves, forgetful, as he says, "*that Rome can not err.*" How can a man, who writes in this manner, be supposed to be in contradiction with our thesis?

Do we not act more prudently and fairly with

this Father, when we interpret declarations made in a moment of excitement, not in themselves, but by the light obtained from declarations made and principles laid down in sober judgment? And did not Tertullian also resist the authority of Apostolical tradition, although he had written a work in its defense? We have in him another sad instance how far one may be misled by prejudice and self-love.

Third—Supposing, again, for the sake of argument, that Cyprian persevered in this particular instance of resistance, it would not disprove our thesis. He did not resist a decision in matters of faith, since St. Stephen had not delivered one, and was not addressing the universal Church. He was, at most, urging that what he regarded as the ancient practice of the Roman Church should be retained. Had there been question of a dogmatic decision, and St. Cyprian had then resisted, St. Stephen, as Pontiff, would at once have excluded him from his ecclesiastical communion. This, certainly, was not done, St. Cyprian remaining united with St. Stephen in ecclesiastical peace and union, as St. Augustin testifies in his book on Baptism.* St. Stephen did, indeed, hold out a menace of excommunication, but

---

* St. Augustin, Lib. de Bap., c. 25.

wisely and prudently forbore to urge matters by a summary decision in regard to such a distinguished prelate of the Church, then laboring under undue excitement. Rome knows how to wait and to refrain from severity so long as there may be hope of prevailing by milder means, as Pope Zosimus acted in the case of Cœlestius. Admonitions usually precede a recourse to more stringent measures. St. Cyprian did all he could to avert such a definitive sentence, but if St. Stephen had pronounced one, no doubt he would have submitted. Stephen had the more reason, then, to proceed with the utmost patience and moderation, dealing, as he did, with men who stood high in the Church—Firmilian and others being involved with Cyprian—and knowing the excitable temperament of the race to which they belonged.

Moreover, it is very probable that Cyprian finally submitted, even without a formal condemnation. There is no historical document to the contrary, while on the other hand, there are some, and of the highest authority, which make such submission more than probable. Those who wish to consult them, will find them in the works of Cabasutius, Baronius, Thomasinus, Ludovicus Bail, and other Canonists. Among other testimonies to this effect, we find those of St. Jerome* and St. Augustin. The latter says that it seems to him very probable, notwithstanding the absence of direct and incontrovertible proof; for, he adds: "Not every thing, which then occurred, has been written, nor has all that was written descended to us."

We must not judge those times, with their difficulties of transcription, and communication, by the standard of modern ages, with their facilities of the press, and their annihilation of time and space.

We may now go one step farther, and say, that even in the supposition that Cyprian did not submit, and really entertained the belief that the Pope was not infallible in his decisions, it is not clear with what hope of success our adversaries could appeal to his authority. Did Cyprian not evidently *err* in matters of faith, when he contended for the invalidity of baptism by heretics, though otherwise rightly administered? If he *explicitly erred* in one point of faith, may he not have done so in another, which was only implicitly denied? Undoubtedly, Stephen was right, and Cyprian, as every one must grant, was wrong, and this circumstance needs must considerably weaken the authority derived from the

* St. Jerome. Dialog.

latter's resistance. We should rather see in this whole case a splendid confirmation of the prerogatives and rights of the Holy See, and a beautiful instance of the prudence, moderation, and firmness with which they are exercised. Besides, our adversaries appear to forget that to make sure their standing against the grave and weighty mass of testimony, which we have adduced in support of our thesis, they must oppose testimony from the Holy Fathers at least as certain and as clear as ours. In this instance it is surely not the case. On the contrary, historical criticism points out doubts so manifold and serious, that there have been theologians, who have not hesitated to deny entirely the fact of Cyprian's resistance. St. Augustin, living but a short time subsequent, after weighing the arguments *pro* and *contra*, could not arrive at a final and definite decision. We are content with saying that there is good ground for suspecting that Cyprian's writings have been tampered with by Donatist interpolators.*

If our adversaries are learned in Patristic science, they must be aware of the difference in this respect between our own times and those in which manuscripts first began to be multiplied.

---

* Aug. l. 2, de Bap. S. Hieronymus. Dialog. contra Luciferum.

Now, that works are so easily and so widely disseminated by the press with its iron hands moved by steam, an interpolation in a recent work is almost impossible, and is easily detected, but in those days of slow and patient scribes it was not so difficult, and especially in a particular province or locality, where the original copies were few and easily altered.

Every theologian can recall analogous examples, as in the works of St. Jerome, and more especially in those of Origen. Nay, men, who are versed in the history of those earlier ages can tell you that the heretical Greeks dared even to change the lists of Œcumenical Synods, and that Photius ventured so far as to send to the Provincial Churches the pretended Acts of a Council of Constantinople, which had never been held.

If then, our adversaries can not clear these letters of Cyprian of suspicions, so weighty and reasonable, that St. Augustin was unable thereby to come to a positive decision, with what face do they oppose them to us as the testimony of this Father, and an argument, *omni exceptione major*, counterbalancing all the Patristic authorities which we have brought forward in proof of our proposition, free from all shadow of uncertainty, and which we could still increase *ad indefinitum*.

One more saying of St. Augustin we here give, to show how little Cyprian's error in this matter, if admitted, availed against the truth in the mind of that great Doctor and Father of the Church. In answer to the Donatists, he says: "Cyprian received the palm of martyrdom, that, by the glory of his blood, he might dispel the mist occasioned by human weakness and passion. Cyprian sinned and expiated that sin with the blood of martyrdom."* This is no allusion to the original error of Cyprian condemned by St. Stephen, but to the resistance which he gave to an ordinance emanating from so high an authority.

We may now conclude our answer to this objection with another passage from the same holy Doctor, in his forty-eighth letter. "*Cyprianus aut non sensit omnino, quod eum sensisse recitatis, aut hæc postea correxit in regula veritatis, aut hunc nævum coöperuit ubere charitatis; quoniam scriptum est: charitas operit multitudinem peccatorum.*" "Either Cyprian did not hold what you charge him with, or afterward corrected it by the rule of truth, or also covered the wrong with his exuberant charity, according as it is written, 'Charity covereth a multitude of sins.''

---

* St. Aug. de Bapt. Cont. Don. l. 1, c. 8.

So far, then, from being embarrassed by the sayings and actions of St. Cyprian, as urged against us by our adversaries, our conviction, must be the more strengthened on finding that objections heralded with such vaunting of victory, on close examination, have proved rather in favor than against our thesis. The like result will be found to attend the discussion of the succeeding objection.

OBJECTION VI.

"*This Objection is derived from the four articles of the so-called Gallican Liberties, laid down by the French Clergy in 1682, and is founded on the authority of the Church, as dispersed throughout the world, that is, not acting in conjunction with its Head. It is as follows: If the authority of the Apostolic See in its doctrinal decisions were infallible, the French Clergy could not have denied it, as they did in the four articles of the so-named Gallican Liberties. This privilege or prerogative is not, then, universally acknowledged by the Church.*"

ANSWER.—First, Were the Bishops assembled in the year 1682, the Church of France, the *Eglise Gallicane*, in the strict sense of the term? We answer, by no means. They were representatives, if you will, but not legitimate exponents of the sense of the Gallican Church. Every one who has read ever so little of French history, knows the influence which Louis XIV exercised over the Bishops of that Assembly. Louis XIV, so wedded to absolutism in government, who said "*l'etat c'est moi,*" was equally anxious to gain a similar control over the Church in France. He was desirous of establishing a National Church, to be governed by himself rather than by the Pope, that his above-cited sentence might have its fellow, "*l'Eglise en France, c'est moi.*" That subtle king endeavored to secure the appointing of Bishops, whose courtly servility he might trust; and believing himself assured of their connivance or coöperation in his schismatical tendencies, he caused them to assemble in 1682, and proclaim the so-called Liberties of the Gallican Church. But these Bishops did not faithfully represent the sentiment and belief of the Church of France, and even though they had, what then? Would that have been to us a law? Then, with the defection of England, a great part of Germany, Sweden, Prussia, Russia, and many provinces in the East, we would have been equally bound not only to abandon our faith in the Infallibility of the Holy See, but in many other doctrines, which, with us, our adversaries claim as necessary articles of the faith of Christ, held by their fathers before them, and positively defined.

Second, The very name given to these four propositions stigmatizes them as ambitious and heterodox assertions, tending to a national schism, thereby showing them in their true nature. *The liberties* of the Gallican Church—what a self-condemning name! Were the framers of these articles blind to the fact, that their very title condemned them as deviations from the otherwise universal faith and sentiment of Christianity, concerning the authority of the Holy See. *Gallican* only, they would be, and therefore not Catholic; *liberties*, and therefore anomalies and contradictions, as regards the faith and obligations of the rest of the Catholic world. Can there be "*liberties*" as opposed to truth? If it be a truth, and of faith, is it not equally so for all? What liberties can a National Church claim for itself in revealed truth, and because revealed, is imposed on all mankind? The very name is more than insolent—it is absurd. If the four articles asserted truths appertaining to faith, were they not the property of all the faithful; and then what special claim did the Church of France possess over them?

Third, But let us consider these declarations of the Bishops assembled in 1682. We shall find them in flagrant contradiction to the teaching and tradition of the Church of France up to their time, and we shall find also that they retracted what they had so rashly advanced.

We have said that they are contradictory to the traditional teaching of the Gallican Church, from the first introduction of Christianity until the holding of the assembly of 1682. To prove this, we have but to recall the long series of quotations given in our pages, from the Fathers, Councils, Theologians, Universities, and even the Princes living in France, and members of its Church, commencing from the Apostolic age. These testimonies are headed by Irenæus, followed by all those who lived after him through the centuries of the Christian era. Were not Hilary of Poictiers, Priccius of Tours, Cassian of Marseilles, Eucharius of Lyons, Avitus of Vienne, of the five first centuries, witnesses to the faith of the Gallican Church of that time? Is not the testimony of Cæsarius of Arles, of the Fathers of the Synod of Orleans, in the sixth century, of Rhegino of *Prum*, of *Lupus* of Ferrieres, of the Synods of Soissons, Douzzi Pontigny, Troyes, and Limes, a luminous witness of the faith of the Gallican Church up to the ninth century, followed by the forcible testimony of an Oddo of Clugny, of an Abbo of Fleury, a Fulbert of Charters, of the Fathers of the Synod of Limoges up to the time of St. Bernard, whose grand and solemn profession of faith we gave, closing with him the tradition of the patristic period?

On this path, following the footsteps of their fathers, the Bishops and Theologians continued to walk, and gave the most illustrious proofs of their submission to the Apostolical authority of the Holy See in matters of faith. So thought and spoke the Bishops of France in the Synods of Bezieres, Valence and Albi. At times, as with William of Dijon, they even gave the Pope to understand that he might make a more vigorous and energetic use of his power, Rome seeming sometimes too slow to act, because prudent and merciful, patient and forbearing.

At the time of the great schism, brought about by the uncertainty of the legitimacy of the Papal elections, French Theologians began, it is true, to speak with Gerson, of the superiority of a General Council over the Pope, but, on a close examination, it becomes evident that they are speaking of those Pretenders to the Papacy, and not of the authority of an undoubtedly elected Pope, Head of the Church, as we have shown when discussing the Council of Constance.

Gerson himself, whose authority our adversaries are so fond of urging, positively asserts that before the Council of Constance, any theologian contending for the superiority of a Council over the Pope, would have been accounted a heretic.* That, after the Council, he himself adhered in this to the primitive traditions of the Church, is proven by the arguments he used in a sermon delivered before Pope Alexander V, when accounting for the privilege of immunity from error in matters of faith existing in the Western Church. He deduced it from the fact, that Peter erected his See in that part of the Church, for whose immutability in the faith He had prayed who was always heard because of His dignity. And even though Gerson had not held to the tradition of the Church of France, our opponents are no better off with his support than when they pretended to shield themselves with that of St. Cyprian. How insignificant are the authority and opinion of one theologian like Gerson, when compared to the testimony resulting from the consent of so many others of far greater reputation in the Church, who preceded or followed the Council of Constance, as Rainald, Milante Duval, Claudius Florins, together with

---

* Gerson, De Potest. Ecclesiæ, Consid. ii.

the clearest professions of the faith, which we have quoted from the Sorbonne of Paris.

More interesting yet are the solemn declarations of the Clergy of France, in the beginning of that very century, toward the close of which were issued the schismatical propositions which astonished the world. That these last were not grounded on the previous teaching and tradition of the French Church, is evident from the Synodical letters addressed to the Clergy in the year 1626. The Bishops teach and ordain, "That all should venerate the Pope as the visible Head of the Universal Church, as the successor of St. Peter upon whom Christ founded the Church, to whom He gave the Keys of Heaven, with that *infallibility of faith*, which we see miraculously preserved in his successors even to our own day." "*Super hunc Christus fundavit Ecclesiam, illi claves cœli tradens, cum infallibilitate fidei, quam non sine miraculo immotam in ejus successoribus perseverare usque in hodiernam diem cernimus.*" In the year 1653, the Bishops of France wrote the congratulatory letter to Innocent X, which we have previously quoted, and in which they say, that a Papal decision in matters of faith *has a divine authority*, to which every body has to submit, not only exteriorly but interiorly, with a sincere assent before God.

More pressing and comprehensive yet, is another declaration and ordinance of the French Episcopate, delivered in the same century. In a circular addressed to the whole Clergy, in 1663, they say: "The submission which we manifest for the Holy Father is, so to say, the heirloom of the French Episcopacy. This is the firm ground on which our honor is established; this is what imparts to our faith invincibility, and to our authority infallibility." *"Quod et nostram fidem invincibilem reddit et nostram auctoritatem, infallibilem."*

If, then, the Bishops of France hold a different language in 1682, is it not plain that they thereby deviate from the teaching and tradition of the Church of France? And does not the fact of such a sudden change, after the lapse of only twenty years, warrant the suspicion that it was induced by some exterior influence? And so it was. It was the influence of Louis XIV, that led them to contradict what their predecessors had uniformly taught, and they themselves, but a few years previous, had solemnly declared. They lived at that time in a feeble subserviency to the desires of his Majesty, the King; a servility which was but too general then in the higher Clergy of France. They had too much of the Frenchman and the courtier. *"Humani, seu po-*

tius, Gallicani quid passi sunt." Finally, however, they returned to their duty by *retracting* their eror, notwithstanding that they had a Bossuet among them.

It pleased Divine Providence to permit that so great a Theologian should try, but try in vain, to undermine the solid rock of argument on which the truth of our thesis is founded, and be compelled to retract. We read in his life that he never ceased, until the hour of his death, to feel remorse for his weakness and his servility to human respect.

On the other hand, it is gratifying to have such a powerful opponent, as Bossuet confessedly is; for, if all his efforts proved to be like throwing pebbles against the iron gates of a fortress, it is very certain that no other antagonist need anticipate a better fate.

And, first, we may say that Bossuet, in his defense of the four articles, was in contradiction with himself, and through human respect was trying to satisfy both parties by distinctions that proved to be vain. That he was contradicting himself, is proved from his previous assertions on other occasions. In his "Meditations on St. Luke," ch. xxii and xxiii, he professed his belief in the infallibility of the Apostolic See in matters of faith. He does the same in his Catechism, when treating of the Festival of St. Peter and Paul; in the two first Pastorals which he addressed to the Clergy of his Diocese; in his refutation of the Catechism of the Huguenots; and, finally, in his "*Expositio Doctrinæ Catholicæ.*" And even, as he was addressing the Bishops assembled in 1682, his conviction again transpires, for he reminded them that the Roman faith must always be the faith of the Church; that St. Paul, returning from the third heavens, went to St. Peter to give an account of his faith, setting in this an example to all future generations; and that, in fact, the entire Church, extending from the rising to the setting of the sun, was of the same belief.

Bossuet tried, it is true, to restrain the Bishops, seduced by the flatteries of Louis XIV, from a schismatic servility, but being himself too much under the influence of human respect, he summoned all his powers and took refuge in vain distinctions when writing his "Defense of the Declarations of the Bishops."

Even in that "Defense" his intimate and previously expressed convictions are still apparent. He rejects with horror the least suspicion that by these four articles the Clergy of France detracted from the strength and dignity of the Head of the Church. "*Neque vero velimus, quod Ca-*

tholici omnes, Summique Pontifices perhorrescant, Ecclesiæ, tanti corporis, imbecille esse caput." He states the reason of this horror to be, "That if that Chair should fall into error, the whole Church would be dissolved." *"Quæ cathedra si concidere posset, fieretque cathedra non veritatis sed erroris, Ecclesia ipsa Catholica esset dissoluta."* Speaking of the formula of Adrian II, and of its subscription as the test of orthodoxy, he says: "By this subscription all the Churches professed their belief in the immutability of the Apostolic See in matters of faith, according to the promise of Christ." To reconcile such assertions with the tenor of the four articles he had recourse to subtle distinctions and explanations.

We must consider, he tells us, all the Popes collectively, not individually, as constituting one with Peter; it is this collective personality which can not err, and whose faith never fails. In other words, faith may waver and even fail in any one Pontiff, but the error can not take root in the Apostolic See. *"Accipiendi sunt Romani Pontifices tanquam una persona Petri, in qua nunquam fides deficiat, atque ut in aliquibus vacillet aut concidat, non tamen deficit in totum."* Is it not strange that so great a mind should fall into so poor a sophism?

No doubt all the Roman Pontiffs represent

Peter, whose authority they inherit; but for that very reason *none* of them can err, because, as all are one and the same person—Peter—the failure of one would affect that person—Peter. Or, in other words, because the individual who fails belongs to this mystical personage, therefore in him Peter fails.

Moreover, Bossuet is well aware that by the formula of Adrian II, which he holds himself bound to defend, whosoever subscribes it is obliged to obey the decisions of the Pope actually occupying the Apostolic See, as "*a rule of faith;*" neither could he be ignorant that the Fathers of the Œcumenical Councils recognized in every individual Pope, the rock upon which the Church is built, the divinely commissioned teacher of the faith, the Vicar of Christ in whom Peter always lives.

In trying to confirm this distinction, the Bishop of Meaux makes use of an illustration, which serves but to exhibit its shallowness. He says, that Peter himself denied Christ in the courtyard of the High Priest, and in the same way every individual Pope may be supposed to err. Who will not be surprised at such a reason, from such a man! Surely he does not mean that Peter was teaching, or giving a decision or definition of faith to the whole Church, and yet he knew that it is only in this sense that we proclaim

Peter and his successors infallible. He sinned as a man, and so, too, is every one of his successors subject to sin; neither he nor they were infallible in their manner of living, but only in matters of faith, when instructing the whole Church.

Moreover, had Bossuet forgotten that when Peter denied Christ, he had not yet become Head of the Church, Vicar of Christ. The promises of Christ were for the future, when "he should be once confirmed," and enter on his office as Visible Head of the Church. Christ said: "*Ædificabo*, . . . *dabo*, . . . *et tu aliquando*." "I shall build, . . . I shall give, . . . and thou being once confirmed." He certainly can not have meant that after the Ascension of our Lord, and the descent of the Holy Ghost, Peter could have erred in matters of faith; such a supposition he could not have made, and yet such a supposition is needed to give any strength to his illustration. The argument bears witness to the desperate nature of the position which Bossuet had undertaken to defend.

This distinction between the individual and collective personality of Peter, logically involves the most striking inconsequences. For, on the supposition that one individual Universal Teacher can err, we may rightly infer that every one could do so, and then where is the collectively infallible person? If not all, then which is to be the infallible one, redeeming the others; is it to be the third, fifth, or tenth? And how many infallible Pontiffs are needed to prevent the collective personality from being affected by the fallibility of the individuals?

Feeling how untenable this position was, Bossuet in his "Defense" is forced to admit the Infallibility of the Head of the Church, when teaching, or defining an Article of Faith for the whole Church, or, as the theologians say, when speaking "*ex cathedra*," but, for this is our thesis, he adds that we can not know that he so speaks, until his decision has received the assent of the Church, as dispersed throughout the world, or united in Œcumenical Council.

This explanation has been already disproved by what we have said, when urging that neither the decision of an Œcumenical Council nor the assent of the *Ecclesia dispersa* was the tribunal constituted by Christ in matters of faith. The reasons which we then gave are equally applicable to this point.

Bossuet strives to justify his assertion by analogy. He says that a General Council, notwithstanding its infallibility, has to wait for its acknowledgment by the *Ecclesia dispersa*, before it is recognized as a General Council; and so, too, the sentence of a Pope, speaking *ex cathedra*, may be infallible, but its reception by the whole Church is required before we can know that he speaks *ex cathedra*.

In this justification, instead of bettering his argument, he abandons it, since he admits the infallibility of the Pope's decision, provided it be certain that he speaks *ex cathedra*. Now, however it may be with a General Council in respect to historical reality, it is certain that the simple fact of the Pope's speaking *ex cathedra* can be certainly ascertained by his teaching, or pronouncing a definition in matters of faith to be believed by all. This fact can be made evident and as historically certain as that the light comes from the sun, by the very terms of the sentence and the declarations of the Holy Father. We will give an instance. When Pius IX pronounced upon the dogma of the Immaculate Conception, at that very moment every Catholic there present was obliged to believe it, without needing or even being permitted to ask what any Bishop present or absent believed, and, still less, without consulting or awaiting the assent of the *Ecclesia dispersa*. It was a decision addressed to the whole Church, and, as a fact, was spread far and wide by steam and electricity, that Pius IX had so spoken, and *ex cathedra* could not be the subject of a doubt to any reasonable man. Now, in regard to General Councils—as, for instance, those of the East—all remained in suspense until it was ascertained that they had been confirmed by the Head of the Church; when this was made known, nothing was more needed to make their decrees and decisions binding. By parity of reasoning, according to Bossuet's own admission, the same holds good as to the Papal definition, with the difference that the latter, if its genuineness be certain, carries along with it the obligation of submission.

We can not but repeat that it is pitiful to see how far human motives, working on the heart, can influence the mind even of such a man as we know Bossuet to have been.

Fenelon was of another stamp, and though he had been the preceptor of two Princes, belonging to the family of Louis XIV, he refused his assent to the four articles, which he contemptuously characterized, "Liberties against the Pope and servility to the King." In a Pastoral to his Clergy subsequent to their promulgation, he says: "We must attend to the promises of Christ as daily proved by facts, for Peter continues to speak from his chair, and whosoever joins in faith with Rome is preserved from danger. This is proved by the formula of faith sent by Pope Hormisdas to the Eighth Council, in which every Bishop was obliged forever to follow in matters of faith the decisions sent forth by the Apostolic See. This was the price by which they gained admission among Catholics." "*Hoc pretio inter Catholicos recensiti.*"

We may hereby understand what Fenelon meant when he gave expression to his feelings in these beautiful words: "*O Eglise Romaine, O cité sainte, O chere et commune patrie de tous les Chrétiens! Il n'y a en Jésus Christ, ni Grec, ni Scythe, ni Barbare, ni Juif; tous sont un seul peuple dans votre sein; tous sont concitoyens de Rome, et tout Catholique est Romain.*" "O Church of Rome! O holy city! O dear and common country of Christians! In Jesus Christ there is neither Greek, Scythian, barbarian, nor Jew; all together form but one people in thy bosom; all are fellow-citizens of Rome, and every Catholic is a Roman."

How deeply these convictions were grounded, was proved to his personal honor and glory in the prompt and entire submission which he paid to the decision of Rome against himself. He had written a book entitled, "*Maximes des Saints.*" In this book there were certain errors concerning the ascetical life, which Bossuet denounced to Rome.

The errors were condemned, and Fenelon gave a heroic example of humility, faith and submission, which shall forever redound to his greater fame and veneration. He, an Archbishop, and once preceptor at the Court, ascended the pulpit, read aloud the condemnation of the errors contained in his book, and forbade it to be read any longer by the members of his flock, adding that he availed himself of that occasion for paying that obedience to the Holy See which was its due, and which he wished to pay even to his last sigh: "*Dont nous voulons vous donner un exemple jusqu'au dernier soupir de la vie.*" A distinguished French author exclaims, in reference to this act of Fenelon: "*Hereux les hommes, si les hérésiarques s'étaient soumis avec autant de modération, que le grand évêque de Cambrai, qui n'avait nulle envie d'être hérétique.*" "How happy for mankind if the heresiarchs had always submitted with the moderation displayed by the great Bishop of Cambrai, who, indeed, had no inclination to be a heretic."

Finally, our adversaries, if they be theologians, must be aware that the Bishops who devised these "Gallican liberties" *revoked* them, sued for *pardon*, and sent a letter of recantation to Innocent XI. In that letter they say: "Prostrate at thy feet, we confess and declare that, from our hearts, and more than we can express, we deplore what we did in that assembly." "*Vehementer quidem, et supra omne id quod dici potest, ex animo dolere de rebus gestis in conciliis prædictis.*" And, therefore, all that was said in regard to the Papal authority, we will and declare should be considered as not said. "*Pro non decreto habemus, et habendum declaramus.*" De Pradt, in his book, "Quatre Concordats," Paris, 1826, IV, 136, gives us the words of Bossuet, when he heard of the condemnation of the four articles at Rome: "*Abeat ergo quocumque voluerit ista declaratio.*" "May the declarations then be gone where they will."

But apart from these retractations, the articles were defeated on their own ground, and with their own weapons. They claimed for the consent of the Church "dispersed" an undue authority as a tribunal in matters of faith, and that very "*Ecclesia dispersa*" no sooner heard of the four articles, than it lifted up its voice and denounced them, by the voices of the Episcopacy of Spain, Belgium, and Italy. In the year 1684, the Primate of Hungary also assembled a National Synod, in which the four articles were unanimously condemned as absurd, detestable, and productive of schism. "*Damnamus has— propositiones absurdas, detestabiles et ad schisma tendentes.*" Even Voltaire observes that the idea of a National Church, originating in an exaggerated love of nationality, came near being then realized, and what else would it have been, but a Western schism? But the Catholic feeling of France, suppressed for a time, soon awakened, and has remained steadfast to the Apostolic See.

We know very well that Gallicanism, fostered by Jansenism, has never been entirely extinguished in France, and from time to time gives faint sparks of life, counting even yet its adherents, but then, too, we find that the old Eastern heresies, Monothelism, Eutychianism, and Nestorianism, though condemned and crushed by the Catholic faith, have left some faint and lingering traces. We should not wonder at the same fact in regard to the four articles, more noticeable than now, up to the time of De Maistre and Lamennais. Since that period, however, Gallicanism has become well-nigh extinct, disappearing with the few adherents of what is styled "*la petite Eglise.*" The great body of the French Episcopacy and Clergy, with scarcely an exception, is eminently Roman. Thus, in 1819, eighty Bishops signed an address to Pius VII, in which they profess it impossible that he should not be the protector of the true faith, who occupies the place of Christ on earth, as the first leader, teacher, and doctor of the faithful. "*Christi fidem non posse non tueri, qui Christi vices in terris supplet, primus dux, magister, et doctor fidelium.*" More positive and peremptory is the declaration of the French clergy to the king, in 1826, in which their faith is thus expressed: "With the whole Catholic Church we condemn those who, under the pretext of preserving the liberties of the Gallican Church, lessen the obedience due by all Christians to the throne established by Jesus Christ, the Primacy of Peter and of the Roman Pontiffs, his successors, and who injure, in the eyes of all nations, the venerable majesty of the Apostolic See, where the faith is taught, and the unity of the Church preserved." "*Ubi fides docetur, et Ecclesiæ unitas conservatur, detrahere non verentur.*" *

OBJECTION VII.

"*We must distinguish between the Apostolical See and those, who occupy it. The See is Infallible, not the Pope.*"

ANSWER.—This distinction is neither reasonable in itself considered, nor sanctioned by the

* See Ziegler Proleg. de Eccle., p. 291, and De Maistre, on the Liberties of the Gallic Church.

Holy Fathers, who have expressly taught the contrary.

Reason does not recognize it, since it were absurd to imagine any other meaning for the Apostolical See than the Apostolic power and authority of St. Peter transmitted to his *successors*. But how can an Apostolic See, apart from the person who legally occupies it, be said to succeed St. Peter? The expression is meaningless, unless we understand thereby the power and authority of St. Peter invested in the person of his successor, the Primate and Head of the Church. It is, apart from him, a *non-ens*, that can do nothing, and define nothing. Melchior Canus is certainly right in saying "reason despises and rejects this distinction." "*Distinctionem hanc ratio aspernitur—rejicit.*"*

The distinction was unknown to the Holy Fathers, who, on the contrary, identified the individual, with the authority of the See he occupied. Thus St. Jerome exclaims: "I am in communion with thee, that is, the See of Peter." "*Ego Beatitudini tuæ, id est, Cathedræ Petri, communione consentior.*" St. Augustin expresses himself in the same manner, using the expressions as being identical with each other, when referring

---

* Melch. Canus de loc. Theolog. Ep. 6, c. 8.

to the condemnation of Pelagianism at Rome. "Now," he says, "that Innocent condemned it, and now that the Apostolic See condemned it." Our readers will remember how the General Councils, and generally all the authorities of ecclesiastical antiquity, in all ages of Christianity, when addressing the Supreme Pontiff, adopted the same expressions as were used by the Fathers of the Sixth General Council: "Peter lives in his See, and through Agatho, Peter has spoken." The very words by which Jesus declared Peter Head of the Church, identify the authority of his office with that of his person, then when he addressed to him the Chaldaic word: *"Tu es Petra"* —not Petrus. Bossuet, in this point, certainly a disinterested authority, says: "We do not pretend that this See can exercise any act of power or jurisdiction, except through its occupant, and neither can we distinguish between the faith of the Roman Church and that of its Pontiff, because the Romans learned their faith first from Peter, and then from the successors of Peter." *"Neque propterea dicimus ipsam sedem aliquid exercere posse potestatis aut jurisdictionis aliter, quam per ipsum præsidentem; neque distinguimus a Romanorum Pontificum fide, Romanæ Ecclesiæ fidem, quam scilicet moraliter a Petro primo, atque Petri successoribus Romani didicerunt."* By the latter part of this assertion, Bossuet indicates another distinction sometimes advanced.

OBJECTION VIII.

"We must distinguish between the faith of the Roman Church, that is, the Clergy of Rome and that of the Pope individually; so that the Roman Church can never err, but the Pope can."

ANSWER.—This distinction, equally with the preceding, is vain and arbitrary, repugnant alike to Scripture and Tradition. To Scripture, because Christ addressed Peter, and not the assembled Clergy of Rome, when He promised and confirmed to him the privileges which constituted him the irremovable foundation-stone of the Church, and its infallible teacher. This authority, conferred by Christ, is transferred to his successor; but that successor is the Bishop of Rome, and not the synodical assembly of the Roman clergy.

Tradition ignores and rejects this distinction, deducing the privileges of the Roman Church from the one fact that its Pontiff is the successor of St. Peter. Apart from this the Roman Church and clergy would be on the same footing with those of Constantinople and other places. The Holy Fathers and the General Councils have yielded submission to the Roman Church, for no other reason than that they acknowledged its Pontiff as the rightful successor of St. Peter, who still lives and speaks in his See, by the authority transmitted through the institution of Christ to his successors, and which was to endure until the consummation of the world. St. Jerome says: "I agree with the successor of Peter, who occupies the chair of Peter, on which I know the Church to be founded." "*Cum successore Petri loquor, qui cathedram Petri tenet, supra quam Ecclesiam œdificatam scio.*" "And, therefore," adds he, "whosoever gathers not with thee, dissipates; whoso is not with thee, belongs to Antichrist." "*Ideo, quicumque tecum non colligit, spargit, qui tecum non est, Antichristi est.*" And Peter Chrysologus, when urging Eutyches to submit, does not give for reason the faith of the Roman Church or of its Clergy, but simply says: "Peter, who lives in his own See, communicates the true faith to those who seek it of him." "*Quia Petrus in propria sede viveus, præstat quærentibus fidei veritatem.*" The Councils have spoken to the same effect. The Fathers of the Third Council of Constantinople do not rejoice because their faith has been approved by the

Church or Clergy of Rome, but because the "Chief Prince of the Apostles is fighting with us; because we have for Patron his successor. Paper and ink it appeared, but through Agatho, Peter has spoken." *"Summus nobiscum certat Apostolorum Princeps, eo quod ipsius successorem habuimus fautorem. Charta et atramentum videbatur, et per Agathonem Petrus loquebatur."*

In the same sense speak the Fathers of the Fourth and Eighth General Councils. They all allege, as the reason of their submission, the promise of Christ, which can never be frustrated: "Thou art Peter, and on that rock I shall build my Church."

What other reason can they allege who hold the Roman Church, as constituted by its assembled Clergy alone, exempt from every possibility of error? Is it that in Rome there are always so many Prelates and highly-instructed theologians, with such facilities of communication with the other Churches, that the faith of the Universal Church may justly be deemed concentered and concentrated in the Synodically-assembled Clergy of Rome?

But if this reason were sufficient, it would also suffice, and even more, to make the decision of a General Council infallible without the confirmation of the Pope· for there the faith of the Universal Church is even more concentrated, and there is a much larger assembly of illustrious theologians; and yet the history and decrees of these same Councils (in our opponents' theory, infallible) tell us that, without the confirmation of the Pontiff, their decisions are not binding on any Christian conscience or intellect.

Again, as the Church of Rome never teaches by definitions sent to the whole Church, except through the Roman Pontiff, and can not be, and never was consulted except by addressing him, it would follow that a belief in the faith of the Roman Church, in the sense of this distinction, as being the faith of the Universal Church, would remain a mere presumption, more or less probable, but would not, and could not, be a rule of faith, a Supreme Tribunal. There is no one to be addressed, to be consulted, to decide, unless it be the Roman Pontiff.

Finally, it is these very Clergy of Rome that specially defends our thesis, and which derives all their distinction in the Church from the presence and dignity of its Primate, the Head of the Church. If there be any disputed truth more strenuously held and defended than another by the Clergy of Rome, it is this very thesis concerning the rights and privileges of the Roman Pontiff, which we are now sustaining; and, consequently, the favorers of this last objection would be obliged, if it have any weight at all, to accept our thesis.

OBJECTION IX.

"But Popes have actually erred in matters of faith, and, by the fact itself, have therefore proved themselves fallible."

ANSWER.—The consequence would be logically correct were the premises true, but we deny the supposition. No Pope has erred in matters of faith.

Bossuet himself concedes that, of all the pretended cases brought forward to prove the supposed fact, there are only two that merit an answer, the others being generally abandoned even by our adversaries. These two cases, to which our adversaries constantly appeal when there is question of the fallibility of the Pope, are those of LIBERIUS and HONORIUS. The former is charged with Arianism, the latter with Monothelism. We shall presently see how little reason there is in either charge.

Before answering the accusation, we must once more remind our opponents that, in order to overturn our thesis, they must prove not merely that Liberius or Honorius has spoken or written what is contrary to faith, or denied it, but that he did so as Pope, teaching in matters of faith or morals, and thereby binding the Universal Church. If they can not prove this, they prove nothing, for the fallibility would then be only personal and private, and would no more affect the infallibility of the Pope as Universal Teacher, than the denial of Peter in the Court of the High Priest injured his infallibility as Prince of the Apostles. They must, then, first produce good, historical evidence of the fact; secondly, they must prove that it was a definition or teaching contrary to truth in matters of faith; and, thirdly, that the Pope intended, by his teaching, to bind the Universal Church to believe it. This, so long as history is history, they never will succeed in doing. It is an impossibility, as we shall demonstrate to our readers.

They tell us that LIBERIUS taught Arianism. We answer that they can never produce historical evidence of such a fact; and, even though they could, they would not be able to prove that he did so, defining it as a matter of faith to the Universal Church.

As to the fact itself, sound historical criticism tends directly to the contrary conclusion, namely, that Liberius did not do what they suppose him to have done. The historical documents to which they appeal are, some of them, of very doubtful authority, whilst the others are evidently false or corrupted. Their first authority is that of the so-called "Fragments," ascribed to Hilarius, which critics generally acknowledge not to have been written by him, but by some unknown author. They also appeal to two letters of Athanasius, which are spurious.

Two passages are quoted from the works of St. Jerome—the one from his book, "*De Scriptoribus Ecclesiasticis*," the other from his "*Chronicon*." Now, St. Jerome has himself complained of the interpolations made in his works, a thing, as we have mentioned, very easily done in the days of manuscripts; and critics prove that this actually occurred with regard to these two works.

They also bring forward four letters ascribed to Liberius himself, which are mere fabrications by the Lucifirians and Arians. Finally, they give a poorly-manufactured account, to the effect that, after his pretended fall, Liberius, on returning to Rome, was contemptuously driven out by the Roman people. This fiction is borrowed from a spurious work of Eusebius the Priest.

It would be too long and tedious to discuss fully the defectiveness of these pretended authorities, and we are obliged, therefore, to refer those of our readers, who would desire to review the whole controversy on this point, to such celebrated critics as the famous Bollandist, Hettingus,* Cardinal Orsi,† to Antonio Zaccharia,‡ in his learned dissertation on the "Fall of Liberius," and Tillemont."§

Against all their corrupted historical sources are arrayed most trustworthy historical documents, clearly showing that Liberius not only never betrayed the truth, but that he was its consistent, energetic champion.

Nobody pretends to call in question the fact, that it was he who withstood the immense number of fallen Bishops at the time of the Council of Rimini, who had suffered themselves to be entrapped by the Arian into subscribing an heretical formula, of which St. Jerome exclaims: "The Christian world was astonished to find itself become Arian." He compares the fall of so many Bishops, at that time, to falling mountains, and to the ruins caused by an earthquake, in the midst of which we witness the majesty and resplendent authority of the Apostolic See,

* Act. Sanct, Tom iv, Sept. 23 c. 9 et 10.
† Hist. Eccles., Sæc. iv.
‡ Thesaur. Theolog., Tom ii.
§ Tillm. Nat. 59 in Arian.

and we find Liberius, the occupier of the Chair of Peter, using his power and privileges as Supreme Pontiff to condemn and cancel the erroneous professions of the wavering Episcopacy, or, rather, in the words of our Lord, to confirm his brethren, whom Satan had tried to sift as wheat.

It was for this heroic resistance that the enraged Emperor Constantine sent Liberius into exile, and harassed him with vexations and persecutions, to escape which, as they pretend, the defender of the faith finally subscribed an Arian formula, and, on his return to Rome, was driven forth again by the Clergy and people. That such a man, after so heroic a resistance, should have fallen so low as to subscribe what he had denounced and condemned in others, is difficult of belief. History tells a different tale.

The oldest and most esteemed historians of the Church, such as Sulpicius Severus, Socrates, Sozomenus, Theodoretus, Menea, Theophanes, Nicephorus, and Calistus, have not a word concerning the pretended fall of Liberius. Even Photius does not speak of it, and he certainly should have known it, and would have used it, had there been any hope of success. On the contrary, all these historians speak quite differently of Liberius, and ascribe his return to Rome to another reason, and describe his reception in a very different way. Theodoretus, who, in his history of Arianism, made use of the writings of Athanasius, calls Liberius an illustrious and glorious champion of the faith. "*Celeberrimum Liberium, gloriosum veritatis athletam.*" He ascribes his return to Rome, not to a heretical acquiescence, but to the petition forwarded to the Emperor from the noble ladies of Rome, and to the acclamation of the people at the amphitheater, urging his recall. "*Post has Christianæ plebis acclamationes Liberium ab Imperatore postulantis in circo, reversus est admirabilis ille Liberius.*"

Sulpicius Severus also accounts for his return by the commotions and revolts of the Roman people, clamorous for his recall, and says that the Emperor did it against his will, "*licet invitus.*" If Liberius had professed Arianism, Constantine would have let him return, but not unwillingly, "*invitus,*" since it would have been for himself a victory and triumph. That this return, however, may have become in time a matter of suspicion and a ground of the accusation, is possible, if not probable. Communications were then difficult and tardy, and the Arians, hearing of his recall, may have spread the rumor that it could only be accounted for by his recantation and his subscription of the Arian formula.

No, the Pontiff who had anathematized the fallen Bishops, and had braved exile and persecution, could not have accepted such ignominy as finally to subscribe what he himself had so lately denominated a blasphemy, *"blasphemiam."*

But should we, for the sake of argument, abandon this point, our thesis would not, therefore, be overturned.

There are two things objected to Liberius: first, that he cut off from communion with himself that hero of Orthodoxy, Athanasius; and, second, that he subscribed the formula of Syrmia, called by Hilarius, *"perfidiam Arianam."*

Could both these assertions be proved, we repeat, they would not affect our thesis.

Not the first, because, to exclude another from ecclesiastical communion is not a definition in matters of faith, still less is it one addressed to the whole Church. Even though such an exclusion should be groundless and unlawful, it would only prove the peccability of the Pope, not his fallibility as Pope. But the fact itself we emphatically deny. It is in evident contradiction with his enthusiastic reception at Rome, where the people and clergy sympathized so entirely with him, and revolted against the false Pope, Felix, intruded into the See during the exile of Liberius, because he communicated with the Arians, the mortal enemies of Liberius and Athanasius.

Not the second, namely, the pretended subscription to the heretical formula of Syrmia, for all critics, even our opponents, are obliged to admit that if Liberius subscribed at all, it was to the first formula of Syrmia, which Hilarius himself admitted, finding fault with it only in this, that it was a *"perfidia,"* the word *consubstantialis* having been purposely omitted. This would not, however, render it heretical, as the same fault could be brought against the *Apostles' Creed*. This omission in the formula of Syrmia was a perfidy in its framers, because it was done for the purpose of suppressing the truth, but not necessarily such in its subscribers. In the subscription there might be matter for scandal, in appearing to agree in matters of faith with the framers, but there can not be a well-grounded charge of heresy. And had Liberius actually subscribed, it would have been through a mistaken judgment, that in thus securing his freedom, through a subscription which bound him to nothing, he was better enabled to aid and defend the Church. This, however, could never be cited as a definition in faith to the Universal Church.

But even a subscription of this kind can not

be proved against Liberius, since, as we have seen, the most reliable historians of those times attribute his return from exile to a different cause. He can not, then, be stigmatized as a traitor to the faith, but must rather be accounted worthy of all those eulogies conferred upon him by the Holy Fathers. St. Ambrose calls him "*Sanctæ memoriæ virum,*" a man of holy memory; St. Basil, "*beatissimum,*" most blessed; Epiphanius and Pope Siricius, the latter in his letter to Himeric, call him "*blessed.*" His name is found in different Martyrologies, as in that of Beda, of Wandalbert, and even in those of the East, the Synaxarii and Menǽis, where his feast is marked for the 27th of August.

We turn now to the case of HONORIUS, first premising, as in that of Liberius, that the documents from which our opponents borrow their accusations, are very open to more than suspicion of fraud and fiction. This was a common occurrence among the Greeks in those days of manuscripts, of slow and uncertain communication, and in a time, moreover, of constantly renewed, though often baffled attempts at schism. From the earliest times, even to our own days, critics have agreed as to the difficulty of verifying such documents. But this we may safely pass over, since our position is too strong to need urging the point. Granting all that our opponents would ask as to the genuineness of their historical sources, and allowing for true all that they object against Honorius, even then the truth of our thesis remains unimpaired. A close examination of the texts, which they advance in support of the charge, suffices to place the truth of our propositions in a clearer light.

The facts are as follows: At the time of his Pontificate, a violent dispute arose in the East concerning the two wills in Christ and their operations. Sergius, the Patriarch of Constantinople, was the originator of the controversy; he contended that in Christ there was but one will, that of the Second Person of the Trinity, the Divine will, which wholly absorbed the human will of Christ, even as the ocean absorbs a drop of wine allowed to fall into its waters.

Our adversaries assert that Honorius participated in this error. We shall see with what right they make the assertion.

In his second letter to Sergius, Honorius says: "In regard to the dogma of the Church, we must confess that in Christ there were two natures joined together in natural unity, working and coöperating in mutual communion, so that the divine does what belongs to God, and the human affects what belongs to the flesh, not diversely.

nor confusedly, not saying that the Divine nature is changed into man, nor the human nature into God." "*Quantum ad dogma ecclesiasticum pertinet*, UTRASQUE NATURAS *in uno Christo unitate naturali copulatas cum alterius communione operantes, atque operatrices confiteri debemus, et divinam quidem quæ Dei sunt operantem, et humanam, quæ carnis sunt exequentem; non divise, nec confuse, aut inconvertibiliter Dei naturam in hominem, aut humanam in Deum conversam, dicentes.*" And immediately after, he says: "That the two natures, of the Divinity and of the assumed flesh, in the one Person of the Only-begotten Son of God the Father, exercise their appropriate acts, without confusion, without division, and without possibility of conversion." "*Duas naturas, id est, divinitatis et carnis assumptæ in una Persona Unigeniti Dei Patris, inconfuse, indivise, inconvertibiliter* PROPRIA *operari.*"

Is not this, we ask, a sufficiently explicit declaration and confession of the true Catholic dogma? Consequently, when in his first letter to Sergius, Honorius spoke of *the one will*, he did not mean the one Divine will; he was speaking of the human will, which he said was not divided by the movements of passion, such as we find it in ourselves through the fall of Adam, and of which St. Paul speaks, when he says: "I see another law in my members, warring against the law of my mind;"* and again, "for the good which I will, I do not, but the evil which I will not, that I do." †

Honorius intended to say that Christ had assumed the human nature, subject to human sufferings, indeed, but not with that division of the will that exists in us as a consequence of the fall of our first parents, and which subjects us to the movements of inordinate passions, and to disorders leading to sin by our rebellious concupiscence. That this was the meaning of Honorius is confirmed by his quotation of the teaching of Leo the Great in his letter to Flavian: "*Agit enim utraque forma cum alterius communione quód proprium est.*" "Each nature acts according to its kind, in communion with the other." Nobody will dare to say that Leo was infected by Monothelism. If, then, his faith be sound and his words correct, as the Council of Chalcedon acknowledged, why is not the same doctrine, in the same form, when employed by Honorius also correct? But it does not rest on mere conjecture, since the meaning of Honorius is attested by his contemporaries, by his successors in the Apostolic See, and by the most illustrious writers of the age. John IV, the second successor of this

* Ad Rom. c. vii, p. 23. † Ibid, 19

Pope, asserts it in the apology which he wrote of his maligned predecessor. St. Maximus, martyr, gives us the testimony of the Secretary of Honorius, the inditer of the first letter, and still living when his words were cited, to this effect: "When Sergius wrote that there were persons who asserted that in Christ there were two conflicting wills, Honorius answered, Christ had only one will, not two conflicting wills, that of the flesh and that of the spirit, as we have since the fall, but one alone which was natural to His humanity. One only, we said, existed in our Lord, not of the divinity and humanity together, but of the humanity alone." "*Quum enim Sergius scripsisset, esse, qui dicerent in Christi duas contrarias voluntates, respondit Honorius, unam voluntatem Christum habuisse, non duas contrarias carnis et spiritus, sicut nos habemus post peccatum, sed unam tantum, quæ naturaliter ejus humanitatem insigniret. . . . . Unam voluntatem diximus in Domino, non divinitatis et humanitatis, sed humanitatis dumtaxat.*"

Now, it is St. Maximus, a martyr,* who attests this declaration of the Secretary, and says of him that he was renowned throughout the West, for holiness. We could desire no better testimony in favor of Honorius.

* Dial. ad Pyrrhum ap. Harduin, Tom. iii.

But if we inspect the letters by themselves, there are expressions that no interpretation can so distort, as to prevent us from finding these the true Catholic dogma. We find him saying: "Because certainly the Divinity assumed our *nature*, not our *fault;* that nature which was created before sin, not that which was vitiated by prevarication." "*Quia profecto a Divinitate assumpta est nostra natura, non culpa: illa profecto, quæ ante peccatum creata est, non quæ post prævaricationem vitiata.*" Is not this a plain profession of Catholic doctrine as against Monothelism? That it was not uncalled for is proved by the fact that even in our own days there are found some, as the followers of Dr. Guenther, who suppose such contradicting wills to have existed in Christ, and even the possibility of sin.*

But they ask us whether Honorius was not condemned by the Sixth Œcumenical Synod, and by Leo II, in his letters to the Bishops of Spain and to the Emperor Pogonatus? We answer, that in the first place, learned and trustworthy authors have proved that these acts of the Council, as well as the letters of Leo, are open to the gravest suspicions of having been fraudulently changed by the Greeks. We might

* See Dr. Pabst, Temptations of Christ.

therefore first require our adversaries to establish their historical sources on a more evident and substantial basis. As they can not do it, we shall pass over the difficulty, and admit, for discussion's sake, the objection as it is proposed by them. Our answer is positive. The Fathers of the Council, and St. Leo, did not condemn Honorius for having promulgated *an erroneous definition* of faith to the whole, Church, nor yet for having professed Monothelism, but simply blamed him for not having used more vigorous means for its suppression, and by imposing silence on the disputants, having rather favored and increased the spread of that heresy. This is the very expression used by Leo in his letters to the Spanish Bishops: "Who has not extinguished the flame of heresy in its very commencement, as in his Apostolical dignity he should have done, but by his negligence favored it." "*Qui flammam hæretici dogmatis, non ut decuerit Apostolicam dignitatem extinxit, sed negligentia confovit?*"

In this light, and in no other, did the Fathers of the Council regard the fault of Honorius. That they did not look upon him as an adherent to Monothelism, is evident from the acts of the Council, which we have agreed to admit as genuine. How, otherwise, could Agatho, in the face of the Council, assert that the Roman See had never deviated from the path of truth? "*Hæc Apostolica Ecclesia nunquam a via veritatis in qualibet erroris parte deflexa est.*" How, otherwise, could he insert, in his instructions to his Legates, that, after the decision contained in his dogmatical letter to the Council, the Fathers could not discuss the dogma, but must simply subscribe it as a rule of faith? "*Non tamquam de incertis contendere, sed ut certa et immutabilia compendiosa definitione proferre.*" We have seen with what joy the Fathers obeyed his decree. If the Fathers of the Council had asserted or believed that Honorius had erred, they certainly would have acted in another manner, and would rather have invited a discussion of the decree, since, if Honorius had erred, the same might happen to Agatho. Nobody suggested such a course—not even the defenders of Monothelism—knowing too well that, when Rome had definitively spoken, all hesitation and doubt had to cease.

There is not, in any act of the Council, any thing that leads us to believe that the Fathers condemned Honorius for having held the Monothelistic error, but only that they blamed him for having temporized with Sergius, and for having listened to his advisers, imposing silence on the discussion, instead of speaking definitively, and teaching the East and the whole Church what they had to believe.

If the Greeks themselves believed that Honorius had taught Monothelism, the Fathers of the Seventh and Eighth General Councils in the East would have acted differently from what they did. And how otherwise, could the Papal Legates, in the presence of the assembled Council, call upon the Fathers to subscribe, for no other reason than that neither reason nor faith permitted the discussion of an irrevocable decision. "*Quoniam de irreformabili judicio quæri, nec ratio nec fides permittit.*"

It is only under the same supposition that we can account for the action of Adrian II toward the Eighth General Council, in the time of Photius, in sending them a letter for their subscription, which contained the following declarations: "First of all, true salvation is found in keeping the right rule of faith, which is to submit to the decisions of the Apostolic See, according to the promises of Christ to Peter, 'Thou art a rock,'" etc. That this is true is proved by the fact that the Apostolic See has always preserved the Catholic religion immaculate, and professed its holy doctrine. "*Quia in Sede Apostolica immaculata est semper Catholica servata religio et sancta cele-*

brata doctrina." Photius certainly was not the man to have been ignorant of the fall of Honorius into Monothelism, and, knowing it, to have foregone the advantage of objecting it against an assertion that silenced him. Yet neither he nor the Fathers of the Council had one word to say of his case, nor objected to the "rule of faith" as proposed by Adrian, but subscribed in the memorable way that history has made known to us.

The Orientals, seeing their Patriarchs from time to time passing under censure for heresy— as well the Patriarch of Constantinople as those of Antioch, Alexandria, and Jerusalem, would have been very glad to make use of such an opportunity, as our adversaries think was presented in Honorius, to reproach the See of Rome with the same fault, especially at the time of the great schism. It may very well be, too, that this was the secret source of whatever blame they attached to Honorius in the Sixth Council.

We believe that we have made it as clear as any historical fact can be, that, whatever our adversaries may object, they can not, at least, adduce Honorius as an instance of a Pope *"teaching an error or giving an erroneous definition, to the whole Church, in matters of faith."* The most they can show is a *negligence*, on his part, in making use of his Apostolic power, under the circumstances in which he found himself. But this does not affect our thesis, which was simply the infallibility of the Head of the Church when teaching or defining a matter of faith as taught by the Church, and explicitly proposed as such to the faithful. That Honorius did nothing to impugn this, is manifest from the very charge which is made against him, the silencing of discussion, and the refusal to define.

We might go even farther and say, that, had the Fathers of the Council called him heretic, it would not have been sufficient to disprove our thesis, because, in those days, that name was given not alone to those who held heretical opinions, but even to such as seemed to favor heretics; and because so long as they attacked Honorius the man, not Honorius teaching or defining *ex cathedra*, it would have been still insufficient.

And, now, we propose to close our discussion of this case, the most difficult and the strongest that our adversaries could have selected from Ecclesiastical History, with these few reflections. So far from having disturbed our thesis, it rather strengthens it by showing how important and necessary such a privilege in the Holy See becomes in times of dangerous heresy, and that the Fathers of the Council looked upon it in this light, and blamed Honorius for not exercising it. And this blame becomes, then, considered in the light of Divine Providence, a warning to his successors to be vigilant in the exercise of the powers intrusted to them. And, should we give full license to suppositions, admitting that Honorius was at heart a Monothelite, though this is impossible, after a consideration of our quotations, it would then show the overpowering direction of the Holy Spirit in the Church, which, in such a case, prevented a definition which would have trenched upon the dogma of Catholic faith. One thing more we would wish to say. Even as the lives of some Popes have been such as were unworthy of the Vicar of Christ, and have thus proved that the veneration and homage, which the Catholic world continued to pay them, were awarded not to the man, but to the office; so, too, the submission and obedience uniformly given to the decisions of the Roman Pontiff, apart from all question of whom he was that occupied the Holy See, should convince us that it is the office, and the prerogatives of that office, that ask for and obtain the acquiescence of Catholic faith to its Apostolic definitions and teachings.

It would be superfluous for us to consider other cases sometimes insisted upon, since our adversaries should be content with Bossuet's opinion, as found in his "Defense," that they are not worth discussing.

OBJECTION X.

"Why has not the Church defined this thesis to be an article of faith?"

ANSWER.—"*Signa Gentibus*"—"*definitiones hæreticis*," that is, as St. Paul tells us, wonders are for the heathen, who, in the beginning of the conversion of the world, needed visible proofs of the Divinity of the Gospel; the faithful do not need wonders, since they possess the gift of faith, they do not need definitions, except on occasions of doubt or discussion; as a general rule, the ordinary teaching of the Church suffices for them. When, however, new errors are springing up, questions never before discussed are agitated, or an obstinate and dangerous denial of truth in matters of faith is prevailing, then the Church defines what is to be believed or rejected by the faithful. But, even then, directed by the Holy Ghost, her counsels are moderate, and her ways are wise and prudent, lest hasty and ill-judged measures should convert erring souls into obstinate heretics. In matters almost self-evident, or so easily deducible from her ordinary teaching, that the least reflecting mind can discern the truth, the Church imitates the examples of the Apostles. In the very outset they defined very few articles—those contained in the Apostles' Creed, and the question agitated in the Council of Jerusalem.

Now, in regard to the Infallibility of the Pope, the Church has not yet met an occasion in which such definition seemed practically necessary, since they who refused obedience to a Papal decision refused it likewise to the teaching of the Universal Church; and they who obeyed the Church have not refused assent to the voice of the Holy See. It has never desired by an uncalled-for decision to provoke an untimely and dangerous controversy, such as threatened, for awhile, to arise in the midst of the Clergy of France.

In the Council of Florence, when there was a fresh attempt to reconcile the schismatical East, the wisest precautions were taken so to express the truth, that while it should not be denied or silenced, it would not be couched in such terms as needlessly to excite the susceptibilities of the Greeks. But even there the definition was such as implicitly to embrace our thesis, since it was declared one of the rights and privileges of the Roman Pontiff, that he should be the Supreme Judge in matters of faith. It says: "That the

Roman Pontiff is the Teacher of all the faithful, and that on him, in the person of the blessed Peter, has been conferred full power, to feed, direct, and govern the Universal Church." "*Definimus Romanum Pontificem omnium Christianorum Doctorem existere, et ipsi, in beato Petro, pascendi, regendi, gubernandi universalem Ecclesiam plenam potestatem traditam esse.*"

We ask whether this definition does not at least implicitly contain our thesis, when it affirms that the Roman Pontiff is the divinely-commissioned Teacher of *all* Christians, of every one, and therefore of the Bishops, who are preëminently Christian. Just as Christ, addressing Peter, said, "Feed my sheep—feed my lambs," He made him pastor of the pastors; words which our readers will remember that we quoted from Eucherius.

The Council, defining, says, that Christ gave to the Pope full power, "*plenam potestatem,*" to feed, to direct, and to govern the Universal Church. If so, then He imposed upon the Universal Church the obligation of following his directions, teaching, and orders, and to the Universal Church, the *Hierarchy* certainly belongs. Now, if with this obligation on the Church, Christ had not conferred upon the Pope an infallible freedom from error when teaching the

Universal Church, it would follow that He had obliged the Church to obey that Roman Pontiff even though he led it into errors. If He conferred the privilege, subject to the assent of the Church dispersed or assembled, then He did not confer, as the Council says, full power, "*plenam potestatem.*"

We may very well conclude, then, that if the Church has not explicitly defined our thesis as an article of faith, it has at least laid it down plainly enough to satisfy any Catholic of clear, logical mind, and of good will.

Well then, they may say, every one who contradicts your thesis should be accounted a heretic? This consequence, in common with all theologians, we deny, because, to become a heretic, the doctrine denied, must have been expressly and explicitly defined to be an article of faith. The Church most wisely and prudently refrains, as we have said before, from some explicit declarations, which might perhaps provoke an evil which she always prefers rather to avert than to repress.

If up to this time the Church, enlightened and directed by the Holy Ghost, has not deemed it expedient to define this Right and Privilege of the Roman Pontiff, it does not follow that that time will never come, and that the present may not be the very one that will induce her to do so. And, indeed, some circumstances might lead us to suppose so, when we consider that the enemies of the Church, now, more than ever, direct their principal fury against the Authority of the Pope. In trying to deprive him of his Temporal Sovereignty they really aspire to weaken his spiritual authority. It would seem, therefore, that every thing should be done to strengthen his position, especially in his Spiritual dominion. And then, even in the supposition which we made in our Introduction, of his losing his temporal sovereignty, the faithful remaining united to him as their Spiritual Head, with increased devotion, obedience, and love, with all the strength of living faith, nothing could happen in the way of salvation, which could endanger their souls, and prevent their final triumph over all the visible and invisible enemies of the Church. Persecution itself would then prove a spiritual advantage, and strengthen them to fight as true soldiers of Christ, members of the Church militant, that glorious battle, the reward of which is the crown of heavenly victory and eternal bliss.

When there is peril of a fearful battle all care should be taken to increase the strength of the army. With regard to the Church, nothing strengthens her more than the closest possible union of all her members, under the safe guidance of her Head. What strengthens his authority, strengthens the Church. Protestantism was well aware of this truth, and, therefore, from its very beginning, directed all its attacks, with relentless violence, against the Pope and the Holy See. Had the great Papal schism not preceded the Council of Constance, whose opening gave rise to the erroneous opinion of the superiority of a General Council over the Pope, Protestantism, perhaps, would never have gained ground nor have celebrated the triumph of apostasy. The present struggle of the Church against Pantheism and modern heathenism, threatens to be still more disastrous. We, therefore, clearly understand why a leading journal in Rome has invited the faithful even to take a vow to defend this essential prerogative to the utmost of their ability. This invitation was certainly not made without the knowledge and consent of the Head of the Church; and we should not be at all surprised to hear this truth of faith defined in the next General Council. Besides this, there is yet another reason, why a definition of this truth seems to be appropriate in our own day. The source of all the disorder and revolutionary spirit, by which society in our time is so awfully agitated, is the utter disrespect of the principle of authority. By defining the infallibility of the Pope, the principle of authority in the realm of the Church would be thereby strengthened, and if duly appreciated, would prove most useful in strengthening all legitimate authority. What a salutary effect, not only for the Church, but for society in general!

We repeat it, the reverence and obedience which we owe to the rest of the Episcopacy, would not thereby be diminished, but increased; for the Pope is invested with all his Authority because he is a Bishop—the Bishop of Rome.

Moreover, it must be a satisfaction to every Bishop, that the world sees, and must see, the reason of his submitting, reasonably and perforce, to the Supreme Pontiff when defining an article of faith; that it is not through human respect or servility, but through a simple sense of duty, based upon a foundation, solid and illustrious, such as we have endeavored to lay bare in this our treatise.

So we think that we have placed the truth of our thesis in the light of evidence so strong, that no logical thinker, who believes in the infallibility of the Church, can ever deny it without throwing himself into the darkness of self-contradiction.

In publishing this treatise, our primary aim was to address the Rev. Clergy; as it is a dogmatic discussion. Nevertheless, the book has an universal interest for all Catholics; because it is so closely connected with the interest and the welfare of the Church, that they call their mother.

Nay, even for the non-Catholics this discussion may be of no little importance and usefulness; because all that we said in defense of our thesis, refers to the great principle of a *sufficient*, *leading*, and *teaching* authority.

This principle, thoroughly understood, settles at once the right of a Divine Church to claim an infallible teaching authority, and, at the same time, shows evidently the obligation on all to belong to this Divine Church.

In proof of this, we have only to call the attention of every logical thinker to the analogy existing between the natural and supernatural order.

Now, even in the *natural* order, man could not believe, as a rational being, without the guidance of a leading teaching authority, which is reason. Every one denying this would condemn himself to the lunatic asylum.

Therefore, by the force of his own reason, man, "*a priori,*" should infer and expect, that if God pleased to communicate, through Revelation to mankind, truths belonging to the supernatural order, that He would have provided also a sufficient leading and teaching authority for his guidance.

But this *sufficient* teaching authority, in regard to truths belonging to the supernatural order, must be of an *infallible* character; because, as the supernatural order surpasses the sphere of his reason, in order to believe reasonably he must have an infallible guide, whom he can trust entirely, as he, for himself, absolutely can not decide on the tenets of revealed truth. An uncertain and fallible authority in this regard would be no authority at all; because, as it could err in one tenet, it could err in another, and so in all.

Therefore, any logical mind must, "*a priori*," expect that a Divine Church, teaching truths belonging to the supernatural order, must bring with it the claims of an infallible teaching authority; and that any Church not claiming such authority gives up at once all right to be considered a Divine Church.

This logical inference, rightly appreciated, may become, for a sincere inquirer after truth, a powerful motive for a serious examination, and bring him finally to the recognition of the Divine character of the Catholic Church, claiming that privilege of infallible authority.

But this result, in favor of the Catholic Church would at once be paralyzed and stopped for a logical mind, if he would be required to adopt the opinion of our adversaries, placing the prerogative of infallibility in the authority of a General Council, or in the consent of the "Church dispersed."

According to what we said, he would have the right to sneer at an Infallible Judge who has no tribunal to which, at all times, the faithful could address themselves, and who has no organ to answer distinctly and with infallible certainty; and hence would have the right to say, that God had provided for man in the natural order far better than in the supernatural. A stringently logical mind would look to such an infallible guidance as mockery; because, the bearer of that infallibility would be, in many cases, without ears to hear, and would never have a tongue to give a final answer.

Moreover, as the Church, claiming to be infallible, has, in the Council of Florence, defined the Pope to be her *teacher*, in case he could err, we would have an infallible Church with a fallible teacher, and the disciple would know more than the teacher, which kind of contradictions and absurdities a logical mind can never admit.

On the contrary, by adopting our thesis, reason admires the wisdom of the Divine founder of the Holy Church, who adapted the means so well and efficiently to reach the end, giving to the Church a visible and accessible tribunal in matters of faith, and an unerring, visible, and accessible Judge.

The reflecting reader will easily perceive, that this our last remark, is an additional argument to the preceding chapter on the "Ratio Theologica," or, "Evidence from Reason," and completes its logical and invincible strength.

All that our opponents object, or can object to our thesis, are but as shooting stars or baleful meteors, gleaming or glaring for a moment in the firmament of truth, then disappearing in the darkness, while the fixed and glowing stars of solid reason and argument, which they seemed for awhile to equal or outshine, remain in all their cloudless brilliancy. And crowning all the glories in that firmament of truth is the steady, brilliant light of tradition—that common living conscience of the Church, of all nations and peoples, succeeding from generation to generation. Nineteen hundred years have almost elapsed, and yet, echoing through the centuries, we hear the hallowed voice of Christ:

"Peter, thou art a rock, and on this rock I will build my Church, and the gates of hell shall not prevail against it. To thee shall I commit the keys of heaven. Feed my lambs, feed my sheep."

And those gates of hell have never prevailed, and still that rock endures, in the time of Pius IX, as in the days of Peter. The keys of Heaven are still held on earth, and now, as then, the faithful turn listening ears and wistful looks to the voice and sign of Pius IX as they would to those of Peter, when he warns them of impending evils or directs them to wholesome pasturage. Still, now as then, Peter confirms his brethren, as when the assembled Bishops raised their acclaim to Pius IX, on the occasion of the proclamation of the dogma of the Immaculate Conception, and used the self-same words: "Speak, Peter; confirm thy brethren."

Now, as nineteen hundred years ago, the Church remains the same, and the reason is found in the words of St. Augustin, of which our thesis is the practical development. Number the Supreme Pontiffs on the Chair of Peter—*ipsa est petra*—that is, the rock on which the Church is built. Thus, and thus only, does the Church remain infallible. Deprive her of her Head, with all its powers and privileges, and all her majesty and intrepid firmness depart with them.

And so long as the Church is permitted to pray, as on the Parasceve, "Almighty and Eternal God, in whose judgment all things are founded, mercifully receive our prayers, that the Christian people who are governed by Thee, their Author, under so great a Pontiff—*sub tanto Pontifice*—may reap the reward of their fidelity"— so long as that prayer is heard, as heard it will be, and the Church enjoys the protection of such a Leader and Teacher, she has nothing to fear— not even in the gloom that shall herald and accompany the great persecutor, Antichrist.

The children of the Church will always look calmly to the future, knowing that the end shall surely come, when all the sons of men shall behold, with the same reverence, the Supreme Pontiff; when there shall be only one fold and one Shepherd, the REPRESENTATIVE on earth of the ONE, INCARNATE, INFALLIBLE, ETERNAL TRUTH.

www.ingramcontent.com/pod-product-compliance
Lightning Source LLC
Chambersburg PA
CBHW020226240426
43672CB00006B/429